'In this engaging and informative book, June Sarpong examines the research behind diversity and discrimination while grounding them in personal narratives, highlighting our common humanity.'

Kofi Annan

'As a survivor of Auschwitz, I sadly lost my father and brother to the brutality of the Holocaust. As a child I unfortunately witnessed first-hand how quickly diverse cities can be hijacked by dangerous demagogues and unravel in the process.

'My experiences during the Holocaust have led me on a lifetime mission to promote the benefits of diversity by travelling the world, bringing people from diverse backgrounds together, telling my story and that of my stepsister Anne Frank, and why civil society must do all it can to protect and celebrate our diversity.

'*Diversify* lays out a practical framework about how we best achieve this and helps us take the first steps on the journey to tolerance.'

Eva Schloss

June Sarpong MBE is one of the most recognizable faces of British television. A media phenomenon, she has interviewed hundreds of people, from politicians to celebrities and members of the public.

In addition to twenty years of television work, June has hosted a wealth of events, including Make Poverty History in London's Trafalgar Square and Nelson Mandela's 90th birthday celebrations alongside Will Smith in London's Hyde Park.

June has worked extensively with HRH Prince Charles for ten years as an ambassador for his charity the Prince's Trust. She is the co-founder of WIE UK (Women: Inspiration & Enterprise) and, in 2007, was awarded an MBE for services to broadcasting and charity.

A former board member of Stronger IN, the official campaign to keep Britain in the EU, June is now a board member of the pro-EU think-tank Open Britain.

She is co-host of *The Pledge*, Sky News' flagship weekly political discussion show.

Diversify

June Sarpong

ONE PLACE. MANY STORIES

HQ
An imprint of HarperCollins*Publishers* Ltd
1 London Bridge Street
London SE1 9GF

This hardback edition 2017

19 20 21 22 LSC 10 9 8 7 6 5 4 3 2 1

First published in Great Britain by
HQ, an imprint of HarperCollins*Publishers* Ltd 2017

Copyright © June Sarpong 2017

June Sarpong asserts the moral right to be
identified as the author of this work.
A catalogue record for this book is
available from the British Library.

ISBN: HB 978-0-00-821704-4
ISBN: TPB 978-0-00-833444-4
Typeset by Palimpsest Book Production Ltd, Falkirk, Stirlingshire
Printed and bound in the United States of America by
LSC Communications

For more information visit: www.harpercollins.co.uk/green

Contents

Contents

To Sammy – love you to the moon and back.
See you next lifetime

INTRODUCTION

THE 'OTHER' SIDE OF THE STORY

'Diversity may be the hardest thing for a society to live with, and perhaps the most dangerous thing for a society to be without.'

William Sloane Coffin

Only Connect

The British humanist and novelist E. M. Forster famously wrote 'Only connect'.* And he was absolutely right. While the Earth is vast, we live in a small world full of opportunities to connect with each other, and it's only when we do this that the walls between us come down. Yet the majority of us seem to find this incredibly difficult, caught up as we are in the things that divide us.

In one sense, of course, we are more connected than we've ever been before. Whether we live in the remotest parts of the world or in great international cities such as London or New York, we can connect across the globe at the click of a button. So it's a great irony that the economic gap between those at the centre of society and those at the periphery is ever-growing. Our great cities of culture and commerce are in fact cities of strangers, where individuals have rejected relationships with neighbours in favour of superficial relationships with an online community. We often ignore passersby as we get on with our lives. We may SMH (Shake My Head) at newsfeeds that show injustice at home and abroad, yet somehow we continue on, unaffected by what happens to 'others'.

And yet, as the MP Jo Cox argued so passionately before she was murdered in 2016, we have far more in common than that

---

* *Howards End* by E. M. Forster (Edward Arnold, 1910)

which divides us. This isn't head-in-the-clouds liberalism speaking; this is scientific fact. Genetically, human beings are 99.9 per cent identical.* Our bodies perform in the same way – we breathe the same, we eat the same, we sleep the same – and yet we choose to focus so much on the 0.1 per cent that makes us different – the 0.1 that determines external physical attributes such as hair, eye and skin colour. This focus has been the cause of so much tension and strife in the world, yet by re-evaluating the importance we place on it, we have the power to change how it affects our future. What if we celebrated that 0.1 per cent rather than feared it? What amazing things might follow for our society? The need to do this has never been so urgent – thanks to the recent political upheavals of Brexit and the election of Donald Trump, the rise of extremism and economic instability, we are now more divided than ever before – but the ability to change this is firmly within our grasp. To heal the wounds that have been exposed, we need to diversify, and we need to do it now. This is an issue I've felt passionate about for a long time: it informs my work, my relationships and my everyday life. And it's more than a question of encouraging human kindness; I've long suspected that there is a hidden financial cost to our lack of diversity. The research that I have undertaken for this book has confirmed that.

I decided to write this book, often drawing on my own experiences, to present the issues that a lack of diversity is causing for us today, alongside the arguments for the social, moral and economic benefits of diversity. You'll also find practical tools and ideas for how we might go about creating a new normal that is equitable, diverse and prosperous.

* *Daily Telegraph*: http://www.telegraph.co.uk/news/worldnews/northamerica/usa/1416706/DNA-survey-finds-all-humans-are-99.9pc-the-same.html

Why now?

On 28 August 1963, Dr Martin Luther King – for me, one of the greatest men of the twentieth century, without question – delivered his iconic 'I Have a Dream' speech. I have always found his words, laying out such a powerful and clear vision for global equality and unity, and delivering a message of hope that we could all be part of, absolutely mind-blowing. He presented a comprehensive vision and framework for the much-needed journey that would get us there, and I firmly believe it's one of the best examples of the type of society we should all be striving to create. Now, over half a century later, where are we on that journey that Dr King laid out for us, and what does this mean for humanity?

The sad truth is, it's a journey that many of us are yet to embark on. Prophesying his own assassination, King ended his last speech with 'I may not get there [to the Promised Land] with you', and indeed he didn't. And there have been claims that if Dr King were still alive he would be incredibly disappointed by what he saw: a world divided by gender, nationality, class, sexual orientation, age, culture, and, of course, the two big Rs of Race and Religion.

I would argue that, actually, Dr King would not be so disappointed in what he *saw*, but rather in what he *couldn't see*. It's what lies beneath the surface and facade of 'tolerance' and political correctness that causes the real malaise – the limiting viewpoints that are hidden inside us, that we rarely speak of but often think about and, worse, sometimes act upon. Whether they are conscious or unconscious, it's these hidden, unexamined attitudes that shape the inequality we see in society.

The evidence of that is clear in the political upheaval that has occurred in both the UK and US recently. There are many parallels between the shock results of Britain's Brexit referendum and the Electoral College victory of Donald Trump in the US in 2016. As a board member of the official Remain campaign, I was certainly not in favour of Brexit and put all my passion and energy into trying to convince the British public that Britain was Stronger IN Europe. The result was a painful and bitter blow, and one that still hurts. We will only see the true fall-out now that Article 50 has been triggered and the negotiations have begun . . .

However, we are beginning to see what this new world looks like. For many, Brexit represented freedom. Yet one of the worrying repercussions of Brexit, which the experts didn't anticipate, is the rise in hate crime and the open season on anything or anyone deemed 'other'. Since the referendum I've heard phrases such as, 'This doesn't feel like modern Britain', 'A victory for xenophobia', and 'The revolt of the working class'. The same seems to be true of Donald Trump's victory in the US, with David Duke, the former KKK leader, celebrating it as 'one of the most exciting nights of my life'. I feel huge disappointment for those who wanted us to stay part of the EU, and fear what might happen to tolerance of the 'other' in the US – but, more importantly, I want to understand why these results went the way they did, shaking up the status quo in response to campaigns which focused on immigration and fear. The short answer is that both Brexit and Trump were symptoms of our failure to address the issues of fairness and inequality in our globalized economy.

The majority of us recognize that there are things greater than ourselves that can unite us: the world we share and our common humanity. We know that the need for understanding, connection and solidarity as one human family is more urgent now than ever. The greatest challenges of our time demand our cooperation. But how do we achieve this? When we have been separate for so long, change is not easy. But it is necessary. That's where this book comes in.

Why me?

The daughter of Ghanaian immigrants, I was born and raised in the East End of London, home to a diverse range of people. The part of town that I grew up in, Walthamstow – or *Wilcomestu*, as the Anglo-Saxons called it – means 'place of welcome'. Coincidentally, the Ghanaian greeting for hello is *Awaakba*, which also means 'welcome', so being welcoming is part of both my British and Ghanaian heritage – literally.

During my early years, Walthamstow more or less lived up to its name. We had the longest street market in Europe, where you could get anything from anywhere. The older generation of market stall-holders were mainly white working-class survivors of the Second World War. They were community-minded, and would call out to you if they knew your mum, chucking you an apple or a bag of sweets from their stall. My school was like a blue-collar version of the UN and proclaimed the belief that diversity was an asset. All the main religious holidays were celebrated – my Indian friends always brought in the best sweets on the Guru Nanak celebration. I was well liked and, being an inquisitive soul, I often found myself at my friends' houses celebrating Shabbat, Eid and Diwali. My best friend, Levan Trong, was Chinese Vietnamese, so this meant free Mandarin lessons and amazing New Year parties.

This multicultural upbringing served as a great basis for my media career, paving the way for me to connect comfortably with people from all walks of life. After leaving school, I started an internship with Kiss FM, a vibrant, fresh radio station that looked to unite the young people of London through music. So wherever I went, it was a given for me that difference was not a problem. In fact, it was cool, and what London was all about. I carried this belief with me from radio to television, to my first presenting job. I was getting to do what I had enjoyed my entire life: meeting and talking to people from anywhere and everywhere.

In 2008 I moved to the US in the hope of finding that holy grail: the secret formula for 'cracking America'. I wouldn't say I 'cracked' America – rather, I made a small dent in her West and East Coast – but with the support and mentorship of Arianna Huffington, Donna

Karan and Sarah Brown, I was able to sample a slice of the American Pie when they helped me to co-found a women's network that was designed to facilitate this generation's female leaders paying it forward to the next: Women: Inspiration and Enterprise (WIE) (www.wienetwork.co.uk).

I was also lucky enough to start working in American TV quite quickly, and one day, when I was filming in Las Vegas, a young sound assistant appeared on set. I noticed him straight away – and immediately felt uneasy around him. He hadn't behaved aggressively towards me, but he was covered in tattoos. And I'm not talking David Beckham-style ink, but rather what looked like gang markings. I suspected he'd probably had a tough upbringing, possibly had a few run-ins with the law in his time. But had I really just painted this picture and gained this insight into another person's life based on some tattoos and a bad ponytail? Yes, I had. And, regardless of the illogic of my assumptions, I began to feel intimidated.

As a woman of colour, I am all too aware of the problems that can be caused by stereotyping. In fact, being excluded as a result of being a woman, and being excluded because of your race, are two forms of discrimination I understand first-hand. So you might think that I, of all people, should know better, and should get over my discomfort and preconceived ideas and just have a conversation with this man. But in that moment I couldn't do it. And in that moment I suddenly understood both sides of this enigma – and how our fear of the 'other' (whatever that 'other' is for you) subconsciously influences our behaviour. Whether we like it or not, 'other-izing' is something we all do, and 'other-isms' are something we all have.

I was about to quietly exclude this young man – not overtly (I'm far too polite and British for that), but subtly, which is even more soul-destroying: no eye contact and false politeness. Basically, I was prepared to pretend he wasn't there so I could feel comfortable. But I'm happy to say that I didn't. In that light-bulb moment, I chose to be my better self and to challenge some of my own limiting beliefs.

Limiting beliefs that I didn't even realize I had. So I went over nervously and did what usually comes very naturally to me: I spoke to him.

As it happens, he had indeed had a difficult start in life. However, he had also done a great deal of studying and self-development, and was now committed to making a better life for himself and was extremely excited about the possibility of a career as a soundman. He was brimming with enthusiasm and full of dreams – dreams that, I sensed, he secretly hoped wouldn't be dashed by those prejudging him. Fortunately, our lead soundman had looked beyond his exterior and taken him on as an apprentice, but I couldn't help but lament what it would take for him to rise above the limiting beliefs of others in order to achieve his full potential. He was truly a gentle soul, yet I could sense the unspoken burden he had to carry because of his appearance and the effect it had on people like me – he had to go out of his way to seem unthreatening, and to overcompensate with helpfulness.

Now, I grew up around men like this, so it was not as if I had never encountered someone like him, but I had never encountered someone like him in this context. I work in an industry that, in both its on- and off-screen talent, is not known for its diversity. I have been a very outspoken critic of this, yet I didn't realize that I had become so accustomed to the lack of diversity at work that when the status quo was challenged, even I had to adjust.

I ended up having one of the most enlightening conversations of my life with this young man – and I realized that, had I not been able to put aside my issues around his appearance, I would have missed out on a defining moment that not only changed the way I think, but also enabled me to truly understand both sides of a problem that affects me personally. It made me wonder how many of us miss out on enriching, enlightening, even magical moments every day due to our failure to put aside our issues with external packaging.

Part of the reason so many of us are reluctant to honestly address our ism's or voice our pain from being otherized is because it involves guilt and shame, two emotions most humans seek to avoid at all costs.

Family issues that involve these emotions often go unspoken and unresolved, and the same is true for societal issues; but, as we know from our personal relationships, ignoring conflicts doesn't dissolve them, it just allows them to fester, breed resentment and then sometimes explode. I still have a funny feeling in my stomach every time I recount this story, because to own the positive outcome, I have to accept that I went into the situation with prejudice. And this is not who I consider myself to be. But this belief is itself limited, because we are all hardwired with stereotypes – perceptions of what looks like safety and comfort, and what looks unfamiliar, something to be kept out. At times these ideas protect us, but they often trap us, too. Stereotypical assumptions on who should lead and who should follow limit potential, which in turn limits us all. Those to whom we mentally close our gates may well possess the answers to some of the greatest challenges of our age: extremism, economic instability, poverty, and the sustainability of the planet itself. To solve these complex problems (which don't appear to be going anywhere), we need to nurture the greatest minds of our age – whatever body they reside in.

Why this book?

The aim of this book is to help people take a more positive view of others and their differences. It is not, by any means, about privileged white male bashing, but rather the opposite. My argument throughout this book is that by operating in a more inclusive way towards *everyone* we will be able to realize the talents and potential of *everyone*. Scapegoating any one group or defining an individual solely by their demographic or otherness blocks us from having the honest and open dialogue we need in order to create a fairer society. To achieve 'business as unusual' we have to make a compelling case that demonstrates that diversity is better for everyone, even those who will need to share a little more than they have previously, thus helping the UK and the US – two of the richest countries on the planet in terms of diversity (and in terms of monetary wealth) – to meet and overcome the challenges of the twenty-first century.

This isn't a book that offers a whimsical argument for being nice to one another. It provides solid evidence of what's going wrong and why, and offers practical tools and arguments for how we can change things. To use a business analogy, even the novice investor knows that the best way to achieve a return on your investment is to diversify your portfolio. If you invest all your capital in one place, you leave yourself vulnerable to fluctuations in that particular market. In the same way, companies need to ensure a diverse mix in their employee portfolio so that new ideas from people with different skill sets give them a competitive edge. Because when everybody thinks the same, we miss out on the opportunity to meet challenges with fresh ideas, we become complacent and we continue to do what we've always done before. The question that every company and every community has to ask is: 'Is everyone in the room?' And this book will try to help make sure they are.

How this book works

In *Diversify*, I will be primarily looking at the social, moral and economic benefits of diversity from a UK and US perspective, arguing that these two nations are probably best placed to lead the way on tolerance and equality. Both nations have 'United' in their title, both countries are born of the concept of 'union', and its essence is in their DNA. And both countries, as we've seen, are at a critical stage politically, economically, and socially.

The Others

You will notice that each section in *Diversify* is titled according to an 'Other'. So what do I mean by labelling a group as 'other'? Well, for the purpose of this book, 'other' refers to any demographic that is excluded socially, politically, or economically because of their difference from the dominant group(s) in society. If you are not a white, non-disabled, educated, heterosexual, middle-aged, middle- or upper-class male adhering to a version of Christianity or atheism that fits within the confines of a secular liberal democracy, then on some level you will have been made to feel like an 'other'. The 'others' that I have chosen to look at here are as follows:

- **The Other Man:** This section looks at disenfranchised males in society: black, Muslim and white working-class men.
- **The Other Woman:** This section explores gender inequality in the workplace, in the media and in wider society, and what the barriers are to female empowerment.
- **The Other Class:** In this section I look at the class divisions that separate societies, in particular the economic gap between the elites and the working classes.
- **The Other Body:** This looks at what society deems as valuable bodies, and how we treat those who don't fit the physical and mental standards of the so-called 'able bodied'.
- **The Other Sex:** This section looks at how LGBTQ communities have been perceived and treated throughout the ages to the present day.
- **The Other Age:** This section covers ageism from the perspective of the young and the old, by analysing the disproportionate value we place on those of 'working age'.
- **The Other View:** This section looks at the divisions caused by opposing political views and the vital importance of listening to the other side of the argument.
- **The Other Way in Action:** The final section will focus on what a fair and inclusive society might actually look like and how we might practically achieve it.[*]

---

[*] You'll notice that there isn't a section called 'The Other Race'. I purposely chose not to create one, as I've included the subject in the sections on gender. Racial discrimination is incredibly nuanced – much like any racial group, the experiences

Each chapter within these sections will feature theories, data and real-life stories that examine the perspective of each of the discriminated groups and the solutions to combat that discrimination. Each one opens with a look at The Old Way for that group – how things are and have been in the past – and closes with a vision of The Other Way – outlining how things could be. And at the end of each chapter you will also find action and discussion points to help you kick-start change in your own life, right here, right now.

The Numbers

Where diversity is concerned we have long heard the moral arguments and the rational reasons for equality, but Western society is primarily financially driven. So, to support my case further, I've partnered with some of the leading academic institutions and organizations in the world, including Oxford University, LSE, and Rice University TX, to provide the cold, hard numbers that demonstrate just what we stand to lose, economically as well as socially, by failing to diversify. Each of these institutions has provided some of the research and data in the book, and the Centre for Social Investigation at Nuffield College, Oxford, in particular, has provided the statistics you will see at the end of each chapter. This data is a combination of both new and existing research that delivers an overview of the challenges facing each 'other' group. Perhaps the most striking data in this book comes from LSE. Professor John Hills and his team at the International Inequalities Institute have calculated what must surely be the most important number of them all: the actual economic cost of discrimination – a shocking figure that brings this book to a close.

of men of colour are acutely different to those of women of colour – and I think it's important to separate the two and address each within its own context of gender.

The Six Degrees of Integration

Finally, you will also find in this book what I'm calling the Six Degrees of Integration. Famously, it is said that there are just 'six degrees of separation' between any two individuals on the planet – from a newborn child in the most isolated tribe of the Amazon to Queen Elizabeth. The concept originates from social psychologist Stanley Milgram's 1967 'small world experiment', in which he tracked chains of acquaintances in the United States, by sending packages to 160 random people, and asking them to forward the package to someone they thought would bring the package closer to a set final individual: a stockbroker from Boston. Milgram reported that there was a median of five links in the chain (i.e. six degrees of separation) between the original sender and the destination recipient.[*]

But while Milgram's experiment proves we may be linked, are we really *connected*? Misunderstanding and strife dominate our world and its politics, and there is now an urgent need for understanding and connection. None of us can be fulfilled in a life alone. We need others in our lives, yet many aspects of modern life are leaving us increasingly isolated. Social networking as we now experience it generally limits us to the people just one degree away, people we already know.

We need a human revolution that opens a world of possibilities for us to connect with the members of our human family who are living beyond our comfort zones and our cultures. So, in order to do this, rather than six degrees of separation, I'm introducing the Six Degrees of *Integration*: six steps or degree shifts in our behaviour patterns that will bring us closer to having a more diverse and integrated social circle. You will find these Six Degrees dotted throughout this book, and each one is a tool that will show you how to break free of prejudice and take action as you go on your journey towards diversity. They are:

[*] Milgram, 2004, p.117

- Challenge Your Ism
- Check Your Circle
- Connect with the Other
- Change Your Mind
- Celebrate Difference
- Champion the Cause

Human beings are notoriously creatures of habit, so change is of course difficult, but my goal in writing this book is to show how change for the willing might be made easier – and my hope is that in choosing to read this book you may indeed be one of the willing. So by undertaking the Six Degrees outlined, you will be changing your behaviour patterns bit by bit, edging ever closer to creating your own truly diverse circle. When this is true for the majority, then we will be able to change the way we think and the way we do things.

Diversify.org

Accompanying this book is www.Diversify.org – a revolutionary online space that opens up a world of possibilities for us to connect with the members of our human family who are living beyond our known horizons. www.Diversify.org is the next generation of social networking – *'emotional networking'* – and breaks the mould as we now experience it: networking that limits us to the people one degree away that we already know. We will use the Internet in the spirit in which it was created – to connect with the lives of others, to promote our own humanity. From our own doorsteps to the most distant horizon, together we can create the unity that eludes the conventional grind of politics and diplomacy. Together we can share. Share information. Share imagination. Share vision. Share a movement that unites us, thus making it that much better and fairer for us all.

As well as being an online community, this innovative multimedia platform will also act as a resource tool for many of the elements I refer to in this book, housing content such as the ISM Calculator, case studies, interviews, videos and campaigning tips.

Remember Anansi

Changing attitudes is not easy to do, and must come from within, but we can draw on inspiration in order to empower us to do this. As a result of my Ghanaian heritage, I have always been fascinated by mythology and the power that storytelling has to shape our image of ourselves and the world around us. Ghanaian culture is steeped in folklore and myths that have been passed down from generation to generation through an oral tradition, one of the most important being the tale of Anansi – or 'Kweku Anansi' as he is called in Ghana – the original Spider-Man! Anansi's story is itself a parable of self-belief and succeeding against the odds. It is a story of hope for anyone with an uphill climb to face between themselves and their dreams.

The story goes something like this: Anansi is a spider and the smallest of creatures, almost invisible to the naked eye. But he has the audacity to ask the Sky God, Nyan-Konpon, if he can buy all his stories. The Sky God is surprised to say the least. Even if Anansi could afford to buy his stories, what was a lowly spider going to do with these stories – the most valuable items in the animal kingdom?

I suppose Anansi took the view that if you don't ask you don't get, and what's the worst the Sky God could do? Say no? At the bottom of the animal kingdom, 'no' is a word Anansi is very much accustomed to.

Still confused, the Sky God asks Anansi: 'What makes you think you can buy them? Officials from great and powerful towns have come and they were unable to purchase them, and yet you, who are but a masterless man, you say you will be able to?' Anansi tells the Sky God that he knows other high-ranking officials have tried to get these stories and failed, but he believes that he can. He stands firm and challenges the Sky God to name his price. Now the Sky God is intrigued, but also slightly on the back foot. When you're a God you don't expect to be challenged by a spider, after all. So the Sky God sets Anansi the same 'impossible' challenge he set the others: to bring him a python, a leopard, a fairy and a hornet. (Yes, we do have fairies in Ghana, just like everywhere else.)

Anansi is not the strongest creature on earth, but he is the most resourceful – he has to be to survive, right? Otherwise he ends up down a plughole or flattened by a newspaper. By using his wit and cunning, Anansi manages to catch all of these creatures. This involves some elaborate hoaxes and traps, but true to his word Anansi delivers to the Sky God the animals, and in return the Sky God gives Anansi the stories. Stories that Anansi goes on to share with the whole of humanity, spreading wisdom throughout the world. From that day on, Anansi grows in stature above all other creatures.

This story is dear to me because it tells us that when you have equal opportunity coupled with purpose and self-belief, anything is indeed possible. Even though the Sky God did not believe Anansi could complete the task, he gave him the opportunity anyway – the same opportunity he had given the previous, seemingly worthier, candidates, who had each failed. Fortunately, Anansi believed in himself, and with a little help from the Universe, he achieved the impossible. It's this theory that I want to explore in more detail in this book – as well as how limiting beliefs about ourselves and each other prevent us all from achieving our full potential, and how society is robbed as a result. It's the equivalent of mining for treasure: we are standing in a vast, mineral-rich landscape, but deciding only to dig a small section of the Earth, and so we're missing out on all the gems the rest of the ignored land has to offer.

We have no template for a truly fair and equal society from any major civilization in recent history. In fact, we have to travel as far back as 7500BC to Çatalhöyük, a Neolithic settlement in southern Anatolia, Turkey, to see an example. Çatalhöyük is extraordinary for many reasons, not least its vast population (over 10,000 inhabitants), which makes it our first known 'town'. However, perhaps its most notable characteristic was its inhabitants' egalitarian ways and their lack of societal hierarchy. The town comprised an enclave of mud structures, all equal in size – there were no mansions or shacks. There was no concept of 'rich' or 'poor', no nobility or slaves, and no separate or lower castes of people. Men and women were considered equal with a balanced distribution of roles and participation in civic life.

Our so-called 'civilized' way of living would have us believe that a fair and inclusive society is wishful thinking – a naive or utopian idea. We are naturally programmed to follow the Darwinian theory of the survival of the fittest – a system that has only worked for a privileged few, caused social polarization and proved unsustainable. But as Çatalhöyük shows, this doesn't have to be the conclusion. Its exact model is perhaps unrealistic in a modern capitalist society, yet we *can* incorporate some of the philosophies of our ancient ancestors and make our communities much more inclusive. We have the chance to change gear and move towards a more meritocratic model – a thrilling and exciting destination.

The old way isn't working; the first country that gets this right will be a beacon to the world. The first economy that is efficient enough to capture the talents of all those available to contribute and utilize its greatest minds will produce a model that the rest of the world will be desperate to emulate.

My sincere hope is that the arguments, evidence, stories and tools in this book will help us to get there – to that Promised Land that Martin Luther King dreamed of. If we remember the story of Anansi, give each other equal opportunities, and believe in ourselves, we can achieve this seemingly impossible utopian ideal. Put simply, to make progress, we must diversify, transcend the six degrees of separation and move towards lives connected by six degrees of *integration*.

Because the world is separate enough.

PART ONE

THE OTHER MAN

'It is easier to build strong children than to repair broken men.'
Frederick Douglass

The Old Way

Making up slightly more than half of the world's population, women are probably the largest 'other' group – but it's the 'other' man that I want to discuss first.

If you genuinely want to identify and understand the 'other' man (and the fact that you have chosen to read this book gives me confidence that you do), he is not hard to find. The 'other' man is a diverse group found across the Western world in working-class communities, blue-collar jobs, and weekend football matches. These are the men I was raised by and raised with. They have been taught from a young age not to cry, not to be a sissy, and to stand up for themselves. They are more likely to have been celebrated by their peers and perhaps even their teachers for their physical prowess than their mental agility. This other man is black, Muslim, or white working class, and each group is the victim of their 'otherness' in a different way. But each will have been taught early on to understand the importance of a man being able to provide for himself and his family – and each will have encountered barriers in trying to achieve this.

Discrimination against men is important to address because of the impact it has on the rest of society. The exclusion of the 'other' man can often have violent and devastating consequences. This isn't always the case, obviously, but men have a different way of dealing with fear and frustration to women, as does each person to the next. Some of this is due to socialization, but some of it is pure biology. Leading neuroscientist Dr James Fallon explained to me that our genetics can result in striking differences in our response to stress, abuse, and rejection: 'People with "vulnerability" forms of genes are extremely impacted . . . while those with highly "protective" [genes] are remarkably resistant.' This suggests that some people are genetically more likely than others to develop damaging responses to environmental stressors, such as depression, PTSD, substance abuse, and personality disorders. And, says Dr Fallon, 'males often [have] poorer mood and personality outcomes than females'. So men are in fact more vulnerable to exclusion than women, and no man – no matter how much he may have been taught to suppress his emotions – is immune to its effect.

We've seen this in action throughout the UK and US in recent years. The failure of these societies to prevent the economic and social exclusion of their 'other' men has weakened and divided communities, and created a ticking time bomb that we must deactivate. It has caused feelings of inferiority and led to a fractured society. It has compromised social mobility and created artificial bubbles whereby the situation you are born into dictates your job and educational prospects. It has opened the doors to radical groups, and nurtured breeding grounds of extremism. In short, it has led to a lack of diversity, which then leads to a lack of empathy on both sides: cue demagogues fanning the flames of division for political ends.

For it has been the exclusion of the 'other' man with muscle where it still counts – at the ballot box – that has had the most profound implications. In the UK, the white working-class male vote delivered the shattering of Britain's 40-year union with Europe; in America, it brought the election of Donald Trump, a President with zero experience in public office and some unsavoury views and conduct. Whatever your opinion on either Brexit or Trump, 2016 provided the two most extreme examples in recent history of how a marginalized group can dictate the social and economic future of society.

And of course, politics aside, the exclusion of any 'other' man impacts more than just him. His family will share the impact of his pain – sometimes literally, if alcohol and low self-esteem are part of the toxic mix. This scenario played out within a family has a multi-generational impact, and can cost the state millions of pounds in welfare and social services professionals, called in to address family breakdown and deprivation. Failing to diversify and include all 'other' men is not something we can afford economically or socially. Quite simply, it will cost a lot less – financially, but also in pain and suffering – to expand opportunities to the 'other' man rather than continue to exclude him.

While preparing to write this book, I wrote to three such 'others': prisoners in the UK with strikingly similar stories; young men – one black, one Muslim, one white working class – who all once had dreams that turned into nightmares. You will find their letters in response to mine at www.Diversify.org. I read their personal accounts of how life had taken them on a path that led to prison, a powerful line from philosopher Susan Griffin's *A Chorus of Stones: The Private Life of War* kept running through my mind: '"There is a circle of humanity," he told me, "and I can feel its warmth. But I am forever outside."' And this 'circle of humanity' excluded for them behind bars, too: The Young Report of 2014 found that: 'Most of the prisoners, said that they experienced differential treatment as a result of their race, ethnicity or faith. Black prisoners felt that they were stereotyped as drug dealers and Muslim prisoners as terrorists.'

These three young men may not possess the tools to express themselves as eloquently as Griffin's subject, but their words of despair and hopelessness are no less powerful. They are men who, thanks to mass social media and globalization, knew what bounties the modern world had to offer, yet felt that they and their kind were not wanted, valued, or needed. Is it any wonder they ended up where they did?

CHAPTER ONE

Colour Is Only Skin Deep

'I refuse to allow any man-made differences to separate me from any other human beings.'

Maya Angelou

A black male child growing up in America or Europe will, by the time he reaches school, already have an understanding that he is different from the majority. Whether it's the images he sees in the media, or family members attempting to prepare him for the exclusion he's likely to experience outside the home, he will know that the rules are not the same for him and boys that look like him. In many cases, he will be told that anything is possible, but that he has to be twice as good and work twice as hard as his white counterparts in order to succeed and be worthy of acceptance. Many will take this message on board and strive for academic excellence in a pressured education system. Others, seeing black role models in sport, music, or some other art form, will pursue a career in that field, hoping that their talent (as has been the case with stars such as Jay-Z, Usain Bolt, Floyd Mayweather, Stormzy and Tinie Tempah) will enable them to overcome discrimination and other obstacles to success.

The men in my family experienced this first-hand. My father was gifted and well educated as a child and rose to become somebody of stature in his native Ghana, but when he arrived in Britain as an immigrant in the 1980s he had to start afresh. A political coup in Ghana meant that he had lost his position and his finances. He still had his education and experience, though, which surely would be enough for him to make a new life for himself and his family? Unfortunately not. In 1980s Britain, his thick foreign accent and skin colour meant he was visibly and audibly different from what employers assumed was right for a job in banking. There was an unwritten understanding that non-white migrants from commonwealth countries could settle in the UK to do menial or low-paid jobs that indigenous people didn't want to do. Immigrants like my father, regardless of education and career experience, were not going to be allowed to just parachute into middle-class occupations like banking.

It soon became clear to my father that Britain was not going to be the land of opportunity he had first hoped, so he decided to take his talents and my brother to America. America did provide more opportunities, and Dad was able to secure a job in banking and then eventually launch his own successful real-estate and construction company. Perhaps America, despite its poorer record on race relations, was more amenable than the UK to the idea of social mobility for an African man.

Starting again for the second time in America was not easy, but Sam Sarpong Sr thrived against insurmountable odds and built a very comfortable upper-middle-class life, and I can't help but beam with pride when I look at the journey he has made. A few years ago I made a pilgrimage to the rural village he was raised in, and I couldn't fully comprehend the vast leap from where my father started in life to where he now resides. I doubt I would have had the same level of grit and strength to overcome such odds.

Life wasn't all smooth sailing for my brother, Sam Sarpong Jr, either. African in parentage, British by birth, and raised in America – as you can imagine, he didn't fit neatly into any particular category. As an actor/entertainer, my brother shared the desire for the visible signs of affluence – luxury cars, designer clothes, and beautiful women.

However, as flamboyant as he was, during one of my visits to America I saw my brother become humble pretty fast. Driving through LA in one such luxury car, Sam was pulled over by the police. This being a regular occurrence for black men in America, Sam had his contrite responses memorized: 'Yes sir, no sir, sorry officer,' etc.

Witnessing this exchange and knowing the type of person Sam was, I felt upset and indignant – especially as he had done nothing wrong and there appeared to be no valid reason for the stop. My friend and mentor Baroness Margaret McDonagh – white and well spoken – was also with us in the car. As Sam delivered his usual routine, Margaret and I weren't so agreeable, as this is not something either of us are accustomed to. We demanded the officer's badge number and a detailed explanation as to why we were stopped. The police officer seemed taken aback, as he hadn't expected to be met by two British women, and his tone changed immediately to become less threatening and more like a public servant. We received the badge number but no valid reason for why we were pulled over.

With US police officers being fully armed, black men in the US have to humble themselves to an almost humiliating degree to ensure their survival each time they encounter law enforcement. Regardless of the outcome of these exchanges, they serve as an overt reminder to all young black men that, whatever your achievements, aspirations, or character, you can be brought down to the level of a criminal at any time. Male pride makes this a difficult reality to live with and can generate anger in the most excluded and vulnerable black men. However, anger and resentment at authority are costly emotions that black men can ill afford in Western society. In both the UK and the US, it's an uncomfortable truth that in spite of claims of equality and calls for fair treatment, young black men continue to be targeted for no other reason than the colour of their skin.

These stories show just how difficult it is for black men – even those of education and affluence – to negotiate life in the UK and US as an 'other'. Their colour is always the first thing people see. But where did this obsession with race and skin colour come from? And why have we allowed it to become such a divisive and alienating factor in our society? These are fundamental questions that scientists may now be able to answer for us. And perhaps, by answering them, we can tear them down.

The false social construct of race

Anthropologist Nina Jablonski has conducted extensive studies into this issue from her research lab at Pennsylvania State University. I've been lucky enough to spend time with Jablonski and listen to her speak about the origins of the social construct of race, and her findings are fascinating. In her book, *Living Color: The Biological and Social Meaning of Skin Color*,[*] Jablonski investigates 'the social history of skin color from prehistory to the present' and finds that, biologically, 'race' simply does not exist. In a separate article she states, 'Despite ever more genetic evidence confirming the nonexistence of races, beliefs in the inherent superiority and inferiority of people remain part of the modern world,'[†] and she goes on to explain that the most influential ideas on the formation of historic racism came from just one man:

> *The philosopher Immanuel Kant (1724–1804) was the first person to classify people into fixed races according to skin color. To him and his followers, skin color was equated with character. People of darker-colored races were inferior and destined to serve those of lighter-colored races. Kant's ideas about color, race, and character achieved wide and lasting acceptance because his writings were widely circulated, his reputation good, and his audience naïve. The 'color meme' was born. The linking of blackness with otherness and inferiority was one of the most powerful and destructive intellectual constructs of all time. Views on the inherent superiority and*

---

* http://www.ucpress.edu/book.php?isbn=9780520283862
† 'Why racism doesn't go away' by Nina Jablonski for the DNA Summit magazine

> *inferiority of races were readily embraced by the intelligentsia of Western Europe and eventually by the general populace because they supported existing stereotypes.*[*]

It's hard to overstate the damage this kind of thinking has done over the centuries.

Geneticist Spencer Wells, founder of The Genographic Project and author of *The Journey of Man*,[†] goes even deeper, using the science of DNA to tell a similar story to Jablonski – that 'we are all one people'.[‡] By analysing DNA from people in all corners of the world, Wells and his team discovered that all humans alive today are descended from a single man (Y-chromosomal Adam), who lived in Africa around 60,000–90,000 years ago, and from a single woman (mitochondrial Eve), who lived in Africa approximately 150,000 years ago.[§] (It's a quirk of our genetic evolution that our two most common recent ancestors did not have to live at the same time.)

Due to this common ancestry, the human genetic code, or genome, is 99.9 per cent identical, which suggests that the 0.1 per cent remainder that is responsible for our individual physical differences – skin colour, eye colour, hair colour and texture, etc – has primarily been caused by environmental factors. Like Jablonski, Wells believes our early ancestors embarked on their first epic journey out of Africa in search of food, which led them to gradually scatter across the Earth. Wells explains that the physical appearance of these early travellers changed depending on which part of the world they migrated to. Those who ended up in Europe – in the northern hemisphere – received less sunlight, so their bodies did not need to produce as much melanin (a natural-forming skin pigment that protects from the sun's ultraviolet rays), and so they developed lighter skin and

---

[*] 'Why racism doesn't go away' by Nina Jablonski for the *DNA Summit* magazine
[†] https://www.amazon.co.uk/Journey-Man-Genetic-Odyssey/dp/0141008326
[‡] 'Why racism doesn't go away' by Nina Jablonski for the *DNA Summit* magazine
[§] http://ngm.nationalgeographic.com/2006/03/human-journey/shreeve-text/2

straighter hair to match their new cold conditions. The same is true for other communities around the world whose appearance adapted to match their new environment. And so our physical differences – once just mutations of survival – became embedded in our DNA, to be passed down through the generations for millennia.

Wells's deep understanding of human DNA has also influenced his views on humanity and the false social construct of race. In an interview with the UK's *Independent* newspaper, he commented: 'It's worth getting the message out, that we are related to one another, that we are much more closely related genetically than people may suspect from glancing around and looking at these surface features that distinguish us . . . Race, in terms of deep-seated biological differences, doesn't exist scientifically.'

Many of us have instinctively felt and argued for a long time that the concept of 'race' is a misleading human construct used to divide us, but it's reassuring to now have the science to back this up. If more of us understood the epic voyage that our early ancestors embarked upon, which led to the rich diversity we see around us today, perhaps we wouldn't be so fixated on race. Indeed, we really are all one, and that oneness began in Africa.

The daily reality

Sadly, this understanding hasn't yet reached everyone. Even when young black men play by the 'rules' today, some find that many of the people they come across are still unable to see their academic and career achievements, but have less difficulty seeing their skin colour. Regardless of their personal journey, young black men learn to take the stop-and-searches in their stride (after all, it's nothing new), as long as it results in their walking away without being too delayed (or physically wounded, as we've seen in the US with the rise of police brutality). At work, he is frustrated with his lack of progress in relation to his contribution, although he is careful in office environments to mask his feelings for fear of being viewed as 'angry', 'threatening', or potentially violent. And he may have qualifications but is unable to get a foothold in the sector he has trained for, or has been given an opportunity and is expected to feel grateful while he remains at entry level and is surpassed by other colleagues, some of whom may be less qualified.

This is the reality for young black men, although it's fair to say that being prepared for the possibility of rejection on account of your colour from an early age does foster determination and can lead to success, as it forces one to develop astounding levels of resilience. Like diamonds, this pressurized environment can produce spectacular gems, such as Frederick Douglass, Martin Luther King, Muhammad Ali, Colin Powell, Barack Obama, Kofi Annan, Sir David Adjaye, Ozwald Boateng OBE and many of the great men of colour who have helped shape our world for the better. However, it can also cause deep-rooted feelings of inferiority and inadequacy. The sense of never fully being accepted doesn't go away, especially as it is reinforced daily, which continuously erodes a sense of belonging and self-worth.

For some black men, this can result in the rejection of education and the world of work, and the pursuit of validation from a subculture where material possessions are valued above those things deemed further out of reach, such as employment and schooling. This route can indeed bring more immediate rewards than academia and employment, where rejection will already have been experienced, but it stands in the way of true social mobility.

Young males in poorer black communities can also fall prey to the trappings of a prescribed form of masculinity that thrives in these subcultures: one in which using violence to defend your reputation is seen as acceptable and sometimes necessary. Men in these environments – gangs, particularly – are often considered weak by their peers if they fail to defend their honour or respond to a slight, the consequences of which can be disastrous. Ironically, the ability to reason oneself out of conflict or to avoid it altogether would be applauded outside of the subculture, but is often seen within the community as cowardice. And the rewards within the subculture – respect, and attractiveness to women – are hard to refuse, especially if escaping the subculture is not seen as a possibility, which makes it pretty difficult to bring about a change in behaviour.

The revolving door

For many black men, this route leads to only one destination: in America especially there is a revolving door from the classroom to the prison cell. Mass incarceration has reached epic proportions, with one in three black men imprisoned at some point during their lives.[*] This has big implications for their futures; the ramifications of a criminal record can be catastrophic for employment prospects and, once the step along the criminal justice path has been taken, it's near impossible to turn back.

When it comes to the American criminal justice system, the odds are stacked against you if you are black. A 2016 report by The National Registry of Exonerations found that 47% of all wrongful convictions involved black defendants. The figures for serious crimes such as murder show that black defendants account for 40% of those convicted, but 50% of those *wrongfully* convicted (in comparison to whites, who account for 36 percent of those wrongfully convicted for murder). It's a similar picture with sexual assault: 59% of all exonerees were black defendants, compared with 34% for white defendants[†].

As well as falling victim to police brutality disproportionately, US blacks are also more likely to be victims of police misconduct, such as 'hiding evidence, tampering with witnesses or perjury'. This may also have contributed to the aforementioned racial disparity; the report concluded that black defendants accounted for 76% of wrongful murder

---

[*] Report of The Sentencing Project to the United Nations Human Rights Committee: Regarding Racial Disparities in the United States Criminal Justice. Published August 2013

[†] http://www.law.umich.edu/special/exoneration/Pages/about.aspx

convictions where police misconduct was involved, in comparison to 63% of white exonerees[*].

50%: the percentage by which US prison populations would decline if African Americans and Hispanics were incarcerated in the same proportion as white people.[†]

Ava DuVernay's powerful BAFTA-winning Netflix documentary *13th* chronicles how the abolition of slavery and the subsequent exploitation of the 13th Amendment, which deemed it unconstitutional to hold a person as a slave, have led to more black men being locked up now than there ever were during slavery. On the surface, the 13th Amendment seemed honourable and straightforward enough. But there was a loophole that excluded 'criminals', and so began the hyper-criminalization of the black male as a means of maintaining the free labour that had been so easily available during the years of slavery. Fast forward to today, and this loophole has morphed to fit the times: from the Jim Crow laws of segregation, to mandatory sentencing and Nixon's 'war on drugs', Reagan's 'war on crime', and, more recently, Clinton's 'Three-Strikes Law'; 150 years of systematic discriminatory policy-making has led us to the black male mass-incarceration epidemic in the US today.

American lawyer and founder of the Equal Justice Initiative Bryan Stevenson has spent the best part of three decades fighting to highlight the plight of those caught in the crosshairs of the US criminal justice system, and he argues that at the crux of the problem is how we treat the marginalized and dispossessed:

Proximity has taught me some basic and humbling truths, including this vital lesson: each of us is more than the worst thing we've ever

[*] *New York Times*: www.nytimes.com/2017/03/07/us/wrongful-convictions-race-exoneration.html?mcubz=3
[†] According to the report, Unlocking America

done. My work with the poor and the incarcerated has persuaded me that the opposite of poverty is not wealth; the opposite of poverty is justice. Finally, I've come to believe that the true measure of our commitment to justice, the character of our society, our commitment to the rule of law, fairness, and equality cannot be measured by how we treat the rich, the powerful, the privileged, and the respected among us. The true measure of our character is how we treat the poor, the disfavoured, the accused, the incarcerated, and the condemned.[*]

Stevenson also states that the criminal justice system unfairly favours those who are 'rich and guilty' over those who are 'poor and innocent' – after all, the poor can't afford a good defence lawyer. It seems prison-for-profit is a very lucrative business, and is now a booming industry – it pays to send people to prison. One of the final acts of the Obama administration was to issue a memo to bring an end to the Justice Department's reliance on private prisons (which now account for approximately 18 per cent of US federal prisons – a figure that is steadily increasing). The memo, issued by former Deputy Attorney General Sally Yates, cited more 'safety and security incidents' in private prisons than public ones as the reason for this change in policy. Unfortunately, a month after Trump took the Oval Office his Attorney General, Jeff Sessions, rescinded this and announced a reinstatement of private prisons.

This, coupled with the fact that a whopping 90–95 per cent of prisoners accept a plea bargain and never go to trial,[†] has created a system where poor people of colour are disproportionately incarcerated. This is not only ethically wrong, but also in the long term it is economically insane. To discard one-third of all black males when they are in their prime and most able to contribute to society is a cataclysmic dent in the moral, social, and economic fabric of America.

[*] *Just Mercy* by Bryan Stevenson (Random House, 2015)
[†] Bureau of Justice Assistance – US Department of Justice, Research Summary: Plea and Charge Bargaining

Yes, we can!

Clearly, this is by no means the story of every black male. The majority will play by rules that are stacked against them and will seek inclusion, complete their education, and make sacrifices in order to achieve this by going the extra mile, conforming to a mainstream culture, and focusing on presenting an acceptable and 'unthreatening' outward appearance, harbouring dreams that this will help people to focus on the content of their character as opposed to their colour.

Having lived in America for eight years, I consider it my second home – and a paradox. In one country, we see dreams and aspirations realised that would be impossible anywhere else. But we also see that the fear and division present at the birth of the nation remains.

For me, the election of the first African American president was a watershed in American and global history akin to the election of Nelson Mandela. I count myself privileged to have played a small civic part in the Obama election campaign, canvassing on the eve of the election in Virginia – a deep red Republican state that had not been blue since Lyndon B Johnson's (LBJ) victory in 1964. And even though LBJ won the state back then, many white residents in Virginia were against his landmark civil rights legislation and had wanted to keep segregation after that point. Virginia would never again be a true-blue state. Or so it seemed.

I had flown out to Virginia with my friends, Labour party strategists Margaret McDonagh and Anji Hunter. At campaign headquarters, I was struck by an elderly white gentleman whose face was badly bruised. Feeling concerned, I walked over to check if he was okay and asked how he had injured himself. With a voice full of emotion, this southern gentleman revealed to me that he was in his nineties and owned a farm that had been in his family for generations. He had fallen over a few days before and had hurt his face on a rake. But, against doctor's orders, he was determined to come and support the Obama campaign efforts.

He explained to me how, as a young man, he had been an ardent segregationist and saw this as a route to some sort of redemption. He never thought he would live to see an African American President, but felt he needed to actively support Obama in order to right some of the wrong doings of his past. After speaking to this gentleman, I felt something momentous was about to happen. That evening, Margaret and I attended the final Obama rally in Virginia. It was a cool, crisp night and the atmosphere was electric as we all sensed history was about to be made.

The then Senator Obama had just lost his grandmother, who had died that day in Hawaii, so he was flown in by helicopter to the rally. There wasn't a dry eye in the house as he paid homage to his grandmother, Toot, and the vital role she played in helping to shape him as a man. He went on to explain the origins of his campaign slogan, 'Fired Up & Ready To Go', which we all were as we left this poignantly magical evening.

The next day, Margaret, Anji and I watched the election results at the home of legendary Democratic pollster and close Clinton confidant Stan Greenberg. His DC townhouse was heaving with guests, many of whom were close allies of the Clintons.

Everyone was jubilant as the results started coming in and it began looking like victory was on the horizon. Once Ohio was called, we knew it was game over. Everyone began cheering – then, we all sat in silence as we watched the footage of the victorious Obamas and Bidens take the stage in Grant Park Chicago, with Oprah and Jesse Jackson shedding tears of joy in the crowd.

As Anji, Margaret and I left Stan Greenberg's house, we were met with cheering and dancing in the streets of DC. Cars were beeping their horns, Obama 2008 signs were everywhere, and a joyful crowd was roaring 'Yes We Can'. The atmosphere was like the homecoming of a winning Superbowl team x10. America was proud of itself because, in that moment, it had chosen to look beyond its complex issues with race and chosen 'change' and 'hope' over the status quo. In doing so, they had done something that, in all likelihood, no other Western country would have been capable of at the time. This is the dream personified by the Obama presidency, which has been both an inspiration and a post-racial challenge to young black males everywhere. If Obama can do it, why can't you?

In the UK, this is certainly easier said than done. A recent study conducted as part of a BBC documentary hosted by British actor David Harewood examined the probability of the UK ever having a black prime minister. Using empirical evidence to project how likely it would be for male children from different backgrounds to make it to the nation's highest electoral office, the findings were shocking, to say the least. Statistically, a black child born in the UK has a 1 in 14 million chance of becoming prime minister, while a white child has a 1 in 1.4 million chance, and a white child with a public school (not state-funded) education and a degree from Oxford University has a 1 in 200,000 chance.* What this effectively means is that we are severely restricting the talent pool for political leadership, and rebirthing the same ideas and thought patterns again and again.

This presents numerous issues, perhaps the most concerning being that by completely excluding 'other' talent pools from the decision-making process, the changes that many of us seek become even more unlikely. With few exceptions, it seems that whichever side of the political aisle they sit on, most of the leaders available to us have all trodden the same path and share a similar worldview. It seems pretty clear that in order for there to be sustainable change, the people leading us need to change, too. But in order for this to happen, the education and employment opportunities for young black men need to be firmly put in place, as well as an atmosphere of real, attainable aspiration – in contrast to what, currently, is often an atmosphere of poverty and lack of opportunity.

Twice as likely: the Pew Research Center in the US finds that African Americans are twice as likely to be in poverty as white people.

* http://www.bbc.co.uk/news/magazine-37799305

Because in reality, regardless of the data suggesting that the odds are heavily stacked against black men becoming president or prime minister, the truth is that most don't want to anyway. The dreams and aspirations of black males are no different to the dreams and aspirations of men in general – the difference is that many will have a shortage of realistic role models in the media or within their own families, who successfully do what is 'expected' of a man (i.e. support himself and his family), are supported by the education system, and are able to work hard, attain the right training or qualifications, prove the right to 'belong', and be rewarded accordingly. For the ambitious, hard-working black male, this unlevel playing field can be extremely demoralizing. He must ask himself: am I the problem? Is it my colour, or am I simply not good enough? Is he one of those men with a chip on their shoulder, imagining prejudice?

Nina Jablonski believes that a new form of education and honest dialogue is needed to turn back this tide of hundreds of years of misunderstanding and mistrust, and I wholeheartedly agree. She argues that endemic racism is holding back not just black people, but the whole of society:

> *Erroneous and deep-seated notions about race persist because we are scared to discuss misconceptions about colour and race in our classrooms and boardrooms. Paranoia about race born of political correctness has led to the perpetuation of misconceptions about colour and race, the cloaking of discriminatory behaviour and language, and the persistence of racism. Racism is probably humanity's single biggest impediment to human achievement.**

Racism is an ancient problem and, thankfully, society has moved on in the last century. We now have anti-discrimination policies and

---

* *Living Color: The Biological and Social Meaning of Skin Color* by Nina Jablonski, University of California Press, 2012 legislation in place, and yet clearly these are not doing enough. The stats prove that a young black man still rarely sees himself reflected in any positions of seniority. He can only hope that things will be better for his son – a hope he believes in as things are certainly better for him than they were for his father. But hope may not be enough. Nina Jablonski is not alone in demanding real, tangible change. 'Race at the Top', a comprehensive study by Race for Opportunity on black, Asian and minority ethnic (BAME) representation in leadership in UK business, concluded that there had been virtually no ethnicity change in top management positions in British business in the five years between 2007 and 2012.* In a letter to the British government, Sandra Kerr – the CEO of Race for Opportunity – urged them to deal with this problem as a matter of urgency before it was too late:

> *By 2051, one in five people in the UK will be from an ethnic minority background, representing a scale of consumer spending and political voting power that business and government alike cannot afford to ignore. The gap must not be allowed to widen further, but without action little will change. I am calling on government for a review to amplify understanding around the barriers BAME employees face in reaching management positions, and for two simple words – 'and race' – to be added to the UK Corporate Governance Code. We urgently need this to happen if we are to ensure that we don't pass the point of no return.†*

---

* 'Race At The Top' 2014 – study by Race for Opportunity, part of the (BITC) Business in the Community: http://race.bitc.org.uk/all-resources/research-articles/race-top
† 'Race At The Top' 2014 – study by Race for Opportunity, part of the (BITC) Business in the Community: http://race.bitc.org.uk/all-resources/research-articles/race-top

94.5%: the percentage of police officers in England and Wales who are white[*].

If governments heed such stark warnings, if we can undo the centuries of false racial programming and teach our children the scientific truth of our common ancestry and foster a wealth of role models for young black men at home and in the media, then maybe, just maybe, the achievements of men like Barack Obama can become the standard, rather than the exception to the rule.

ACTION POINT: Watch Ava DuVernay's documentary, *13th*
DISCUSSION POINT: Should positive discrimination be employed to ensure ethnic minorities are represented proportionally in the police service and justice system?

---

[*] *Guardian*, October 2015 https://www.theguardian.com/commentisfree/2015/oct/05/racist-racism-racially-white-ethnic-minorities

CHAPTER TWO

Brown Is the New Black

'Conquering others shows strength, but conquering one's self shows true power.'

Lao Tzu, *Tao Te Ching*

If the Obama presidency has been the modern defining global event for aspiring black males, then terrorism has been the defining dictate of the Western view of 'other' Muslim men. It has arguably led to Muslim men overtaking black men as primary figures of fear: 'brown' has become the new 'black'. This group is the most diverse of the 'other' male groups, covering a wide variety of ethnicities, national-ities, and socioeconomic groups, with Islam being the world's second biggest faith. However, in the modern collective Western psyche there are only really two kinds of Muslim men: those who will harm us, and those who probably won't. And nobody seems to know the difference.

Integrate or separate?

Though the religion's main presence has been in the Middle East, Islam has had a longstanding presence in the West, predominantly in mainland Europe, where rulers and warlords of Muslim faith ruled over Christian populations before extending to parts of Asia and Africa. This led to periods of Holy Wars in the medieval era, as well as phases of coexistence between Muslim and Christian populations. Fast forward to the twentieth century – post Second World War – and we have Muslims migrating from Africa and Asia to Christian America and to Christian/secular Europe.

Muslims, for the most part, hail from countries that were less dominated by the West. So, unlike most colonized communities, Muslims were able to keep their language, faith, and customs rather than adopting European equivalents. This is something they were also able to maintain during modern migration, still retaining their faith in predominantly Christian and secular societies. Many also chose to retain the language and style of dress of their country of origin, protecting, in theory, a clear cultural identity and sense of belonging. So we have a scenario in which the British Muslim male child finds himself in a Western society where he is visibly different, sometimes in dress as well as beliefs and complexion, and with a family at home who often wish to retain many aspects of their original culture. As is the case with most immigrant communities, Muslim families wish their young men to gain acceptance and develop the ability to pursue success and support a family of their own. To this end, many young Muslim men will study diligently and embark upon a career path and seek the same respect, recognition, and acceptance that we all strive for.

For some it's not acceptance at any cost, however, and as we've seen with black men, when 'other' men feel excluded by the main culture, they form a subculture. British Muslim communities tend to be close-knit, and they have a strong economic presence, especially in London, that provides a back-up option for those who may fall outside the confines of wider society.[*] So the question for these young

---

[*] 'Muslims add over £31 billion to UK economy', The Huffington Post, 2013: http://www.huffingtonpost.co.uk/2013/10/29/uk-muslims-economy_n_4170781.html

British Muslim men is in fact not so dissimilar to the one the British people have recently faced in their relationship to their European neighbours: integrate or separate?

15%: the proportion of Muslim prisoners in 2015 (up from 8% in 2002)*.

Let's be clear: the vast majority of Muslim men have chosen integration, while still proudly retaining their Muslim identity. There is not a one-size-fits-all approach, and nor should there be. Keith Ellison, Mahershala Ali, Aziz Ansari, Hasan Minhaj, and Reza Aslan in the US, Zayn Malik, Rageh Omaar, Mo Farah, Sajid Javid, Riz Ahmed, Adil Ray, and London's mayor Sadiq Khan in the UK are all examples of Muslim men who have made a contribution and commitment to their respective countries, while celebrating their Muslim identity.

However, on 11 September 2001 the question of the integration of Muslim men suddenly became acutely urgent. If you happened to be a Muslim man – indigenous or otherwise – failing to display visible signs of integration into Western society, you immediately became an object of suspicion and fear. In fact, you didn't necessarily have to be Muslim – just of a light brown complexion and rushing to work, as in the tragic case of Jean Charles de Menezes, who, on 22 July 2005 (two weeks after the London 7/7 bombings), was mistakenly identified as a potential suicide bomber and shot dead by a team of armed police at Stockwell Tube Station in London. We have reached a point where society has demonized these people in the worst possible way, assuming Muslim men are a threat to our lives and the lives of others.

The backlash against Muslims following the rise of terrorist incidents by Muslim men born in Western countries has been phenomenal,

---

* Official UK Prison Population Statistics, researchbriefings.files.parliament.uk/documents/SN04334/SN04334.pdf

and is probably the greatest challenge to date to our Western model of secular multiculturalism. In response, both Muslim communities and the Western societies they are part of have become vulnerable to extremist views from each side of the argument. The rise of populism has destabilized the political and liberal centre ground in many Western countries, and Muslim men across the socioeconomic groups find themselves on the fault line. For all our sakes we must face the epic twofold challenge in front of us: to tackle the root causes that lead Muslim men to become radicalized in the first place, and to quash the Islamophobia that has reared its ugly head in response.

Five times: the amount more media coverage a terrorist incident receives if the perpetrator is Muslim.*

The route to radicalization

We know that poverty, lack of employment opportunities, and alienation from wider Western society offer a more direct route to radicalization. When disenfranchised young Muslim men, who do not identify with their parents' interpretation of their faith or with mainstream Islam, can opt for a political extremist interpretation, which resonates with their anger over Western foreign policy towards Muslims around the world, everyone is at risk – especially the young men themselves. Our lack of diversity has a lot to answer for.

However, poverty and lack of opportunity is not the only route to radicalization, as well-educated and relatively affluent Muslim men have also embraced and acted on extremist views. This is difficult for liberals and centrists in the secular West to reconcile. How can Muslim men who have been afforded the opportunity to be part of

* Muslims carried out just 12.4 per cent of attacks in the US but received 41.4 per cent of news coverage – *Independent* http://www.independent.co.uk/news/world-0/terror-attacks-media-coverage-muslim-islamist-white-racism-islamophobia-study-georgia-state-a7820726.html

Western society and been rewarded for their contribution opt to actively work towards the destruction of that society? Indeed, the destruction of their neighbours, colleagues, and fellow citizens who, you would assume, are also friends and acquaintances? You'd think that religious freedom, democracy, and the opportunity to achieve prosperity is a pretty good deal. We've covered all the bases, right? All the things that should matter to them? What are we supposed to do?

Sadly, it's never that simple. Growing up in East London, I witnessed the insidious creep of radicalization and its divisive effects first-hand. I had friends at college who I suspect became radicalized before I even knew what that meant. They became estranged from their friends, were told they needed to separate themselves from 'infidels' in order to get closer to God. Their style of dress and patterns of behaviour changed, and they became strangers, while we became 'others' to them. These were young men we had all previously socialized with and considered friends. Our teachers had no idea how to reach out to them, and neither did we. But we shrugged our shoulders and continued on our life journeys, as it's only natural that some friends will drop off as we progress from adolescence to adulthood. So what if those who 'dropped off' happened to be disenfranchised Muslims with an underlying resentment of Western foreign policy? Who cares?

Well, Londoners did on 7 July 2005 when our citizens were killed and maimed by fellow citizens, for whom Britain was their home but no longer where their hearts resided. I would later discover that two of the bombing suspects had attended a mosque not far from where I grew up.

Twelve years later, London and its global visitors would face the same horror again, but the Westminster terror attack on 22 March 2017 forced us to rethink our assumptions of those most likely to do us harm. We'd always thought young Muslim men were the danger – radicalized, impulsive, and with not too much to lose – but this time the perpetrator was not a young man and neither was he born a Muslim. He was a 52-year-old mixed-race male born Adrian Elms, and was a late convert to Islam. Having previously been imprisoned at Her Majesty's pleasure several times for violent attacks, he drove a car into pedestrians on Westminster Bridge and went on to stab Police Constable Keith Palmer, killing four people in total.

This atrocity, as well as the murder of MP Jo Cox in June 2016 by 52-year-old far-right extremist Thomas Mair, and the Finsbury Park attack on 19 June 2017, perpetrated by 47-year-old Darren Osborne – both middle-aged, non-Muslim men – have proved that radicalization in all its forms – be it Islamism, far-right extremism, or Islamophobia – is equally dangerous and that the profile of a 'terrorist' is far broader than we thought. It seems some men do not grow out of violence but rather into it, and isolation and exclusion from society leaves them and us vulnerable to the impact of the indiscriminate violence of terrorism.

The multifaceted threat we all now face, not just from terrorism but from extremist responses to it, became disturbingly apparent just two months after the Westminster attack, when the city of Manchester fell victim to perhaps the most heinous of terror attacks so far; this time the target was children – mainly young girls attending the concert of pop sensation Ariana Grande. The devastation resulted in 22 fatalities and 59 injured. And to make matters worse, following the Manchester atrocity there was a reported 500 per cent surge in Islamophobic attacks in Greater Manchester. This is something we must denounce with all our might. We have to stand up for compassion and the rule of law, even when it is hardest to do in the face of hostility – in fact, this is when it's most important. Less than two weeks after the Manchester attack, London was hit again, this time on London Bridge and in nearby Borough Market, where people were enjoying a night out in cafés and restaurants. The attack lasted just eight minutes, thanks to the brave and speedy acts of the police, but in that short space of time, three young Muslim men armed with knives were able to murder eight innocent victims – from Britain, Australia, France, Canada, and Spain – and injure an additional 48. And again, the police reported a 40 per cent increase in Islamophobic attacks immediately afterwards. London still stands as the multicultural jewel in the United Kingdom's crown – but the threat to our unity remains.

This is where we must consider the devastating effects of a lack of diversity not only on the minority who are excluded, but also on wider society. And of course the problem is not unique to the UK and US. In recent years Europe has also experienced numerous horrific incidents of Islamist terrorism that have left the world stunned and citizens traumatized. The civil wars in Iraq and Syria have been used by purveyors of a fundamentalist interpretation of Islam to attract young European Muslim men and women to travel to these war-torn regions, and this in turn creates a challenge for the authorities: what to do with returning citizens who may pose a terrorist threat following weapons training and potential involvement in atrocities? Some suggestions I've heard here in the UK have been that we should remove passports, revoke citizenship from dual nationals, or imprison without trial. I understand the desire and the need in some cases for harsh measures. But these are short-term responses when what we need is a long-term solution: prevention. We must explore other options, since marginalizing these men and allowing them to be 'other' exposes them to the very extremism that many would not turn to if fully accepted and supported by society.

The route to integration

So what can we do to tackle this proliferation of radicalization? How about the tough love approach? What about banning burkas and burkinis (French proposals) and enforced English language tests for Muslim mothers (a British proposal advocated by David Cameron)? Oh wait, all those proposed measures, supposedly aimed at dealing with the threat of extremist Muslim men, target Muslim women instead – how unfortunate. How about a 'Muslim travel ban', as ordered by the Trump administration in early 2017? Well, according to UK Home Secretary Amber Rudd, this gave ISIS a 'propaganda opportunity' – and the evidence suggests that the more we isolate or alienate a particular group, the more vulnerable to extremism they are. Again, all these measures are short-term and short-sighted, and motivated as they are by Islamophobia and prejudice, they relegate all Muslim men to the category of 'other'.

We have allowed this fear to prevent us from applying the one thing we haven't yet tried: diversity, inclusion, and tolerance – allowing these men to truly belong. Surely, to transform the minds of these radicalized young men we must create a powerful and undeniable counter-narrative to extremism? Believe it or not, some political decisions can be guided by compassion and love as much as self-interest, even though we shy away from this in the face of right-wing pressure. This is where we offer something the extremists can't.

A brilliant initiative that shows how this can be done is currently underway in Denmark. After Britain, Denmark has the second largest number of its citizens fighting in Syria, and Steffen Nielsen – a crime prevention adviser in the country – is trying a fresh approach to reach out to them. He has helped develop an innovative rehabilitation programme for young radicalized Danish Muslims, offering them a second chance and the opportunity to be reintegrated back into Danish society. The programme runs in collaboration with welfare services and police in Aarhus, Denmark's second largest city. Ex-radicals are offered intense therapy and psychological treatment, mentors, and assistance with rebuilding their lives by finding work or accessing further education. The programme also provides support for their families.

Nielsen is the first to admit that the programme is still 'trial and error'. However, he is committed to this rehabilitative approach, even though not all of the political class in Denmark approve. 'We are experiencing more political pressure to do something more like the British stuff,' said Nielsen – revoking British passports, etc. 'The entire political debate is rife with simplifications. You can choose to shut them out and say, "Okay, you chose to be a jihadist, we can't use you any more." Or you can take the inclusive way and say, "Okay, there is always a door if you want to be a contributing member to society." Not because we are nice people, but because we think that is what works.'*

It's an important point. The problem is far too complex to try only one approach, and we cannot assume there is no way back for those young European citizens who feel disenfranchised and have chosen hatred as a means of finding purpose and meaning. Men who perpetrate violence are, after all, themselves victims of their own violence, whether they die by their own actions – flying a plane of innocent people into a building or detonating a suicide bomb – or are killed or imprisoned by the authorities.

Prominent anti-extremist campaigner and LBC presenter Maajid Nawaz, a former jihadist himself, has clear views on what needs to be done and believes it's a process we all need to participate in: 'The only way we can challenge Islamism,' he says, 'is to engage with one another. We need to make it as abhorrent as racism has become today. Only then will we stem the tide of angry young Muslims who turn to hate.'

Maajid is not alone. British Muslim businessman Iqbal Wahhab, has put this idea into practice and made it his personal mission to help rehabilitate disenfranchised men by giving them work and responsibility. Through his thriving restaurant Roast (which coincidentally is based in Borough Market, the second location of the London Bridge attack), Iqbal hires ex-offenders and helps train them for a career in the food industry. You can read about one of his most

---

* From an interview on Channel 4 News: https://www.channel4.com/news/can-returning-jihadis-be-reintegrated-into-society

heartening success stories, Mohammed, a young Muslim who now manages a chain of busy cafés, at www.Diversify.org. It's a clear example of the key role the business community can play in helping to steer at-risk men onto a productive path.

It's ironic that the day after the Westminster attack we buried former IRA commander and Deputy First Minister of Northern Ireland Martin McGuinness – initially a man of violence and a former terrorist who then became a statesman and a man of peace. It took many years to end the violence in Northern Ireland, precisely because we weren't prepared to examine and address the causes of it. I recognize that reaching out to men of violence is never easy or palatable, but violence comes from vulnerability and the inability to achieve aims by other means, so we need to recognize this in potential perpetrators and work with them to achieve much more benign aims, so that we're not all left to deal with the tragic aftermath of their frustrations.

Of course, when faced with destructive acts of terror, there is an understandable urge to err on the side of enforcement. Those involved in such heinous crimes obviously must be severely prosecuted – but we cannot ignore that there is also a contingent who have lost their way and have not yet reached the point of no return. These young men are British citizens. So what do we do with them? This is the question that determines who we are. Which path do we choose? Rehabilitation or retribution? Our future safety depends on how we answer.

ACTION POINT: Find out when the next #VisitMyMosque day is, go along and meet local Muslims (if you are a non-Muslim yourself).

DISCUSSION POINT: How would Trump's 'Muslim ban' have been received if it had been proposed before 9/11?

Whitewashed Out

'A working-class hero is something to be.'

John Lennon

The last of the 'other' men I am going to look at is by no means the least. They are probably the most powerful group politically and, unlike black and Muslim men, they are not a minority. In fact, they are a sizeable voting bloc who, when mobilized, have the ability to swing a referendum (as we saw with the Brexit vote in Britain) or take over a political party that is the bastion of the elite, as we saw with Trump's triumph in the Republican primaries. This group has the potential, perhaps more than any 'other', to cause waves of social, political, and economic change: 72 per cent of non-college-educated white men voted for Trump[*], and 70 per cent of those with only GCSEs or less voted to leave the EU.[†] Their status as 'other' comes not from their race or religion, but from that age-old British institution: class.

Both votes were an expression of white working-class men's frustrations over globalization and the decline in their living standards.

---

[*] FiveThirtyEight: https://fivethirtyeight.com/features/clinton-couldnt-win-over-white-women

[†] 'How Britain Voted', YouGov: https://yougov.co.uk/news/2016/06/27/how-britain-voted

The winners on both sides of the pond were able to link this decline in living standards and employment opportunities to immigration. They successfully promoted fear of the 'other', inciting a revolt against the establishment by white working-class men in the UK and US – resulting, in some extreme cases, in violence.

Fear of the 'other' is not endemic or inevitable. The UK has not had the same history of segregation as the US, and 'other' ethnic groups in the UK have lived alongside the white working class for decades. White working-class men in the US even helped to elect the first African-American president in US history. So what's changed?

White working-class men have been manipulated and discarded for political and economic expediency for longer than any of the other groups. They've been conscripted to colonize the Earth, to fight wars, and to fuel the industrialization of the West. And the reason they have endured these hardships and the exclusion from the full bounties enjoyed by the elites until recently is the unspoken agreement of entitlement – the idea that they, like the people who rule them, are the indigenous group, and are therefore entitled to a modest but credible standard of living, provided they are willing to work. It's not an unreasonable expectation by any means, considering the contribution they and their predecessors have made to their nation's prosperity, but somewhere along the way that unspoken agreement has been broken by the ruling class, and it's left a lot of working-class white men behind. So how exactly did this happen, and what can we do to heal these wounds and regain the trust that has been lost?

The lost world

If you were lucky enough to grow up in a white working-class area in East London as I did, you will have experienced a real community. This area endured the Blitz during the Second World War, so I grew up among a community of elders for whom being a good neighbour was part of survival. If a bomb dropped on your home, it was one of your neighbours who would shelter you and your family. Britain survived the war, and this is a badge of pride among white working-class men, especially if your grandfather served. And this pride and strong sense of community, along with standing up for yourself and your country, doing a good day's graft (usually manual work), and a willingness to appreciate your lot, were values instilled in white working-class males as standard.

And so they just got on with it. The blue-collar vocations laid out for them did not require higher education, focusing much more on practical and skills-based learning. Back then, the economy had a clear place for this group of men – there would be a job at a local factory where many of their mates worked, and there they would stay until retirement. A lack of social mobility was not a deal-breaker for white working-class men as long as they had employment and their way of life remained unchanged.

But change was in the air, whether they liked it or not. As soon as the elites in Europe and America came to realize that the movement of industry and people was required to maintain their margins as the rest of the world started to develop, the argument that the indigenous population should be entitled to work for a fair day's pay became worthless. The need to meet the demand for labour after the war ushered in immigration, nearly always in working-class communities. Some working-class men did resent the newcomers, fearing change as many people do, but most welcomed migrants into their homes, local pubs, and families. Some even marched in solidarity with these new immigrants against far-right groups. It's fair to say that the response to *Windrush*, the ship that brought one of the first groups of post-Second World War immigrants to the UK, and the subsequent waves of immigration that followed, was mixed across the country. But unlike in America, the overarching moral response was always 'live and let live', enabling Britain to claim the mantle of being a bastion of tolerance and diversity. However, this was based on the expectation that the 'agreement' between the working class and the elites would be upheld.

But as infrastructure in other parts of the world developed, it was no longer necessary to import labour and skills to the West, since we could just as easily export the working-class *jobs* to the rest of the world where costs (wages) were cheaper. Great for bosses and those with capital to invest; not so great for the white working-class male.

Fast-forward a few decades to the twenty-first century, and working-class neighbourhoods have experienced yet more dramatic change. The Thatcherite revolution in the UK, and Reaganomics in the US, oversaw deindustrialization of their respective industrial bases, resulting in the erosion of traditional white working-class jobs. Economically, the decline in manufacturing has hit the working-class male the hardest, demoting him in many cases from full-time bread-winner for his family and household. His jobs have been replaced by less well-paid and often part-time service sector jobs that (from a traditional male perspective) require skills aligned more with female workers. Many of these jobs are paid as zero hours contracts intended to supplement the family income, as opposed to replacing a bread-winner's salary, yet in many cases this is exactly what has happened. The result is quite a come-down for the white working-class man: as a factory worker he took pride in the goods he made, which were shipped across the globe, but somehow making and serving lattes for a minimum wage doesn't quite match up.

If white working-class males wanted to maintain their standard of living they would need to do what 'foreign' parents were demanding of their kids – work hard at school. But by now, white working-class males had the lowest levels of educational attainment and parents without a traditional reverence for higher education, and this trend continued.

A white working-class boy is *less than half as likely* to get five good GCSEs, including the core subjects, as the average student in England.[*]

At present, white working-class boys have the lowest literacy levels in British schools and are the least likely group to attend university. Throw in the free movement of higher-educated and skilled multilingual migrants from former communist Eastern Europe, with a couple of colourful demagogues who can spice up discontent with provocative statements, and we have ourselves a working-class populist revolt seasoned with an unfortunate taste of resentment. As an ardent pro-EU campaigner, I am disheartened to see the results of this shift to the right in Western democracies – but I also understand the legitimate concerns of those communities that have been failed by globalization. I have no criticism for the victims – they are the symptom, not the cause – and until we treat the cause, the symptoms will just get worse.

Toxic masculinity

A key exacerbating factor in the populist revolt we are now witnessing is the disenfranchised white working-class male's notion of traditional masculinity. Within this subculture, authority tends to be spurned, and violence – often in the form of hooliganism – is deemed acceptable. Males in academia and office jobs are not viewed as 'proper men': they have soft hands, never break a sweat, and don't build or make anything. They put on 'airs and graces' and work in offices where political correctness wins the day. The white working-class male prefers blunt straight-talking.

But what happens when the world moves on from this version of masculinity? Professor Michael Kimmel, a sociologist at Stony Brook

[*] *New Statesman*: The Lost Boys http://www.newstatesman.com/politics/education/2016/09/lost-boys-how-white-working-class-got-left-behind

University in New York, is one of the world's leading authorities on masculinity. He examines the parallel phenomenon happening in the US in his book *Angry White Men*, and writes that many of the white working-class men from forgotten Rust Belt communities feel 'betrayed by the country they love, discarded like trash on the side of the information superhighway'. In many ways the plight of the white working-class male may perhaps be the easiest to dissect in terms of understanding where the growing dissent comes from. According to Kimmel, the men he studied see positions that were once their birthright disappearing, and are no longer sure where they fit in the societal pecking order. They are white and male in a society that values those two attributes above all others – yet being white and male no longer has the same guarantees, at least not for white men who look and sound like them.

In adult men this state of confusion can lead to what Michael Kimmel describes as 'aggrieved entitlement', and the need for scapegoats in the form of 'feminazis' like Hillary Clinton or Mexican immigrants, who need to be 'walled' out of America in order to make the country 'Great Again'.

This is not a new phenomenon: Kimmel's book was written in 2013, long before the 2016 US election, and documentary filmmaker Michael Moore also tried to alert Liberals and Democrats about the anger that was building in rural communities up and down the country,[*] even predicting in his 2016 film, *Michael Moore in Trumpland*, that Trump would win. But it's only now that the real scale of the problem is making itself apparent. Aside from the obvious political ramifications, in America it has also resulted in an alarming increase in early death rates among the middle-aged. This growing pandemic has been termed 'deaths of despair' by Princeton economists Anne Case and Angus Deaton.[†] They argue that there is a direct correlation

---

[*] https://michaelmoore.com/trumpwillwin

[†] https://www.brookings.edu/bpea-articles/mortality-and-morbidity-in-the-21st-century

between the economic decline of this group and a sharp rise in deaths caused by drugs, alcohol poisoning, and suicide.[*]

In part, the growing pushback against patriarchy and 'toxic masculinity' has made politicians reluctant to address the issues of white working-class boys in our education system. In a warped kind of way it's easier to acknowledge inequality where women or people of colour are concerned, and harder to have that same level of concern for white males in a society that was designed to promote their dominance and progress. What we mustn't forget is that not all white males have been beneficiaries of this system.

Daily Telegraph reporter Martin Daubney has been a passionate advocate for tackling this emergency. He believes the problem is in part due to a breakdown in the family structure in many of these communities, with high numbers of absent fathers and a serious lack of positive male role models.[†] Daubney also thinks that we need a larger number of male teachers from this background who can fill the void – currently 85 per cent of teachers are female. The general consensus is that 'boisterous' masculine energy is often viewed as 'disruptive or destructive' in the classroom, and cuts to physical activities in our schools mean we no longer have an adequate outlet for this energy. Daubney advocates a similar programme to the 'Young Men's Initiative' in New York, designed to train and promote more black male teachers in New York schools. He believes it is vital that we encourage more white working-class men into teaching.

Indeed, had a concerted effort been made by governments through education and training to ensure that white working-class men (and

[*] From 1998–2015, the mortality rate for white men aged 50–54 with a degree fell from 349 per 100,000 to 243, but for non-educated white males the figure rose from 762 per 100,000 to 867. And poverty is not the only deciding factor here. Thirty years ago whites without a college degree were 30 per cent less likely to die in middle age than their African-American equivalent. Today the reverse is true and they are 30 per cent more likely to die.

[†] http://www.telegraph.co.uk/men/thinking-man/stop-the-pointless-gender-war-and-get-behind-our-men--boys-coali

in fact all 'other' groups) were adequately equipped and able to benefit from globalization rather than becoming victims of it, this erosion of faith in the system and anti-establishment rage in the West could have been averted. Had the impact of migration been more evenly distributed and integration more carefully managed in the UK, so that traditional white working-class areas had not changed beyond recognition, this could have addressed the resentment.

And lastly, if a genuine effort had been made to accommodate and accept working-class values and culture rather than neglecting them, we may have achieved a much higher degree of social mobility within this group. Instead, we have marginalized frustrated young white men, who have gone from being part of the national culture to a subculture wrapped up in a crumpled English flag, unfairly characterized as work-shy, nostalgic, and parochial.

The rise of extremism

The crisis that this subculture is in has reached fever pitch in recent years, and the urgency with which we must deal with it has become painfully apparent, not just because of the political ructions it's caused with Trump and Brexit, but because of the alarming rise in far-right extremism that we've seen come with it. Who could forget the horror of 16 June 2016, when the MP Jo Cox was murdered by far-right extremist Thomas Mair, shouting 'Britain first'? Before his wife was murdered, Brendan Cox had actually been studying this frightening trend. Speaking a year after Jo's passing at the 2017 Amnesty International General Meeting, he warned of the grave challenge facing us and issued a clarion call to all those who believe in a fair and inclusive society:

> *We are facing a new threat today – one that we still haven't fully appreciated. We have got into the absurd position of celebrating fascists coming second in national elections, rather than first, as if that is a great outcome.*

I'm not suggesting that we become defeatist, but unless we are clear about the size and scale of the challenge, we will be defeated by it.

As well as understanding the scale of the problem – we must also call it what it is. Populism is too kind a term. In fact, in most countries these groups we refer to as populist are consistently unpopular.

More importantly, the people who lead these movements are not populists – they are racists, bigots, and xenophobes, intent on tearing our communities apart. And we should call them out for what they are.

The threat of rising far-right extremism is real and it isn't going to go away quickly. But with resolution, a concerted attempt to reach out, and a focus on building closer communities, we can and we will defeat it.

These so-called 'populist' leaders have manipulated and exploited the genuine concerns of a group who are witnessing their traditional way of life evaporating in front of their eyes, and who haven't been given the right tools to adapt to this change. Fuelled by a 'Cause Conspiracy' ignited by the dangerous rhetoric of a new breed of charismatic social-media-savvy demagogues, there has been an exponential increase in far-right membership and incidents. In the UK alone, the 'suspected far-right extremists flagged to the Government's key anti-terror programme soared by 30 per cent in the past year'.[*]

Having a cause to get behind is one of the most powerful of all callings, especially for men who are often lacking in words and therefore prefer action. Our 'other' young men who are excluded due to race, class or religion are all more vulnerable to radicalization

[*] http://www.independent.co.uk/news/uk/home-news/finsbury-park-attack-far-right-extremist-rise-year-statistics-prevent-terrorism-scheme-referrals-a7798231.html

and the rhetoric of causes, which will supposedly give their life greater significance while at the same time putting it in jeopardy.

America is facing its own issues with a rise in white supremacy movements. Having experienced first-hand the uplifting feeling of unity in Virginia during Obama's 2008 election, watching the clashes between the far-right extremists and anti-racism protesters in Charlottesville on the news 10 years later filled me with dread; it felt like America had gone back in time, to racial tensions and the strife of the sixties. We had reverted to arguing over whether to celebrate Confederate generals who fought to keep slavery. We were, once again, seeing the KKK marching with lit torches – only this time the marchers were brazen enough to do so without hoods.

This against a background of the mass incarceration of African Americans and their falling victim to countless acts of police brutality and shootings. The one difference with the 1960s is that the then President Lyndon B. Johnson, when faced with the decision of whether to pander to his core base or lead the country to better tomorrow, chose the latter. He paid a price in losing the support of some Southern states, but he took an important step in America's redemption and progression.

Unfortunately, the current President's response to overt racism has been tentative at best. He took 48 hours to condemn the violence of the white supremacist protesters and the senseless murder of 32-year-old Heather Hayer, an anti-racism protester, at the suspected hands of James Alex Fields Jr, a far-right extremist and accused domestic terrorist.

Many of these far-right extremists were courted shamelessly by Trump during his campaign as they lapped up his rhetoric on Muslims and Mexicans. However, once in office, his chickens had come home to roost and he found himself in the difficult position of having to denounce them, albeit two days too late. Trump must now address the real issues affecting white working-class men in America: the fears from a changing world where their dominance is diminishing.

What's needed are realistic solutions that allow everyone to thrive in the modern world rather than return America to an older, more racist and less progressive nation. The country has come too far to turn back now.

And there are of course many correlations between radicalized Islamists and radicalized white supremacists. If you explore the lives of many of the perpetrators, it is clear that they were excluded men looking for deeper meaning in their lives, even if that meant ending it and hurting countless innocents in the process. Their lives, as they were, were clearly not worth much, and this was the only way to give them purpose. Radicalized men from opposing sides, ironically working towards the same aim.

A different script

If the Finsbury Park mosque attack (when, targeting a Mosque on 19 June 2017 in the ethnically diverse North London neighbourhood of Finsbury Park, which was over 300 miles away from his home in Wales, Darren Osborne acquired a van and drove it into Muslim worshippers during early-morning Ramadan prayers) showed us one thing, however, it's that we can change the prescribed narrative surrounding this pattern of behaviour. According to the existing script, the enraged mob at the Finsbury Park mosque, fuelled by fear and a desire for revenge, should have then butchered this lone assailant, fuelling more fear and mistrust. But that's not how it happened. Mohammed Mahmoud, the imam of the mosque, calmed and reasoned with the crowd and protected the terrorist from attack until the police arrived to make an arrest. Mahmoud was later dubbed a 'hero' by the British press and was personally thanked by Prince Charles when he visited the mosque days after the attack. Thousands of Londoners would also show their solidarity with the Muslim community by participating in a flower march the following evening and delivering thousands of bouquets to the mosque.

This is a prime example of how extremism can be fought. This was homegrown terrorism that failed to divide society because good Muslim men were prepared to stand up for compassion and the rule of law, and because the people of London came together in support of this 'other' community. Where radicalization is concerned, there is more than one side involved. The conspirators show no sign of quitting, so neither must we in fighting for the values we hold dear.

It's clear that we can no longer sit back and ignore the disintegration that is brewing in white working-class communities both in the UK and US; it's their values that for centuries have been the bedrock of British and American society, after all. The traditional values of the white working class are translatable into any setting: loyalty to a cause, hard work, and a grim determination; they are attributes that we want not only in our employees and citizens, but in our leaders and bosses, our friends and family. If we can harness these qualities, equip these men with the education and skills they need to contribute to this new globalized world, and show that they are valued, then the damage that is currently being wrought at every level can be prevented and reversed. Now that's a cause worth pursuing.

ACTION POINT: Find out how many university degrees are open to applicants without A-levels.

DISCUSSION POINT: What job do you instinctively think of a white working-class man doing?

The Other Way

'If you treat an individual as he is, he will remain how he is. But if you treat him as if he were what he ought to be and could be, he will become what he ought to be and could be.'

Johann Wolfgang von Goethe

If you are one of the 'other' men reading this, then I thank you for persevering in the face of life's obstacles. I hope I have given an accurate account of your plight – generalizations notwithstanding. To the rest of us who regard these 'other' men as 'them' rather than 'us', I would say this: there is another way.

To create a new normal, each of us must change the way we see, treat and include the 'other' man – to break down the stereotypes that we ourselves have created based on nothing more than outward appearances. Equally, we must turn our attention to class: in a report entitled 'Elitist Britain' by the UK Government's Mobility and Child Poverty Commission, it was concluded that elitism was so ingrained in British society 'that it could be called "social engineering"'. Too often, this is at the expense of the 'other' man.

And across all three of these 'other' groups, we must reassess our understanding of 'masculinity' in the round. As we've seen, these men inhabit their respective subcultures where their own rules and norms apply, which will often conflict with mainstream values — particularly the acceptance of violence as being part of a man's DNA. If we can help change the script within these subcultures about what a man 'ought' to be, then we can surely help to stem the flow of violence that often spills out into the world as a result of their frustrations.

On a wider scale, the issues society has with its 'other' men are ingrained and complex, and we require effective leadership to fully address them. We need politicians and policy makers who are not just driven by self-interest, but are willing to make tough decisions and take the long-term approach needed to fix these problems. Our 'other' men trigger three of the toughest issues that society is yet to reconcile: race, religion, and class. However, there are countless examples of regeneration and integration programmes that have been proven to work (go to www.Diversify.org to see the remarkable case study of Braddock, Pennsylvania, where Mayor John Fetterman is spearheading a fantastic regeneration drive of this ailing steel town). What they show is that it's only by turning our attention to marginalized groups such as the 'other' man that we can reach our full potential as a society, and that when we get it right, we all benefit.

THE OTHER MAN:

The Numbers

Disparities in earnings and unemployment in the UK and the USA*

UK	All men	Black men	Muslim men	White Working Class men
Unemployed	7%	11%	10%	7%
Weekly earnings 2015£	603	395	495	570
USA	All men	Black men	Asian men	Hispanic or Latino men
Unemployment	5%	9%	4%	5%
Weekly earnings 2015$	895	680	1,129	631

* USA Bureau of Labor Statistics 2015; Centre for Social Investigation using UK Household Longitudinal Study 2015. White working class defined by family background

Disparities in rates of incarceration[*]

UK	% of UK population	% of UK incarcerated population
Christian	61%	49%
Muslim	4%	15%
White	88%	74%
Black	3%	12%
USA	**% of US population**	**% of US incarcerated population**
White (non-Hispanic)	64%	39%
Hispanic	16%	19%
Black	13%	40%

Facts and figures

- **15%**: the proportion of Muslim prisoners in 2015 up from **8%** in 2002.
- The Young Report of 2014 found that 'Most of the prisoners we met with all said that they experienced differential treatment as a result of their race, ethnicity or faith. Black prisoners felt that they were stereotyped as drug dealers and Muslim prisoners as terrorists'.
- **50%**: according to Unlocking America, if African American and Hispanics were incarcerated at the same rates as

[*] USA Prison Policy Initiative; UK House of Commons briefing paper

whites, today's prison and jail populations would decline by a half.

- **12%**: the percentage of drug users in the USA who are African American, but **38%** of arrests for drug offences and **59%** of those in state prison for a drug offence are African American.
- **Twice as likely**: the Pew Research Center finds that, in the USA, blacks are twice as likely to be in poverty as whites.
- **50%**: the percentage of Muslim households in poverty in the UK, according to the Joseph Rowntree Foundation, compared to the national average of **18%**

THE FIRST DEGREE OF INTEGRATION

Challenge Your Ism

'Not everything that is faced can be changed, but nothing can be changed until it is faced.'

James Baldwin

We all have so many 'isms' that keep us apart; isms that are buried so deeply within us that we are unaware of them and their ramifications on ourselves and others: race-ism, sex-ism, class-ism, sectarian-ism, age-ism . . . the list is endless. And all of us are guilty, myself included (mine, of course, being tattoo-ism).

If you had asked me five years ago to name my ism, I would genuinely have told you I didn't have one. This, in fact, was one of the things I prided myself on the most: my self-perceived 'open-mindedness'. For most of my life, I have happily revelled in this bubble of self-satisfaction, and never felt the need to partake in an inventory of my own limiting beliefs.

How many of us question our beliefs and the way we see the world, and whether or not these beliefs prevent us from being the best we can be? Are these beliefs even our own, or have they been passed down to us by our parents and our surroundings? Are they logical? And, most importantly, do they best serve us, society, and humanity? How often do we ask ourselves, 'Should I hold these beliefs? If not, do I want to do anything about it?' These questions are much deeper than surface prejudices – they go to the core of the way we think.

Having said that, isms are a two-way street, and the responsibility for change does not solely lie at the door of the instigator. Isms require both parties to subscribe to the stereotype. It takes one party to apply the label, but it can only hold relevance if the other side accepts the label. In the words of Eleanor Roosevelt, 'No one can make you feel inferior without your consent.'

Recognizing half-truths and our role in perpetuating them is at the core of Degree One in the Six Degrees of Integration. Accepting our individual responsibility for stereotypes gives us the power to challenge them. So, what are your isms? Are you sexist? Are you class-ist? Do you have a race-ism? A gay-ism? The Ism Questionnaire below has been put together by the Centre for Social Investigation at Nuffield College, Oxford, to get to the heart of your beliefs.*

So take five minutes to reflect – and be honest in how you answer the questions, no matter how uncomfortable or embarrassing it may be. Only by identifying our prejudices can we confront them. If you turn to page 381 you'll see that, whatever your view, you are not alone. Absolute honesty is the only way to begin the process of change.

---

* The questions have been compiled using the British Social Attitudes survey 2012, the European Social Survey 2014–2015, and YouGov/ *The Times* 2016

The Ism Questionnaire

Attitudes towards other political views

1. As far as you are concerned personally, how important is it to try to understand the reasoning of people with other opinions?

   Choose a number between 1 and 7, where 1 is 'Not at all important' and 7 is 'Very important'.

2. How would you feel if you had a son or daughter who married a Conservative?

   Not upset at all
   Somewhat upset
   Very upset
   Not sure

3. How would you feel if you had a son or daughter who married someone who was Labour?

   Not upset at all
   Somewhat upset
   Very upset
   Not sure

Attitudes towards ethnicity and race

4. Do you think some races or ethnic groups are born less intelligent than others?

   Yes/No

5. Do you think some races or ethnic groups are born harder working than others?

   Yes/No

6. Would you say that some cultures are much better than others, or that all cultures are equal?
    Some cultures are much better than others
    All cultures are equal

7. How much would you mind or not mind if a person from another country who is of a different race or ethnic group was appointed as your boss?
    Choose a number between 0 and 10, where 0 is 'I wouldn't mind at all' and 10 is 'I would mind a lot'

8. How much would you mind or not mind if a person from another country who is of a different race or ethnic group married a close relative of yours?
    Choose a number between 0 and 10, where 0 is 'I wouldn't mind at all' and 10 is 'I would mind a lot'

Attitudes towards gender, family life, and sexuality

9. All in all, family life suffers when the woman has a full-time job?
    Disagree
    Agree

10. A man's job is to earn money; a woman's job is to look after the home and family.
    Disagree
    Agree

11. A working mother can establish just as warm and secure a relationship with her children as a mother who does not work.
    Disagree
    Agree

12. One parent can bring up a child as well as two parents together.
    Disagree
    Agree

13. A same-sex female couple can bring up a child as well as a male-female couple.
    Disagree
    Agree

General ism questions

14. Do you think your opinion of people might be swayed by social class, even if in subtle ways (style of dress, way of talking)?
    Yes/No

15. Would you have concerns if a girlfriend of yours starting dating a Muslim man?
    Yes/No

16. Imagine you are a businessperson about to negotiate a deal with a company: would you rather deal with a businessman or a businesswoman in your negotiations? If you have a preference, why?
    Businessman/Businesswoman
    Reason:

17. Would you want to make friends with someone with different political beliefs to you? If not, why not?
    Yes/No
    Reason:

18. Can you remember any moments in life that changed your worldview? Were you influenced by someone 'other' from outside your social circle?
   Yes/No
   Details:

19. Imagine you meet a friend's 3-year-old daughter for the first time: would you compliment her for wearing something pretty? Is there something better to say?
   Yes/No
   Details:

20. Have you ever made a judgement about someone based on their appearance and been really wrong?
   Yes/No

Additional questions can also be found at our website: www.Diversify.org

PART TWO

THE OTHER WOMAN

'Stereotype of females begins when the doctor says: 'It's a girl'.'
Shirley Chrisholm

The Old Way

In 1969, Congresswoman Shirley Chisholm delivered a powerfully emotive speech to the House of Representatives demanding 'Equal Rights for Women'. She remarked:

> *The emotional, sexual, and psychological stereotyping of females begins when the doctor says: 'It's a girl.' At present, our country needs women's idealism and determination, perhaps more in politics than anywhere else.*[*]

Heeding her own advice, three years later Chisholm would become the first woman to run for the Democratic Party's presidential nomination, and the first African-American to run as a major party's nomination for President of the United States.

It was 1972 and, alas, America was not yet ready for a woman, let alone a black woman as bold as she; her presidential bid was ridiculed, laughed at, and met with cynicism and disdain by most of the elite. But even so, Chisholm still managed to secure 151 delegates in the Democratic primaries. As a prominent member of both the civil rights and women's movements, her courage and belief in the

---

[*] Equal Rights for Women speech by Shirley Chisholm to the House of Representative 1969: Congressional Record – Extensions of Remarks E4165-6. Also available online at http://scriptorium.lib.duke.edu/wlm/equal

possibility of change helped pave the way for a Barack Obama and a Hillary Rodham Clinton. She most certainly lived up to her gutsy tagline of 'Unbought and Unbossed' – she famously espoused that 'if they don't give you a seat at the table then bring a folding chair' – but Chisholm was the exception and, unfortunately, her remarks are still as relevant today as they were in 1969. Because it's true that when a child is born and the doctor says, 'It's a girl', that tiny, innocent miracle already has the odds stacked against her and will have to play on a field that most certainly isn't level.

Women are the largest oppressed group in the world, and the degrees of subjugation vary from country to country, with women in the West faring much better than their counterparts in developing parts of the world. In their 2008 Pulitzer Prize-winning book *Half the Sky: Turning Oppression into Opportunity for Women Worldwide*, Nicholas Kristof and his wife, Sheryl WuDunn, argue that: 'In the nineteenth century, the central moral challenge was slavery. In the twentieth century, it was the battle against totalitarianism. We believe that in this century the paramount moral challenge will be the struggle for gender equality around the world.' A struggle it may be, but it's one that will be 100 per cent worth it, given the rewards that are to be won. So, in this section, I will challenge the idea of women as 'other', and argue that the results – personal, cultural, and economic – of diversifying gender will be spectacularly beneficial, for women, for men, and for society as a whole.

CHAPTER ONE

In the Boardroom

'Our deepest fear is not that we are inadequate. Our deepest fear is that we are powerful beyond measure. It is our light, not our darkness, that most frightens us.'

Marianne Williamson

On 29 May 1851, a heckler disrupted the Ohio Women's Rights Convention, leaving the room stunned with a speech that would go down in history as one of the most iconic feminist speeches of all time.

The heckler was Sojourner Truth. Born a slave 54 years earlier, she was the complete antithesis of the aristocratic women who had gathered there to discuss female emancipation. Her 'Ain't I a woman?' speech was unapologetic, courageous, and humorous, and it brought the audience to their feet with rapturous applause. Sojourner Truth's powerful words of female empowerment were a clarion call then as they still are now:

That man over there says that women need to be helped into carriages, and lifted over ditches, and to have the best place everywhere. Nobody ever helps me into carriages, or over mud-puddles, or gives me any best place! And ain't I a woman? Look at me!

Look at my arm! I have ploughed and planted, and gathered into barns, and no man could head me! And ain't I a woman? I could work as much and eat as much as a man — when I could get it — and bear the lash as well! And ain't I a woman? I have borne 13 children, and seen most all sold off to slavery, and when I cried out with my mother's grief, none but Jesus heard me! And ain't I a woman?

Then they talk about this thing in the head; what's this they call it? [A member of the audience whispers 'intellect'.] That's it, honey. What's that got to do with women's rights or negroes' rights? If my cup won't hold but a pint, and yours holds a quart, wouldn't you be mean not to let me have my little half measure full?

Then that little man in black there, he says women can't have as much rights as men, 'cause Christ wasn't a woman! Where did your Christ come from? Where did your Christ come from? From God and a woman! Man had nothing to do with Him.

If the first woman God ever made was strong enough to turn the world upside down all alone, these women together ought to be able to turn it back, and get it right side up again! And now they is asking to do it, the men better let them.

Those final words are still being quoted centuries later. Sojourner Truth's breathtaking performance at the convention would thrust her into the limelight and turn her into an icon for both gender and racial equality. A year later, she would meet Harriet Beecher Stowe – one of the celebrated abolitionists and feminists of the day – and these two great women would discuss women's rights. In 1863, Beecher Stowe wrote an article in the *Atlantic Weekly* about their encounter, entitled 'Sojourner Truth – the Libyan Sibyl'. She quoted Truth as saying: 'If

---

* Sojourner Truth Memorial: http://sojournertruthmemorial.org/sojourner-truth/her-words

women want any rights more than they's got, why don't they just take them, and not be talking about it.' If only it were that simple.

Imposter syndrome

The truth is, the gender confidence gap is real. For centuries, women have been told that they are not good enough to receive an education, not good enough to be able to vote, not good enough to have the same jobs, power, and pay as men. They have been told this so often that deep down they have learned to believe it, even though their conscious mind knows it isn't true. So sometimes we women are our own worst barrier to change due to our learned self-criticism, our internalized misogyny, which cements our status as the 'other' woman – someone who never feels quite at home with success. As a starting point, we must learn to confront this self-criticism in order to embrace a diverse society.

Introducing Agyness

Truth's courageous attitude in relation to equality is way ahead of many twenty-first-century women, even though we have far more opportunities than she could ever have dreamed of. So many of us still suffer from 'Imposter Syndrome', perfectly described by Sheryl Sandberg in her 2013 book, *Lean In*:

> *Many people, but especially women, feel fraudulent when they are praised for their accomplishments. Instead of feeling worthy of recognition, they feel undeserving and guilty, as if a mistake has been made. Despite being high achievers, even experts in their fields, women can't seem to shake the sense that it is only a matter of time until they are found out for who they really are – impostors with limited skills or abilities.*[*]

* *Lean In: Women, Work and the Will to Lead* by Sheryl Sandberg (Knopf, 2013)

This form of female professional insecurity is something I thoroughly relate to. I spend hours on the phone with one of my dear friends, dissecting the multiple layers of this syndrome, which can manifest in a range of ways – from simple self-deprecation to all-out self-sabotage.

We decided the best way to tackle our Imposter Syndrome was to name and shame it, sort of like Beyoncé–Sasha Fierce in reverse. The only name suitable for such a destructive foe? *Agyness* (with no offence to any Agynesses out there). And the funny thing with Agyness is that she is unpredictable; you have no idea when she is going to rear her pernicious head. And, when she does, she can wreak havoc.

70%: the percentage of girls who believe that they are 'not good enough' in some way (including looks, education, and relationships).[*]
4%: the percentage of CEO positions held by women across Fortune 500 companies.[†]

I remember, a while back, Agyness had tricked me into believing she was finally gone for good. I had been overdosing on 'you can do it' books and thought I was permanently rid of her. While riding this Agyness-free wave, I was invited by Bill Clinton's team to present at his annual Clinton Global Initiative (CGI) opening gala. The line-up included Matt Damon, Eva Longoria, Angélique Kidjo, Carlos Slim, and many more luminaries from the worlds of business, public life, entertainment, and philanthropy. I was brimming with excitement, and felt no nerves as I casually made small talk backstage with former president Clinton, then San Francisco Mayor Gavin Newsom, and the actress Rosario Dawson. I felt a million dollars as I waltzed

[*] Parent 24: http://www.parent24.com/Teen_13-18/Development/70-of-girls-feel-theyre-not-good-enough-20160629
[†] *Fortune* http://fortune.com/2016/06/06/women-ceos-fortune-500-2016

onto the stage in a black-beaded evening gown to introduce Seal, who was performing that evening. Perhaps, I thought, I was finally worthy enough to rendezvous in these revered circles . . . Wrong!

The next day, during the CGI preliminary session, Agyness returned with a bang. President Obama was delivering a speech on women and gender equality, so the room was packed full. Even so, somehow among the 600 or so people, I managed to sit next to Jochen Zeitz, former CEO of Sport & Lifestyle for the Kering Group (owners of luxury fashion brands such as Gucci, Puma, and Alexander McQueen). Jochen has been a real pioneer in ethical fashion and is the co-founder of The B-Team with Sir Richard Branson – an organization that is committed to business fairness. So, needless to say, I'm a huge fan of his work. For months I'd been trying to secure him as a speaker at a conference I was organizing and was having difficulty finding the best route to reach him – and here it had been handed to me on a plate.

As I opened my mouth to introduce myself, Agyness took over and I froze. I couldn't speak, my palms began to sweat, and I was overcome with insecurity and self-doubt. Agyness was on a roll, bombarding me with numerous reasons as to why I shouldn't ask him to speak at our next event. An hour passed, he even smiled a few times, but I averted my eyes and looked to the floor. Eventually he and his team left.

I was furious with myself for not having seized the opportunity that was right in front of me. I got up to leave and bumped into an old work colleague in the seminar foyer. As my colleague and I chatted, Jochen and his team walked past and stopped yards away from where we were standing. They say there are no second chances in life, but here I was, being given one just moments after I had blown the first. This was my opportunity to take the reins from Agyness and redeem myself *to* myself. But, unfortunately, Agyness overpowered me and I froze again as Jochen and his team left the building.

That was a pivotal moment for me, a moment when I let fear win the day. What was different this time, compared to when I was walking onto that stage? Why did I make a choice to play it safe rather than risk rejection? On another occasion, there could have been an entirely different outcome – there have been plenty of times in my life when opportunities have presented themselves and I've jumped at them, because in that particular moment I was feeling confident and sure of my abilities.

I've nicknamed this moment a 'Jochen Moment' – basically the opposite of a light-bulb moment. Fortunately, 'Jochen Moments' do not occur as much as they used to, but when they do, Agyness is usually lurking somewhere not too far away.

I'm pleased to say this story has a happy ending: a few years later I did manage to summon up the courage to ask and, yes, Jochen did end up speaking at one of my events. In this case opportunity actually knocked thrice, but obviously this is by no means the norm. I got lucky.

I encourage you to muster up the courage to seize all good opportunities when they arise. Courage requires risking failure and rejection, but it's a muscle that needs to be regularly exercised in order to develop core strength.

The Agyness Challenge

My cousin Reg has an interesting theory about women and fearing rejection – he believes that part of the reason men are better at dealing with rejection is because of the practice they get in the dating arena. According to Reg, from the time boys hit puberty and start asking girls out, 'no' is a word they become well acquainted with. Therefore they take 'no' less personally, and see it as a numbers game. As far as Reg is concerned, for every ten women he asks out at least one is bound to say yes – two if he's lucky. Those aren't bad odds.

And he might actually have a point. The research suggests that in the workplace men *are* better at dealing with rejection than women, and certainly don't judge themselves as harshly. Sharon Vosmek, founder and CEO of Astia (a US not-for-profit organization that supports women-led businesses), cites a study by Professor Shelley Correll at the Clayman Institute for Gender Research at Stanford University, which monitored the reactions of 'C' grade calculus students. This is what Vosmek discovered:

> *The men were perceiving they had passed and were wizards, and would potentially use it to go on and negotiate a higher salary. Women in the same calculus class – the majority would drop the course, perceiving they had failed and never mention it again. So what happens when women are rejected? They are already rejecting themselves.*[*]

My 'Jochen Moment', it turns out, was a classic female response, hardwired from centuries of gender conditioning. It forced me to face my insecurities and stop avoiding the fact that they existed, something I had been doing my whole adult life. And using Reg's theory as my guide for healing, I decided to develop my own 'Agyness Challenge' based on Jason Comely's 'Rejection Therapy'; I suppose this is a sort of Degree for the Others. Comely, a Canadian entrepreneur, devised a social self-help 'game' for overcoming a fear of rejection, whereby to 'win' required you to receive at least one rejection each day for a period of time, with the intention of training yourself to overcome the fear through extended exposure.

---

[*] *Telegraph*: http://www.telegraph.co.uk/finance/businessclub/8010710/Do-women-fear-rejection-more-than-men.html

Do this today: the five objectives of Rejection Therapy

1. Be more aware of how irrational social fears control and restrict our lives.
2. Smash the tyranny of fear and reap the treasures (treasures include wealth, relationships, and self-confidence).
3. Learn from, and even enjoy rejection.
4. Do not be attached to outcomes, especially when it involves the free agency of other people.
5. Permit yourself to fail.

My challenge involves me journaling which of my career choices have been led by Agyness, and which by my confident self. I also do simple things, like seeking advice or mentorship from people I admire – this can be by cold email, or by approaching them at events and seminars.

I force myself to do this much more than I am naturally comfortable with. Even though I work in television and on the surface seem to be very much an extrovert, I am actually quite shy, so this is a real effort for me. However, the benefits far outweigh the safety of staying in my comfort zone.

One example of this is a friendship I now have with Simon Collins, former Dean of the Parsons' School of Fashion in New York. I wanted Simon's help with Ldny.com, a fashion social enterprise I was launching. I emailed him more than five times and he ignored me on each occasion. Something similar happened with Ed Burstell, then CEO of Liberty.

Usually, I would have let Agyness's fear of rejection win, but this time my challenge meant I couldn't. So even though it wasn't exactly a boost to my ego, I refused to give up, and persisted until both of them responded. I can now confidently say they are both glad they did. We've gone on to work on some great projects together as well as to form great friendships, all of which we would have missed out on had I not persisted – which causes me to ask myself: what have I lost on those occasions when Agyness has prevailed?

So, I urge women and other 'others' everywhere to challenge their own Agyness. We have to learn not to take rejection personally, and rather view it as part of the pathway to success. Once women allow themselves to fear that they are not pretty enough, not clever enough, not strong enough, they behave in a way that limits themselves and makes their dreams less likely to come to fruition. I don't know if it's ever possible to rid ourselves 100 per cent of our Agyness – a lifetime of conditioning cannot be erased overnight. However, facing rejection head-on means you become desensitized to it and better equipped to rise above it, which will help level the playing field not just for ourselves but for future generations.

Having it all

The payoff, for ourselves and for society, when we push beyond our worthiness barriers is priceless. Through my work, I've been fortunate enough to come up close and personal with some of the most inspirational women of our time – women who fearlessly embody the Sheryl Sandberg philosophy of 'leaning in'; women who defy (present-day) expectations and limitations.

These women are creating a *new normal* – one that is centred around female-friendly working practices – and it's being led by women like Mary Callahan Erdoes. As chief executive officer of J.P. Morgan Asset Management, Callahan Erdoes is one of the most important people in finance and supervises over $2.2 trillion in assets. A wife and mother to three children, she explained to me how she used her seniority to make it easier for other working mothers within her organization. She leaves the office early enough to collect her children from school every day, and loudly announces it daily to her team: 'I'm leaving to go and pick up the kids.'

Another leading working mother who is unapologetic about it is

Helena Morrissey, former CEO of Newton Investment Management, a £51 billion Bank of New York Mellon European fund. Morrissey is also the co-founder of The 30% Club, a campaign to make UK FTSE-100 boardrooms 30 per cent female. She is a trailblazer and has risen to the top of the UK finance industry. However, she is almost as famous for her professional achievements as she is for her nine children, who range in age from seven to twenty-four.

Morrissey leaves the office every day at 6 p.m. to be home in time for family dinner and the odd bit of ironing. She credits part of her success to having a stay-at-home husband, Richard: 'The idea that a woman can have a family and friends and hold down a difficult, high-octane job when both partners work full-time – that is a very tall order. I am not saying it's impossible, but it's a bit unrealistic.'

Morrissey believes that the key to having it all is for modern couples to determine which career should take precedence while the children are young. And, crucially, this doesn't have to be the man's. In Morrissey's case, after their fourth child was born she and Richard, then a journalist, decided he should stay at home and she should continue with her career – a decision that has paid off considerably. The return on investment (ROI) has not only benefited their family (as Morrissey is one of the highest paid executives in the city), it's also benefited British society – for, in this couple, we have a high-profile example of what The Other Way could be.

Obviously, Callahan Erdoes and Morrissey are unique examples, as these two women are at the very top of their industries. Parent-friendly working practices are easier to implement when you are the boss. However, if more women rise through the corporate ranks, from VP level to the coveted C-suite (Corner office), these sorts of flexible working patterns will become more and more commonplace – because they will have to.

A new kind of role model

Role models are important, for women and men; they give us a glimpse of our possible futures and can keep us on track when our dreams seem out of reach. I remember having a conversation about this with my friend Toby Daniels, founder of the highly successful Social Media Week conferences. I've often chewed the fat with him regarding gender equality, as I do with all my male friends and colleagues, and on one occasion Toby made a point that stopped me in my tracks: 'Men don't see women as role models.' In an attempt to halt my jaw from hitting the floor, he went on to explain:

Mark Zuckerberg grew up wanting to be Bill Gates, Mark Dorsey grew up wanting to be Steve Jobs, Marissa Mayer probably looked up to the same male role models as Zuckerberg and Dorsey with a few female ones too. I doubt Zuckerberg and Dorsey would have had female business role models. When we have a woman who creates and is credited for the next groundbreaking innovation that moves humanity forward, such as the next Internet or the next Apple, then there will be a generation of boys and young men wanting to emulate those women.

I had never even thought about whether or not boys, or indeed girls, grew up with any female business role models. I've always had a slew of male business icons I've looked up to and whose biographies I've devoured. As it stands, women have many professional male role models, but the reverse is seldom true.

I have no idea if Toby is right about Marissa Mayer growing up inspired by Bill Gates and Steve Jobs, but I do know that Mayer has a surprising female role model whose 'against all odds' story deeply resonates with her own – the 2002 Olympic Gold medallist Sarah Hughes. In a 2013 interview with *Bloomberg Businessweek*, Mayer likened her appointment as CEO of Yahoo to Hughes's unlikely winning performance. 'No one thought Sarah Hughes had a chance to win. Afterward, Hughes said that she didn't quite know how she had done it and she wasn't sure she would ever be able to repeat it. It was the routine of her life . . . I feel like Sarah Hughes. Actually, I still have her performance saved on my TiVo.'

At 37 and seven months pregnant, Mayer managed to pull off an incredibly impressive career move and leapfrog from vice president, location & local services at Google, to president and CEO of Yahoo. Many industry insiders were stunned, as there were numerous tech execs who were more senior and would have seemed more likely candidates for the job, but Mayer had something these didn't: the power of the personal brand.

While at Google, Mayer carved out a stellar profile for herself as spokesperson for the company. She was also well known and respected outside of tech circles and able to explain complex technologies to the masses via the mainstream media. Undoubtedly her public profile would have played a role in helping the board of Yahoo in their decision. They would have been savvy enough to know that not only did Mayer have the ability to do the job, she also had the brand to sell the company to shareholders and potential advertisers. Even though Mayer's tenure at Yahoo has been viewed as mixed, she undoubtedly brought something extra – something unquantifiable on a CV, but nonetheless impactful in real life.

Every female in a leadership position is a role model for a new generation of both men and women about what is possible. One such woman, who's always been one of my favourite role models, is Clare Boothe Luce, a woman who carved out a phenomenal life for herself in mid-twentieth-century America, then very much a man's world.

A *Vanity Fair* excerpt from the second volume of Sylvia Jukes Morris's biography of Boothe Luce opens with: 'What Clare Boothe Luce wanted, Clare Boothe Luce got: a man, a seat in Congress, an ambassadorship.' All this was true, but Boothe Luce also managed to achieve so much more. She was able to soar to great heights in three distinctly different careers. Starting out as a journalist, she rose to become managing editor of *Vanity Fair* in 1930, aged 24, making her one of the youngest magazine editors in history. She then tried her hand at playwriting, penning the smash hit *The Women* in 1936, and later the screenplay for the movie *Come to the Stable*, which earned an Oscar nomination in 1949 for Best Story. After writing came a foray into politics, where she became one of the first women in Congress after running as a Republican and winning what was then a safe Democratic seat. She rounded out her political career as an ambassador to Italy for the Eisenhower administration.

Boothe Luce was very much aware of the double standards women of her day faced, and that her success or failure would affect not just her personally but the perception of female ability in general. 'Because I am a woman, I must make unusual efforts to succeed. If I fail, no one will say, "She doesn't have what it takes"; they will say, "Women don't have what it takes."'

Any woman who works knows that Boothe Luce's words are as true today as they were when she uttered them over four decades ago. Even so, she never let the barriers she faced prevent her from succeeding. Instead, she used them as motivation to defy expectations for women of her day. Hers was a life well lived and a life that has inspired generations of women who have followed in her footsteps.

The American Dream seems to provide a better breeding ground for these kinds of entrepreneurial women. By default, American women benefit from this system more than their UK counterparts. British women are still so underutilized, especially once they become mothers, when we still have so much more to add to the British economy. In a 2012 speech about female economic empowerment, then Deputy Prime Minister Nick Clegg declared that the 'absence of women from our economy is costing us dearly. If the United Kingdom had, for example, the same proportion of female entrepreneurs as the United States, we would see an extra £42 billion on GDP. In the words of the World Bank, gender equality is "smart economics".' He closed with, 'Greater equality, a fairer society, a stronger economy too.'

Having lived in both the UK and US, I've seen for myself that this is an area US women excel in. And it's not just about the job, it's about what you stand for. Across the pond, being of service is very much expected – even in the case of Sheryl Sandberg herself. Becoming a fearless spokesperson for female professional empowerment has opened countless doors and brought all sorts of new opportunities to her and to others, and has also helped to establish Sandberg as one of the most admired women of our day. She and others like her have proved that when we leap over the barriers within as well as without ourselves, we can achieve incredible things. This new normal hasn't yet filtered all the way up to influence the top job, as we know, but as Hillary Clinton said after her defeat in the 2016 presidential election: 'The future is female.'

ACTION POINT: Take the Rejection Therapy Challenge for seven days.

DISCUSSION POINT: What if Steve Jobs had never tried again – and never gone back to Apple?

CHAPTER TWO

In the Media

'You can't be what you can't see.'

Marian Wright Edelman

Throughout the ages, from paintings through to magazine covers and the movies, society's beauty standards have been represented via images that have been heralded as the 'ideal' of the day. Women in particular have been subjected to this relentless objectification and anyone falling short of these standards is either denigrated or ignored, leaving millions of young girls and women feeling unworthy, unrepresented, and fearful of rejection. Women are held to an entirely different set of standards than their male counterparts – we are valued by the way we look and how young we are; the 'prettier' and younger the better – and the mental pressure this creates wreaks havoc on our self-esteem. As a result, women are plagued with a level of self-doubt and self-criticism (myself included) that men do not have to face. And it's led to a narrow representation of women, not just in the visible media but behind the scenes as well.

As someone who has worked in the media for almost 20 years, I am very much aware of the power of image and the impact it has on how we value ourselves. I've even experienced its discriminating effects first-hand. So now, with ordinary women drastically under-represented, with actresses frequently flagging up the gender pay gap in the film industry, the proliferation of misogynistic trolling on social media and the easy access to online porn, it's become blindingly obvious that unrealistic, unrepresentative, and sometimes unhealthy images of women are projected into people's homes and minds on a daily basis. To counter this, we clearly need our media to start involving and portraying women in a more balanced and affirming manner.

Leading ladies

The Oscar-winning actress Geena Davis has become a leading advocate for the better representation of women in the media: her Institute on Gender in Media is doing a stellar job of holding Hollywood accountable by monitoring the representation of women both in front of and behind the camera.

I was fortunate enough to discuss this issue in detail with Geena when she delivered the keynote address at the WIE New York 2012 that I helped to organize, and some of the data from her research is quite startling.

- Only 16% of protagonists in film are female.
- Only 7% of film directors and 10% of writers are female.
- There were only 13 female protagonists in animated movies between 1937 and 2005.
- The female characters in G-rated family movies are just as likely to wear revealing clothing as in R-rated (effectively 18-rated) movies.
- More than 70% of the women on TV are in their twenties and thirties.[*]

---

[*] Geena Davis Institute on Gender in Media

The Institute's findings point to a systemic problem at the very core of the industry: the decision makers in the commissioning meetings, and maybe even the writers and directors themselves, are unwilling to put women at the heart of their stories. Geena is very frank about the problem: 'All of Hollywood is run on one assumption: that women will watch stories about men, but men won't watch stories about women. It is a horrible indictment of our society if we assume that one half of our population is just not interested in the other half.'

In some ways, we are trapped in a vicious circle here. Boys see from early on that male superheroes have a wide range of abilities, but the female's superpower will primarily be that she looks good in a tight outfit. That may well be nice to look at, but it can't be called *interesting*. In a world where women on screen are idolized primarily for their appearance and rarely given stories of much depth or complexity, it's no wonder that it's been hardwired into all of society that women are not interesting to men.

In all of the myths that the American writer Joseph Campbell examined in *The Hero with a Thousand Faces*, his seminal 400-page study on world mythology, none of them featured a female protagonist or 'hero'. He simply said he couldn't find any and that perhaps women didn't need mythical heroes as they didn't need to embark on a hero's journey in the same way as men. Author Elizabeth Gilbert addressed this on *The Oprah Winfrey Show* when she said: 'Men have a 30,000-year head-start over women in role models.'[*] And it's true. From culture to culture, women have been excluded as leading protagonists in the many stories that have shaped humanity.

We now need the support of men to create new, more inclusive stories, because of course part of the issue is undoubtedly that the decision makers, writers, and directors are – as the stats above confirm – also predominantly men. But even the female creatives who do

* Elizabeth Gilbert – Guest on *Super Soul Sunday*, Season 5 Episode 527. Aired on 10/05/2014 | tv-14. Read more: http://www.oprah.com/own-super-soul-sunday/elizabeth-gilbert-give-yourself-permission-to-honor-your-life-video#ixzz4oszUeGzl

manage to make it to the top industry jobs face a whole raft of unexpected barriers. The actress Anne Hathaway bravely admitted to an example of this in an interview with ABC News. Describing her treatment of Lone Scherfig, the female director of Hathaway's film *One Day*, Hathaway said: 'I really regret not trusting her more easily.' She went on further to explain: 'I'm so scared that I treated her with internalized misogyny. I'm scared that I didn't give her everything that she needed or I was resisting her on some level.' Hathaway is not alone in this pushback against female authority. Living in a patriarchy means most of our psyches have been conditioned to mistrust and sometimes punish women in leadership roles. And women can often be even harsher to their own gender because of their internalized insecurities, which can be triggered by other women who are brave enough to break through gender boundaries. Hathaway conceded that: 'It feels like a confession, but I think it's something we should talk about . . . I had actively tried to work with female directors. And I still had this mindset buried in there somewhere.'

We all need to challenge our internalized misogyny. Gender discrimination can sometimes be insidious and a little more difficult to detect because it doesn't carry the same level of guilt as racial or disability discrimination. We inherently know racial discrimination is wrong, even if we are guilty of it, but with gender our ideas about what constitutes sexism are warped, and therefore diagnosing misogynistic behaviour can be difficult and confusing. The level of self-reflection and analysis Hathaway underwent is not something most of us are prepared to do – in that same situation most of us would have put it down to a clash of personalities or just maybe a simple dislike, whereas Hathaway was able to explore the roots of her resistance to Scherfig and honestly challenge herself to explore if she would have behaved in the same antagonistic way towards a 'normal' male director.

The challenge, therefore, is manifold. As well as conducting a bit of self-analysis into our own internalized misogyny, we also need to work together with men to create stories around women, and to make sure women have the opportunity to tell those stories themselves.

Until women see more balanced and inspirational images of themselves, the journey to reach the level of unwavering self-belief required to fulfil our potential will be all the harder. As it stands, only the exceptional can get through. Unfortunately, by the mere definition of the word, most of us are not exceptional.

Cover girls

The film industry is not the only culprit in the media, of course. Unfortunately, a lack of diversity is still very much prevalent in mainstream women's magazines, too. Despite it being a female-centric industry, the images that make it onto the pages of our glossy magazines have long been notoriously homogenous – the women are reliably young, thin and, more often than not, white.

In the US, however, Anna Wintour, the legendary former editor-in-chief of American *Vogue*, has been at the forefront of addressing this. Over the last few years she has broken the mould and produced covers that feature leading women of colour such as Rihanna, Michelle Obama, Serena Williams, Zendaya and Beyoncé. Franca Sozzani, the late great editor of Italian *Vogue*, also made it her mission to make her pages more inclusive – her famed 'Black' issue, which featured the most iconic models of colour, past and present, is to date one of the biggest-selling editions of that magazine. Unfortunately, the UK still lags seriously behind on this issue, though there could be sunshine on the horizon as we again turn to *Vogue*. The appointment of Edward Enninful as its first editor of colour (who also happens to be a man) could result in the UK's most trusted and elite fashion bible becoming a publication that all women can see themselves represented in.

Women's magazine editors in particular have a very important role to play in ensuring their women's empowerment message includes all women – they can't create beautiful images of just one type of woman. What women read and see can very much influence what they believe they can be. A perfect example of this is the pivotal role magazines like *Ms* and *Cosmopolitan* played in the women's movement. Editors like Gloria Steinem and Helen Gurley Brown changed the way women saw themselves, and helped to liberate them both professionally in the boardroom and personally in the bedroom. Women's magazine editors have a clear choice to either be a part of the problem or take brave steps to becoming part of the solution. Publications that claim to be committed to female empowerment do so under false pretences if they continue to exclude women based on race, age, or size. And as we saw with Dove's 'Real Beauty' campaign, if done right, inclusivity can also be very lucrative.

The double struggle

The fight for gender equality often crosses over into, and sometimes clashes with, the fight for racial equality, and black women are at the epicentre of these two struggles. They have a fight on two fronts: they must negotiate a society that discriminates against them because of their gender, and also imposes upon them a standard of female beauty that is at the other end of the spectrum of what they represent. And as we've seen, in a patriarchal society, women are judged primarily by their appearance before they even say or do anything.

It is in this context that we find the labels of the 'strong black woman' who overcomes opposition and adversity, and the 'angry black woman' who is loud and unreasonable. But before we resort to labels we should examine the details of the black female experience more closely. Raised in the US and UK, they will soon become aware that they were not meant to be the delicate damsel rescued by the hero. In fact, in order to be worthy of acceptance they need to become as close as they can manage to their white counterparts by suppressing the essence of their authenticity, i.e. their 'blackness'. Black females in corporate front-of-house roles are often told that their natural Afro hair or braided styles are unacceptable, and that chemical treatments or weaves and wigs that give the appearance of straighter hair are preferable. And even then, wigs and weaves can become a means of denigration, as black US congresswoman Maxine Waters found when US political commentator Bill O'Reilly of Fox News claimed he 'couldn't hear what she was saying because of her James Brown wig!'

Waters responded defiantly as a 'strong black woman who cannot be intimidated or undermined'. She also made a rallying statement to *all* women: 'Don't allow these right-wing talking heads, these dishonourable people, to intimidate you or scare you. Be who you are. Do what you do. And let us get on with discussing the real issues of this country.' The congresswoman's response resonated with many professional black women around the world, who tweeted stories of routine and systemic disrespect at work, ranging from having their authority undermined to being mocked over their appearance. The hashtag #blackwomenatwork trended all over Twitter. These jibes may appear like harmless humour to some, but in actual fact they're an acute reminder of the real power relationship in the workplace in a society where black women have always been at the bottom of the hierarchy.

As a black woman in the media, I have my own wounds and scars from some of the prejudice, rejection, and subtle slights I have faced throughout my career. I learned very early on that the rules were not the same for me, and that my point of difference, although an asset in most cases, was also sometimes a liability.

One incident that comes to mind was when I was around 21. I had not long been at MTV, yet had one of the highest-rated shows on the network: *MTV Dancefloor Chart*. I was succeeded by Russell Brand when I went to co-present *MTV Select* with British comedian Richard Blackwood. It was a great time in the channel's history – I was part of a wave of MTV VJs (video jockeys) that included

Cat Deeley, Edith Bowman, Donna Air, and Sara Cox. We were young, hip, and the voice of Generation X. MTV had just newly rebranded in the UK and Ireland, and the network comms team embarked on an extensive marketing campaign to promote the faces of the channel. This involved a *Sky Magazine* cover titled 'MmmmTV . . . Delicious Reasons to Watch MTV'. The cover was a substantial beauty spread that included every female MTV presenter, except me – even though, at the time, my show was riding high in the ratings and I was a firm favourite with the viewers. My heart sank as I walked past newsstands and saw the cover glaring at me. I was happy for my colleagues but couldn't help crying at the fact that I'd been excluded.

What happened next completely raised my spirits, though. Because it was such a big cover story, the viewers of MTV started calling the network to ask if I had left the channel. The news soon spread that I hadn't left, I just hadn't been included in the shoot. It would later transpire that it wasn't *Sky Magazine* that had vetoed me – rather, it was the MTV PR team, who didn't think I was right for the feature so hadn't put my name forward. I have always been a glass-half-full type of person, and always look for the silver lining where possible. This rejection, painful as it was, ended up working in my favour – more and more viewers kept calling the MTV switchboard to complain. As a result, the MTV press office devised a marketing campaign specifically for me and I ended up shooting a piece for *Sky Magazine* with the legendary David Bailey. As they say, when life gives you lemons – make lemonade!

Incidents such as these would continue throughout my career. Many times I would agree to a cover shoot, only to be bumped off at the last minute – something fuelled by the general unspoken belief in the industry that women of colour do not sell magazines, which as demonstrated by Italian *Vogue*'s bestselling 'Black' issue, clearly isn't the case.

0: The number of Black Women CEOs in Fortune 500 & FTSE 100[*]

It's fair to say that women of colour have a double dose of discrimination: we are often ignored and excluded or, worst still, insulted in the media – and sometimes that insult is at the hand of our colleagues.

Such was the case for stalwart Labour MP Diane Abbott, following the Article 50 vote that awarded Conservative Prime Minister Theresa May the authority to begin the process of leaving the European Union. The Brexit Minister David Davis allegedly attempted to hug Abbott for voting with the government, but apparently her response to his show of affection was a strong verbal rejection. Davis then proceeded to inform a 'friend' about this exchange via text, remarking that he would have to be blind to hug Diane Abbott. Fortunately this 'friend' leaked Davis's text to the press. As hurtful as this was for Abbott, it was important that Davis's disgraceful disrespect was exposed for all to see.

No doubt critics on the other side of this argument will claim that this was merely a joke, and that chastising David Davis is just another case of political correctness. Well, in this and many other cases, politics needs correcting, as too many women, especially those of us who are black, have been expected to tolerate 'jokes' that men would not want directed at their wives, daughters, or sisters. This very public example of misogyny in the workplace helped shine a spotlight on the ways in which black women are stereotyped and denigrated on a daily basis.

This treatment can prompt a heightened sensitivity, especially when your experiences have taught you that this type of unfair abuse can come from anywhere at anytime. With no expectation of being defended by wider society, many of us are left with no choice but to

[*] https://hbr.org/2016/07/getting-more-black-women-into-the-c-suite; http://www.telegraph.co.uk/women/work/just-who-are-the-7-women-bosses-of-the-ftse-100

defend ourselves, sometimes robustly, hence the term 'angry black woman', which is propagated in the media and society generally. This can be the case even when we have broken barriers and succeeded against all odds, whether it be Michelle Obama being branded an 'ape'[*] or Venus Williams being called a 'gorilla',[†] or Viola Davis deemed 'less classically beautiful' by the *New York Times*.[‡]

I unwittingly once found myself witness to a media firestorm around the issue of the so-called 'angry black woman'. As a regular presenter for Sky TV, I was asked by their PR team to moderate a panel for the premiere of the TV show *Guerrilla*, which was soon airing on Sky Atlantic. *Guerrilla* is a story about the British Black Power movement, and the panel included the Oscar-winning writer/producer John Ridley, actor/producer Idris Elba, and other cast members, who were taking questions from an invite-only audience. Members of the audience, including Dominique Hines from the *Express* newspaper, organizer Imani Robinson, and activist Wail Qasim, questioned Ridley on why he had decided to cast an Indian woman (Freida Pinto) rather than a black woman as the female lead. His response was that historically Asian women had been prominent in the UK Black Power movement; this is true and was corroborated by audience member Neil Kenlock, the official photographer of the British Black Panther movement. Ridley then went on to explain that he had also been an activist in an interracial relationship, just like the show's lead character, and had also received prejudice from some in the African-American community. The black women and men in the audience argued back and accused Ridley of 'black erasure', meaning he had chosen to disregard the contributions of black women in the movement.

[*] BBC: http://www.bbc.co.uk/news/world-us-canada-38301808

[†] http://www.news.com.au/sport/tennis/venus-williams-called-gorilla-in-espns-australian-open-commentary/news-story/1b70be84a4fd3c820ecc67ae5f0f7cf9

[‡] *New York Times*: https://www.nytimes.com/2014/09/21/arts/television/viola-davis-plays-shonda-rhimess-latest-tough-heroine.html?_r=1

Freida Pinto became visibly upset at the questioning of her casting and the media story the following day was that aggressive Black Lives Matter activists had reduced her to tears.[*] Great for reinforcing the image of the angry black female, but not so great for addressing the pertinent issue of the representation of black women in the media. As a black woman, I understand that history and experience can make us focus our frustrations where it helps us least. I understand how it feels as a black woman to have your contributions overlooked in the media, in the professional world, and in history in general; the visceral feeling of humiliation yet again as your role in a story is demoted or 'erased'. But challenging the creative licence of a writer to tell a story in the way they want to is the fight that reinforces the stereotype.

The wider argument is the representation of BAME individuals in the creative industries, rather than in one piece of work. I would have liked to see that passion directed towards the government when they decided to cut funding to Creative Access, an organization that has been working to increase diversity in the creative industries through internships, apprenticeships, and other entry routes for young people from under-represented backgrounds. Of course, this didn't get the same media attention as the story about 'angry black protestors', so it wasn't widely known, but this is clearly where the protests need to be directed: making sure there is increased diversity in the rooms where projects are greenlit.

Michelle Obama eloquently discussed this issue with Oprah Winfrey in her final TV interview before leaving the White House. When she addressed how she dealt with being labelled an 'angry black woman' in her early days as First Lady, and how she rose above this to change the hearts and minds of America and show the world who she really was, she told Oprah, 'I don't hold on to the bad stuff. As black women,

[*] *Sun*: https://www.thesun.co.uk/tvandshowbiz/3283150/freida-pinto-cries-sky-drama-guerrilla

there's so much that comes at us all the time, every day, in subtle ways that could tear your soul apart if you let it. My mother taught me: you better keep it moving. You have to brush it off.'*

She is completely right that one has to adopt an extra layer of resilience in order to deal with this kind of discrimination. The one benefit of not receiving adequate or equal validation from the outside world is that it means you go inside yourself to draw upon your own self-esteem, and, in the end, that is the only thing you can truly rely on anyway. This applies to *all* women. When we learn to feel good about ourselves in spite of what the outside world might say, eventually that level of authentic confidence, whatever your gender or hue, is undeniable and the outside world eventually follows suit. It's infectious – we all know it when we see it and can't help but want to be around it. In the end self-love and self-acceptance trump sexism and racism.

But that fact cannot absolve the media of its responsibility. It is imperative that industry bosses change their thinking and ensure that everyone is in the room when the decisions are made, and that they are reflecting and including their audience – *all* of their audience. At the very least this is good business sense, as women will be encouraged to consume the stories that they can see themselves in, but it's also sound moral sense. Harbouring unrealistic ideals of women or a lack of interest in their lives denigrates men as well as women, and can only lead to dissatisfaction, on both sides, with the real thing.

ACTION POINT: Choose a book/film with a strong female protagonist the next time you need to buy a present for a young boy or girl.
DISCUSSION POINT: Who is your favourite female fictional character?

---

* Oprah Winfrey CBS Special with Michelle Obama, 27 December 2016

CHAPTER THREE

In the World

'If you want to go *fast*, go alone. If you want to go *far*, go together.'

African Proverb

Socially and culturally, we are limited by a shocking lack of gender equality on the global stage, be it in business or the media. To do my bit to address this, in 2010, with the support of Sarah Brown, Arianna Huffington, and Donna Karan, I co-founded alongside Dee Poku Women: Inspiration and Enterprise (WIE), a women's conference in New York City.* How WIE came about was really a case of being in the right place at the right time. I had not long moved to America when, in November 2009, Sarah Brown (wife of then UK PM Gordon Brown) invited me to a women's empowerment dinner she was hosting in New York with Queen Rania, Indra Nooyi (CEO of Pepsico) and Wendi Murdoch. Really, the evening was the Oscars of women's empowerment – and one of the most A-list rooms I have ever seen in my life. Guests in attendance included everyone from Nicole Kidman to Ivanka Trump (pre her father becoming President),

* Dee and I parted ways in 2012 – she continued with WIE New York, and I went on to create WIE UK. The two organizations are unaffiliated.

from Naomi Campbell to Jessica Alba, from Martha Stewart to Tina Brown and Shania Twain, and many more.

Sarah Brown delivered a heartfelt speech where she urged every woman to commit to doing something to help another woman. I was lucky enough to be sat next to Brigid McConville, the UK CEO of the White Ribbon Alliance, and – in a momentary Agyness-free second – we stood up and said we were going to organize some sort of event. Afterwards, Sarah Brown walked over to our table to discuss it further, and said she would provide whatever support needed – and she did.

Because we had made the announcement to this esteemed room (without really knowing what we were letting ourselves in for!), it felt like there was no turning back. Months later, we were organizing a press conference with Sarah, who had roped in her friend, Arianna Huffington, and Donna Karan, who had been roped in by a friend of mine. Now there really *was* no turning back.

WIE was conceived with the ethos of women inspiring women and developing a dialogue on how we can all be our best selves. The aim was to create a forum in which this generation's leaders could empower the next generation and then pay it forward to women in the developing world.

The focus of the first two years of WIE was to highlight the phenomenal work of the White Ribbon Alliance (WRA), a global charity committed to reducing maternal mortality. As global patron of the WRA, Sarah Brown and the White Ribbon Alliance have been instrumental in getting this issue on the global agenda and included as part of the UN Millennium Development Goals. Their groundbreaking work also encouraged Bill and Melinda Gates to start investing heavily in the fight against maternal mortality.

Dee and I had a magnificent time working alongside the senior WRA team, which included Betsy McCallon, Brigid McConville, and Jo Cox. The lead-up to our first NYC WIE conference was some of the most fun I've had in my working life. We were a team of five women, all committed to creating an event that would uplift and inspire, while also raising awareness for a great cause. The atmosphere was collaborative and one of female camaraderie. I was able to experience first-hand what a female-engineered professional environment looks like, as for almost ten months we all worked remotely on the event. I was in LA, Dee was in New York, Betsy was in Washington DC, and Brigid and Jo were in London. We were a team of novices on a very tight budget, so there were many close calls, but we handled and solved them together via our weekly conference calls and flurry of daily emails.

I still remember with fondness the day we were all actually in the same room. It was a hot September evening in New York during UNGA (UN General Assembly) week. I already knew Brigid and Betsy well, but it was my first time meeting Jo in person, who was heavily pregnant at the time with her first child. She was a bundle of energy, whose fierce intellect, wit and cheeky grin were simply infectious. She was carrying a boy and we all agreed that this WIE baby would one day become the type of feminist man we were trying to promote with our conference, the like of which we've seen in Jo's gracious and noble husband Brendan since her tragic passing. None of us knew back then in 2010 the tragic turn of events that would cut Jo's magnificent life short six years later, but what is certain is that she didn't just talk the talk – she lived it and inspired everyone she encountered to do the same. She was the living embodiment of the message from her House of Commons maiden speech, and truly believed that we do have 'more in common with each other than things that divide us'. She was, and remains, an inspiration to all women who want to go out there, take a running jump over the hurdles, and make a difference in the world.

He for she

Turning now to the wider and more objective arguments for diversifying gender, we must look at one of the abiding hurdles that women frequently come up against: men. Again, I must stress that this is not an opportunity for male-bashing. On the contrary, we must ensure that men are our partners in this process, not our antagonists. Up until now work has been the main source whereby men have obtained their self-esteem, and we must ensure that women sharing that work-space are deemed collaborators rather than a threat. Women can be as guilty of doing the opposite as anyone when it comes to what (or who) we deem as 'eligible' or 'a catch'. A report by the Institute of Fiscal Studies (IFS) found that poor men in their forties were twice as likely to be single as men from richer backgrounds.* So-called unsuccessful men are made to feel less of a man and less desirable. So, when you weigh it up, on the surface it looks as if men stand to lose a lot more from equality than women – and we haven't yet figured out what the emotional or egoic pay-off will be for them.

As the world changes, modern men are facing a challenge to their roles at home and in the world at large. Political changes have given women the right to challenge male dominance and to compete with men in what was once considered their domain. For boys in the playground who have always been socialized to be competitive go-getters (after all, that's what you need to be in a capitalist economy), there is no greater shame than 'losing to a girl'. Men are used to competing with other men but don't know what a 'fair fight' with a woman looks like. Do they keep them at arm's length, or try to recreate an environment of traditional male supremacy and hope that the woman reverts to type? Neither of these approaches works.

Socially and culturally, we have moved far away from the tradi-tional definition of the male with his angled jaw and broad shoulders. Men now share their gender space with those who don't have old-fashioned male attributes but may well be more successful than the 'traditional' men. Creative men, so-called 'effeminate men', trans-gender men, gay men, designers, artists, chefs, performers, and, of course, models, have all challenged the traditional view of what a

* BBC: www.bbc.co.uk/news/business-40894089

man should be, which for some men has created a crisis of identity and image. What should the twenty-first-century man be able to do? What should he be able to acquire? What should he look like? Who should he love? How should he love?

The man in the house is no longer the man *of* the house in the traditional sense. He may not be solely responsible for providing financial security, the home may not even be in his name, and the children in it may not be biologically his. Being a father was always about providing for your children, not so much about how you interacted with them, and being a husband was about protecting your wife rather than supporting her, but with those certainties no longer certain, what then is the man's role in that house?

Since women stand to be the immediate beneficiaries of gender equality (even if we know that in the bigger picture society as a whole benefits), we need to help shape a new narrative for these men and how we are going to relate to them. Things are going to change for both genders, and how we value men in society has to change to reflect this. Our idea of success needs to be redefined; women have the opportunity to lead the way on this and show our male counterparts that they need not fear a successful woman. This is not a zero-sum game.

We all have men in our lives over whom we have some influence. And we all need to hold these men accountable by encouraging and celebrating their progressive practices at work and at home, thus enabling our husbands, partners, brothers, and sons to see the advantages to a workplace of ambitious and effective female colleagues.

So if men have nothing to fear, then what do they have to gain? Other than, of course, a level playing field for their wives, daughters, sisters, and friends. We will see later in this chapter just how much society as a whole has to gain, economically and socially, from the rise of empowered women, but there are benefits on a smaller scale too. Women are usually the *de facto* operational managers of a home. An ability to manage a budget, resolve conflicts, and inspire excellence come as standard. This skill set is an obvious advantage in management and should not be overlooked or undermined. That is not to say these attributes are exclusive to women, but those who are able to demonstrate these transferable skills are undoubtedly an asset. For the male boss above her, she brings a safe pair of hands, and for the male subordinate, possibly an encouraging style of leadership that fosters progression and development. And for colleagues – yes, an element of competition but also an opportunity to learn alternative styles of working and thinking. Women have shaped the template and culture of the home for centuries; it's now time for us to add a lasting feminine dynamic to the workplace, and reap the social and economic benefits of doing so.

The power of the female workforce

The influence that working women can have on the fortunes of a nation cannot be overstated. The presence or absence of a strong female workforce has a far wider-reaching effect than most people realize. Surprisingly, Communist China is an interesting case study to draw on here. After all, it was Mao Zedong who originally said: 'Women hold up half the sky.'

A few years ago, I was filming in China and interviewed a 90-year-old Wey Chinese woman. The Wey are China's Muslim community and, traditionally, they have been somewhat discriminated against by wider Chinese society. This woman was alive pre-communism, and recounted to me how she felt that, as a woman, she'd had more opportunity under communism than she had before. This was in part due to the 1950 Land Reform Act.

Being a proud and firm believer in democracy, I was surprised to hear this – and keen to hear more of her story. So I learnt how the Land Reform Act was devised to improve the economic conditions of peasant workers through land redistribution – and how, as a result, women were able to own property and have equal rights to work the land. This changed tremendously the role of women in rural Chinese society.

And there was more. During China's 'Great Leap Forward' (1958–1960), the government's industrial push demanded that large numbers of men and women work in the newly formed state-owned industries. During this time, the Chinese government also supported women to establish 'Small and Medium Enterprises' (SMEs) in their local communities. These female-owned enterprises and new government initiatives provided jobs for over 180,000 women in Beijing alone.

However, long-term, this didn't make things easier for women. A few decades of policies that advanced women could not alter centuries of Chinese preference for boys. And, as the Chinese population grew exponentially, the government was forced to implement a one-child-per-family policy, which resulted in mass illegal sex-selective abortions and the abandonment of millions of baby girls. Those of age during the 1980s and 1990s will remember seeing the startling images of Chinese baby girls left by the roadside to die, or the numbers of unwanted Chinese girls discarded in orphanages for Westerners to adopt.

China is still reaping the rewards of its earlier female-friendly policies and is expected to overtake the USA as the world's largest economy in around 2027, with some economists predicting that this could happen as soon as 2020. However, the unforeseen side-effects of the one-child policy and the gender imbalance it has caused means that, long-term, China's dominance is precarious. It is estimated that there are 120 boys for every 100 girls – far above the global average and leaving this vast country with 50 million fewer women than men. This has left the economy short of millions of workers. Citigroup economists warn that this in turn could cut 3 per cent off China's GDP.[*] China is going to have to develop emergency measures to

[*] *Telegraph*: http://www.telegraph.co.uk/news/worldnews/asia/china/10484993/Why-Chinas-boom-may-be-coming-to-an-end-and-the-50-million-women-shortage-is-to-blame.html

tackle the potential economic and social havoc that could be created from its female shortfall. Traditionally, China has not been pro-immigration, but soon it may have no choice – there will be jobs that need filling and men who need marrying.

So what can we learn from China? When you create an environment that favours one group, you of course get inequality and under-representation of other groups within elite sectors. This means that you miss the chance to witness the might of human potential and what is possible for all groups if all are afforded the same opportunities and supportive treatment. Some gatekeepers – the influencers and decision makers – may still believe in the innate superiority or suitability of one group over others. But the irony here is that unless you, as a gatekeeper, are prepared to be proved wrong, you will never know for sure.

One country that has certainly proved this theory is Rwanda. It has one of the largest female workforces in the world and, as a result, now has one of the fastest-growing economies. Sadly, this shift towards women in the workplace came as an unintended consequence of a horrific civil war. The rise of women in Rwanda was out of necessity rather than design, after the 1994 genocide wiped out a considerable slice of the working-age male population – many of whom were the senior leaders and officials. A report by the Harvard Kennedy School Review states: 'Prior to 1994, women only held between 10 and 15 per cent of seats in Parliament. Out of sheer necessity, and a desire to rebuild their country, women stepped up as leaders in every realm of the nation, including politics.'[*]

Therefore, Rwanda had no choice but to develop and promote its women into the highest levels of commerce and power. But the benefits have been huge – not only economically, but also socially and politically. Rwanda is the only nation in the world to meet the UN MDGs (Millennium Development Goals), and its Parliament is

* http://harvardkennedyschoolreview.com/rwanda-strides-towards-gender-equality-in-government

now 64 per cent female. My personal view would be that this is a shift too far – male dominance should not be replaced with female dominance, but rather with gender parity. But it's a huge step in the right direction.

Women are good for business

There is much to be learned from the economic promotion of women in Rwanda and China, but our mature democracies mean that we in the West can lead the way in creating a truly gender equal society. All the recent data shows that women are good for business. A 2015 McKinsey report entitled 'The Power of Parity' found that by closing the gender pay gap and unleashing the full power of women, an additional $12 trillion could be added to the global GDP.

The report went further, to suggest that: 'In a "full potential" scenario in which women play an identical role in labor markets to that of men, as much as $28 trillion, or 26 per cent, could be added to global annual GDP by 2025.' [*]

Nicholas Kristof and Sheryl WuDunn also come to the conclusion that the economic benefits of female empowerment are incontrovertible in their book, *Half the Sky: Turning Oppression into Opportunity for Women Worldwide*: 'It's no accident that the countries that have enjoyed an economic take-off have been those that educated girls and then gave them the autonomy to move to the cities to find work.'

In the UK, a female executive coaching practice called Pipeline, founded by Labour peer Baroness Margaret McDonagh and entrepreneur Lorna Fitzsimons, publish a comprehensive study on the bottom-line numbers regarding senior female executives of FTSE-350

[*] McKinsey report 2015: http://www.mckinsey.com/global-themes/employment-and-growth/how-advancing-womens-equality-can-add-12-trillion-to-global-growth

companies, entitled 'Women Count'. The topline findings of the 2017 study summarized that:

- Women make up only 16% of executive committees.
- Women make up just 8% of executives on main PLC boards.
- Profit margins are almost double in companies with at least 25% females on their executive committee, compared to those with only men.
- Women help other women. Female CEOs on average have twice as many women on their executive committees than their male counterparts.[*]

These stats speak for themselves: the numbers of women reaching these powerful positions are low, but when they do, they are of huge economic benefit to the company.

Despite all our progress, the statistics are still depressingly low. But given the financial rewards that would be reaped, it's clear that the future of business must involve the full and equal inclusion of *all* women.

The disparity between gender pay despite legislation and much debate remains an unresolved issue. The BBC found itself as the national symbol of this debate when the alarming pay disparity between its male and female top earners was released earlier this year. The figures revealed that it's highest earner male, Chris Evans (annual salary between £2.2m and £2.25m in 2016/2017), earned more than four times that of the Corporation's highest female earner, Claudia Winkleman (annual salary between £450,000 and £499,999).[†] The figures were even bleaker in its news department, which had numerous

---

[*] http://www.execpipeline.com/research/women-count-2017
[†] http://metro.co.uk/2017/07/19/bbc-salaries-report-reveals-women-are-paid-four-times-less-with-claudia-winkleman-the-highest-earning-female-star-6790566

male presenters earning over £100,000 more than their female colleagues for doing exactly the same job. The BBC was heavily criticized once the salaries of its top earners was made public, and the fallout has been immense, with many of its female onscreen talent threatening legal action. Unfortunately, the BBC gender pay gap appears to be a microcosm of the society it serves as it also reflects a class bias where 45% of the highest paid were privately educated – so they too are recruiting for the highest-paid positions from a pool of 7%.*

When you factor race into the gender pay gap, women of colour fair even worse than their white counterparts. There were just five black or ethnic minority women on the list of the ninety-six stars who earn more than £150,000. This is an issue that Serena Williams has made it her mission to highlight. Williams, arguably one of the most successful athletes in the world and definitely at the pinnacle of her sport, has spoken up about gender and racial disparity in pay not just in her own sport but in society in general:

> *The cycles of poverty, discrimination, and sexism are much, much harder to break than the record for Grand Slam titles,' said Williams, decrying statistics showing 'women of color* [sic] *have to work on average eight months longer to earn the same as their male counterparts do in one year.*

Her concerns are backed up by many studies, both in the UK and the US, looking at income inequality, such as the Fawcett Society, which highlighted that Black women were among some of the lowest paid females, with Pakistani and Bangledeshi women earning the least among all groups.† This is clearly not where we want to be as

---

* https://www.metro.news/diversity-in-the-bbc-the-11-who-made-it-to-the-top/680354

† https://www.fawcettsociety.org.uk/2017/03/many-minority-ethnic-women-left-behind-pay-gap-progress

a society. But we sleepwalk into the situation by disregarding 'others' even when they are successful (like Serena), and then wonder why we have endemic issues with pay disparity.

In a moving personal essay, published by *Fortune* magazine, the 23-time Grand Slam champion writes that for every dollar a white man earns, black women make just 63 cents, while white women earn 80 cents. Ultimately, on a political level, additional legislation is also needed to ensure that companies are unable to get away with this unfair practice. At a more personal and professional level, the gender pay gap is something that all women need to come together to address while also enlisting and challenging male gatekeepers to adequately compensate for the efforts of men and women equally.

One man who understands the societal and economic benefits of investing in and adequately compensating women is Swiss industrialist Yann Borgstedt. Borgstedt spent the first part of his career building his own business and after a successful exit, he 'wanted to share his good fortune and make a positive impact on society', so he used part of the proceeds to create The Womanity Foundation. Womanity is dedicated to empowering disadvantaged women and girls all over the world. Founded in 2005, the Foundation has gone on to change the lives of thousands of women and girls globally in countries including Brazil, the Middle East, Africa, India, and Afghanistan. Listed among the UN's top 500 NGOs, the foundation focuses on girls' education and helping to end violence against women, which unfortunately is still the top cause of death for women globally and 'one of the biggest economic costs to society – £30 billion per year in the UK alone,' Borgstedt explained when I interviewed him.

Borgstedt is now dedicated to helping close the gender equality gap: 'As a man I could not sit by and let others get the short end of the stick because they were born a woman.' Like many thought leaders and change agents, Borgstedt obviously has a TED Talk, and his is titled 'Why Men Should Invest In Women', which was filmed in London at a TEDx event. Opening boldly, Borgstedt states that his mission is to help 'create a society where men and women are given the same rights and chances'. The passionately reels off stat after stat: 65 countries lose $95 billion in GDP by investing less in girls' education than boys; 70 per cent of the world's poor are women; only 1 per cent of property ownership is in the hands of women. As he continues he then jokes: 'I'm going to bore you with statistics, but I know if I need to change men's minds then I need to bore them with statistics.'*

Borgstedt has a point. One thing that is certain is that when it comes to gender equality the numbers don't lie, both in terms of the severe levels of inequality, the sheer costs financially, and the immense gains, economically and socially, when we get it right. So why are some people so afraid of this? What is the threat inherent in gender equality? Men do not lose from female emancipation. This is something Borgstedt is adamant about: 'Gender equality creates a society that is more prosperous, so the whole society benefits, including men.' Because in the end what is good for Womanity is good for Humanity! The successful man in the twenty-first century is enhanced by female success. It shouldn't be a competition at home or at work. In both spheres men and women have a part to play, and both bring an added dimension that complements their respective roles.

Power couples – collaboration of the sexes

The same goes for relationships between men and women. At this point I would mention the Obamas as a particularly strong example of a couple who have redefined what a truly equal partnership looks like. Barack Obama is one of the few men in the public eye over the past decade to have presented a response to the question of the new

---

* Yann Borgstedt's TED Talk: https://www.youtube.com/watch?v=4gpW9haB5nE

male identity for the twenty-first century. Yes, politically he was the first African-American president, but almost as radical was his portrayal or interpretation of what it means to be a modern man. A man who had not served in the military, as many previous presidents had, but who positioned himself to be judged not only on his performance in his job but as a husband and a father, indicating that his ability in those areas was an equally important measure of a man. He would routinely reference the impact of his decisions as a father of two daughters, and gave a clear message that his wife Michelle was his equal and partner in his role as POTUS, and that it was his role to support and honour her as FLOTUS as much as it was hers to support him.

Michelle in turn often had her own platform and spoke out on many issues, which complemented and enhanced her husband as a president and a man. It was clear that she had been his constant collaborator in his unlikely journey to the White House. Clearly as a man he had been discerning in his choice of partner and not been afraid of intelligence, ambition, and strong opinions when he encountered them. He did not view these as a threat to his masculinity, but rather as an enhancement. As a couple and a true equal union, the Obamas present a redefined view of masculinity and femininity within the context of traditional marriage, and are a living embodiment of Margaret Mead's powerful quote: 'Every time we *liberate a woman*, we *liberate* a *man*.'

Real wonders can be achieved when men and women work together, utilizing each others' strengths and even compensating where the other may be lacking. Great dynasties, empires, and companies have been built, maintained, and expanded through such collaborations. Any entity or venture that interacts with people to persuade them to act in a particular way will be dealing with both men and women, so to have an understanding and empathy of both is essential to success. This might seem obvious, but in many cases the greatest collaborations have been obscured from our view as the female in the partnership has played a hidden role, which suits our preconceived ideas of a male/female partnership.

I believe this is in part why society is so obsessed with 'power couples' – high-profile couples, where a man and a woman become more than the sum of their parts. They are 'all good' by themselves, but a force when they're together. There are many examples in today's media – Jay-Z and Beyoncé, the Beckhams, William and Kate, to name a few – but we can also go back over a century to one of the most effective power couples of all time: Queen Victoria and Prince Albert. Theirs was a unique relationship in an era when men were shaping the world and women still couldn't vote: a queen who ruled over an empire, and her husband, who was her consort but also her subject. This, as you might imagine, must have been a very delicate situation for Albert's male ego. But rather than compete with one another, Victoria and Albert celebrated each other's strengths, and together this formidable pair were great patrons of science and the arts, and their shared vision helped to ignite a century of innovation while also securing the future of the British monarchy.

It's clear that where men and women complement and balance each other, partnerships flourish and great things can happen. This is not only the case in the romantic arena; the same is true in business. One such example is the professional partnership of Angela Ahrendts and Christopher Bailey. During their successful reign at Burberry, this dynamic duo turned a failing British heritage label into one of the most successful and innovative fashion brands in the world.

Hidden figures

Relationships such as these, however, seem to be the exception rather than the rule. The real crux of the problem is how men and women relate to each other in general: how we are socialized and schooled as children, and how this impacts the way we interact as adults. If we drill down a little further, most leadership positions are still the domain of an elite group of privileged men. Many of these men have been educated in the private system, which tends to separate boys and girls. If you haven't grown up collaborating with girls on your end-of-year science project, then you're less likely to feel comfortable collaborating with women in your adult life.

As a state-school-educated woman of colour, I have been negatively impacted by these institutionalized standards that benefit white men from privileged backgrounds. But I've benefited, too – we all have. We can't deny that some of the world's most innovative inventions have been created by this small, elite group and their equivalents from the rest of Europe and the US. For example, many of us today are able to enjoy travelling by land, sea and air, thanks to the endeavours of Henry Ford, John Fitch, and the Wright Brothers.

However, there is a plethora of unsung female inventors who have helped to move society forward, too – and there would undoubtedly be even more if women had historically had the same access to education and opportunity as men. Women such as Maria Beasley, who saved millions of lives with her invention of the life raft in 1882, and Mary Walton, who created several key air- and noise-pollution-reducing devices and mechanisms, also in the late nineteenth century. Or Stephanie Kwolek, one of the first female research chemists, credited in 1971 with the invention of Kevlar®, a synthetic material five times as strong as steel that is the main ingredient in bulletproof vests. Or 12-year-old Rachel Zimmerman, who, in the 1980s, developed a software program using 'Blissymbols', which enabled people who have difficulty speaking – such as those with severe physical disabilities like cerebral palsy – to communicate.

Then you have women such as Katherine Johnson, Dorothy Vaughan and Mary Jackson, three African-American NASA mathematicians whose unsung genius was vital in getting the US into the space exploration game. Their groundbreaking story was depicted in the 2017 movie *Hidden Figures*, which to date has grossed over

$224 million worldwide at the box office[*] and inspired a generation of young girls to study STEM (Science Technology Engineering and Maths).

48: the number of women who have been awarded a Nobel Prize between 1901 and 2016.
833: the number of men awarded a Nobel Prize between 1901 and 2015.[†]

In Britain, one of our own hidden figures marks perhaps one of the greatest injustices in scientific history. When it comes to the discovery of DNA, many people have heard of James Watson, Francis Crick, and Maurice Wilkins – the three male scientists who shared the Nobel Prize for momentous scientific breakthrough – but few have heard of Rosalind Franklin, the woman whose work in the area of crystallography and X-ray diffraction provided the image of the famed 'Photo 51' that Watson and Crick used as the basis for their now-iconic model of DNA. Franklin had innocently given Wilkins, her colleague at King's College, access to the image, not knowing that he would later reveal it to her Cambridge rivals, Watson and Crick. When they published their findings in the scientific *Nature* magazine in April 1953, they downplayed their use of Franklin's research. Sadly, Franklin died from ovarian cancer in 1958. She was only 37 and her vital contribution to the discovery of DNA was never fully recognized in her lifetime. Fortunately, her brilliance was not overlooked permanently and history has been kind to her legacy – she is now regarded as one of the most important scientists of the twentieth century.[‡]

By highlighting the scientific achievements of women like Rosalind Franklin, we can encourage more young girls to develop a passion

[*] Box Office Mojo, April 2017
[†] http://www.nobelprize.org
[‡] PBS's NOVA television episode entitled 'The Secret of Photo 51'/*Life's Greatest Secret: The Race to Crack the Genetic Code* by Matthew Cobb (Profile Press, 2015)

for STEM and to believe that women have a vital role to play in the area of science and technology.

I'm sure no one would dispute that all the aforementioned women, though perhaps not so well known as their male counterparts, have made an equally invaluable contribution to our modern world. These women were exceptional, not because their gender lacked ability, but because they managed to thrive in industries where progression might be restricted or prohibited due to their gender. Imagine how much faster and more innovatively we could progress without those barriers in place!

If all gatekeepers – the educators, the decision makers, the employers, and the influencers – had the same visionary approach that enabled these women to progress, imagine how much richer our world would be. Unfortunately, not all gatekeepers do, which begs the question: what has been the cost to us all? Or, to put it another way, how much longer will we have to wait for a cure for AIDS, a solution to our environmental issues, or a resolution to today's geopolitical and socioeconomic concerns if men and women fail to work together and allow mutual progression? That is the real cost of holding back or denying potential brilliance, because it comes in unexpected packaging.

ACTION POINT: Choose to donate to a charity teaching young girls to code.

DISCUSSION POINT: What if Albert Einstein had been born a girl?

The Other Way

'Human rights are women's rights, and women's rights are human rights.'

Hillary Clinton[*]

One might assume that women would be the 'other' group with the best chance of overcoming prejudice and achieving equality. After all, they are the only group not to be a minority and can be found within every family.

Unfortunately, the very idea of a woman as a leader still faces opposition – from women as well as men. You could argue that race rather than gender was the biggest dividing line in America, but Americans have twice voted in a black president, and they didn't vote in a woman when they had the chance. Hillary Clinton did, of course, manage to win the popular vote by almost 3 million in the 2016 US election, but she failed to secure the votes from the majority of her own demographic. Donald Trump received 53 per cent of the white female vote in the presidential election,[†] and his campaign was anything but female-friendly. He advocated that women be punished

---

[*] Hillary Clinton's remarks to the Fourth Women's Conference in Beijing, China, 1995

[†] https://fivethirtyeight.com/features/clinton-couldnt-win-over-white-women

for choosing to terminate unwanted pregnancies, and during one of the presidential debates, when asked about a recording in which he bragged about sexually predatory behaviour against women, his response was that the US had a problem with political correctness and his comments were just 'locker-room talk'. Over a dozen women accused him of sexual assault, but even this, it seems, did not deter female voters from choosing him over Hillary Clinton.

There are a multitude of reasons why people vote the way they do, but the fact that the majority of white females voted for a man with a very narrow view of the value of women over a female candidate with much more experience suggests that in America it's not only men who have an issue with a female commander-in-chief. This may be the most powerful example we've yet seen of internalized misogyny. America may be the leader of the free world, but in terms of female leadership it still has a long way to go.

In 2017, the UK is on its second female prime minister and has had a female head of state for the last six decades, but there is no cause for congratulations or complacency in gender parity here either. We don't yet have a level gender playing field anywhere in the world, and America, in particular, is yet to reconcile its mistrust of overtly strong women.

And yet the argument for parity for women is overwhelming. We've seen the evidence that it is essential for economic growth, for technological advancement, and for stronger, happier, and more powerful relationships between men and women. We've seen that the misrepresentation and exclusion of women in the media feeds unhealthy stereotypes, encourages insecurity in women and leads to a narrow demographic appeal and a lack of relatable role models for women and for men. We've seen that they can excel in the boardroom as much as men, while still maintaining their role in family life. And we've seen that this parity would in fact benefit men, not detract from them. So everyone really is a winner.

We have already made great headway on gender equality — in the last 50 years especially, the landscape at home and at work and on the global stage has changed significantly for women. But there is still a lot of work to do if we are to continue making progress and, crucially, if we are to prevent it from rolling backwards. Astrologists say we've now entered the Age of Aquarius – the feminine age when women will step into leadership roles like never before, and a feminine dynamic will begin to balance the scales of power. These are indeed very exciting times for women, but to navigate them to our fullest potential, we need to decide how we're going to shape and influence the workplace and power structure in a way that is authentic to who we are as women rather than stepping into the male template, just in higher heels. For decades women have fitted themselves as square pegs into male-designed round holes, but what does success on female terms look like? How will women redefine the attributes society considers successful, and how will we select what those attributes are? To answer these questions in the twenty-first century, gender equality has to be at the forefront of government social policy.

Gender mainstreaming is about making women's issues into men's issues, too. And this has to be a goal that men and women work together on, so that the outcome leads to shared success, rather than resentment or emasculation. This will set the framework for how we create a society in which women are valued just as much as their male counterparts.

The Numbers

Top five professions with the largest male and female gender pay gaps, 2016[*]

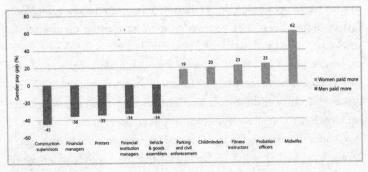

The proportion of women on the boards of FTSE-100 companies in Britain, 2016[†]

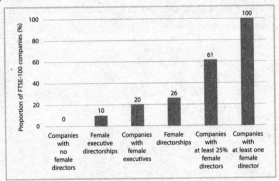

[*] Office for National Statistics
[†] Cranfield University

Average percentage return on capital in FTSE-350 firms, 2014[*]

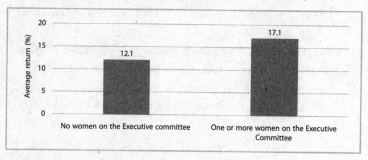

Need-to-know Facts and Figures:

- **54%**: the proportion of the Civil Service who are women and **39%**: the proportion of senior Civil Service roles occupied by women[†]
- **39%**: the proportion of people living in poverty in the UK who are women and **37%**: the proportion of people living in poverty who are men[‡]
- **15%**: the proportion of US women living below the US poverty line in 2015 and **12%**: the proportion of US men living in poverty[§]
- **30%**: the proportion of seats held by women in the House of Commons (195/650). To date, there have only been 455 women MPs – fewer than the number of men currently in the Commons[¶]
- **64%**: the proportion of people paid below the National Living Wage in 2016, who were women. This is largely because women and part-time workers are over-represented

[*] *The Pipeline*. Based on firms where executive committee details and returns on Capital are known
[†] UK Civil Service
[‡] Women's Budget Group
[§] Census Bureau
[¶] House of Commons Women and Equalities Committee

in low-paid industries including hairdressing and childcare, where the highest percentages earn below the National Living Wage[*]

- **Fourth:** The UK's ranking among G20 countries on the proportion of women in senior public sector roles (39%), after Canada (46%), Australia (40%), and South Africa (40%), but ahead of Brazil (35%) and the US (34%)[†]

[*] Office for National Statistics
[†] EY

Check Your Circle

'Playing it safe is the riskiest choice we can ever make.'
Sarah Ban Breathnach

There's an old proverb in Ghana that says, 'Show me your friends and I'll show you your character.' The people we choose to surround ourselves with give an insight into who we are, not just because they may be a reflection of our own character, but because they represent what we feel comfortable around. We design our personal circles inspired by our own image, and in doing so we produce a microcosm of our own society.

So, in creating your circle or mini-society, are you outward-looking or insular? Do you need to hire, befriend, or even love people who feel familiar in order to feel safe? Or are you someone who looks beyond what is visibly different to find commonality? The second of the Six Degrees of Integration asks you to examine your 'circle' and if it needs diversifying, to reach out to those beyond it and find common ground – the point at which all humanity meets – with people with whom you thought you shared nothing.

I saw this principle in action when I moved to America. My first stop was LA, and upon arrival I quickly integrated myself into the British ex-pat community, which is now over 750,000 strong (to my dismay, my British accent had no extra currency at all!). I quickly realized that the City of Angels should be renamed the City of Contradictions. Extreme wealth and excess are blocks away from deplorable deprivation; macrobiotic restaurants and green juice bars sit next door to In-N-Out Burger joints; nobody walks and yet people drive themselves to the gym; hedonism is juxtaposed with yoga and spirituality.

A walking, breathing embodiment of this hybrid of hedonism and spirituality is the 12-Step community – people who have taken their hedonistic pursuits to the point of destruction and have turned to spirituality in order to try to heal and overcome their addictions by using the 12-Step recovery program.

Now, I don't drink – I'm completely teetotal and have only ever been drunk once in my life – yet a large chunk of my friends are in Alcoholics Anonymous (AA). (I wonder what Freud or Jung would make of this . . . though I would add that this comes with the territory of being in the entertainment world.) One day, one of these friends convinced me to go to a 'meeting' with her. What she forgot to mention was that this meeting didn't allow 'outsiders' (non-addicts) to participate, so in order to gain entry I had to pretend to be an addict. Next thing, I found myself standing up before the group, announcing, 'Hello, my name is June Sarpong and I'm an addict.' I have never received so many hugs and good wishes in my life! Little did they know that my addiction was not alcohol but high-heeled shoes, but hey, both bring you excessive amounts of pain for short-term pleasure!

I had no idea how much I would enjoy the 12-Step meeting, so much so that I went back a few more times. I found the whole 12-Step process fascinating, not least because it brought together all manner of people from a diverse range of backgrounds. As well as being a city of contradictions, LA is a divided city – divided by race, religion, income, age, agents, and, most of all, cars! At least in New York different worlds will collide on the subway – even if they don't speak.

If a Wall Street banker takes his kids on the train from Tribeca to their Upper East Side prep school, the ride will comprise Brooklyn residents, both original and new, on their way to work, students on their way to NYU, immigrant nannies and the odd homeless person who's blagged a freebie ride. This journey alone gives these privileged children a snapshot of a world that is very different to their own, and vice versa. This doesn't happen in LA, and yet in this divided city, the 12-Step community manages to move beyond societal divisions to connect on a human level, bringing people together through a need to heal their emotional pain. At the meetings I attended, I saw some of the wealthiest and most powerful people in Hollywood sitting side by side with blue-collar ex-convicts and those discarded by society. What struck me most was the lack of hierarchy and the genuine form of connection that existed in that room. Hearts were open because they had been broken, and each person had their part to play to help reassemble the pieces. Each had their own story, one they were able to share without the fear of judgement, reprimand, or reprisal.

I couldn't help but wonder why it would take reaching such depths of despair for human beings to see each other as just that: human. To see themselves as one rather than the 'other'. And indeed, after the meeting the majority of these people would return to their 'normal' lives and probably revert to the acceptable norms of their socioeconomic group. How many of those Hollywood moguls would actually invite the ex-convicts over to their Bel-Air mansion for dinner? And would an ex-con feel comfortable inviting a mogul to visit their 'hood, as it were? Probably not. Yet in the safety of the meetings, these people knew more about each other than most of their closest family members and friends; they had shared and revealed their deepest, darkest secrets.

I feel there are two main reasons why the 12-Step program is one of the most successful long-term human transformational programmes of all time. Firstly, users are allowed to share honestly in a judgement-free environment; and secondly, sponsorship and community support is key. The 12-Step program understands that lasting change cannot happen in isolation; using 'sponsors' (a more experienced person in recovery who guides the less-experienced aspirant), the programme gives one-on-one accountability as well as communal support at group meetings. To bring the power and the benefits of the 12-Step program out into the wider world, we need to do the same, and maybe then we will make some headway in empathizing with each other's plight.

So, if you live in a diverse neighbourhood, you have the opportunity to discover so much about others as well as yourself. By actively engaging in your community, striking up friendships, or volunteering to mentor or help a stranger, you will gain an understanding of others and exchange valuable skills and experiences. All or any of these actions will enhance your life by teaching you something you might otherwise have been ignorant of. There are of course risks with moving out of our comfort zone, but the risk of failing to do so is that we lead narrow, comfortable lives and miss out on so much of the variety that humanity has to offer.

I believe most of us want more enriching lives, where we can feel we have had an impact beyond our circle. With the Internet and our innate ability to communicate and connect with each other, the possibilities for cross-cultural connections are boundless. With the click of a button, we have the ability to spread ideas and impart change within our local communities, our nations, and even the world. So, check your circle. Does it reflect the full richness of what is available to you? If not, then perhaps it's time to add someone new and different.

PART THREE

THE OTHER CLASS

'An imbalance between rich and poor is the oldest and most fatal ailment of all republics.'

Plutarch

The Old Way

In the UK almost everything is seen through the prism of class. Where you are from is unfortunately often more important than where you are going, and predetermines the likelihood of you getting there, and your social status, education, and wealth are more highly prized than your talents and personal merits.

The famous 'Class Sketch', originally aired in 1966 on *The Frost Report* hosted by the late Sir David Frost, is a hilarious comedy sketch that most Brits over the age of 40 can quote line by line. This frighteningly accurate satire of the British class system stars John Cleese, Ronnie Barker, and Ronnie Corbett, and depicts a hierarchy that most British people can relate to, wherever they fall in the pecking order.

Cleese, tall and patrician in appearance and demeanour, represents the upper class; Barker, of average height, the middle class; and Corbett, short in stature, the working class. Each in turn describes their social advantages and disadvantages, and contrasts them with their neighbours, an effect emphasized by the actors' relative heights as they look downwards or upwards to each other:

'. . . *Barker: I look up to him [Cleese] because he is upper class, but I look down on him [Corbett] because he is lower class . . .*
Corbett: I know my place.'

As this sketch suggests, the generally accepted sweetener to the bitter pill of class inequality has always been social mobility. The excluded accept their exclusion today for the possibility that they, or at least their children, may have the opportunity to transcend their class tomorrow. Emotionally, they accept a degree of inequality as much as they accept that competition and financial rewards for success are part of a fair and free society; because they can aspire to the position of the man above them and hope that they will be better off.

And for a while this seemed to work. In the wake of two world wars in the first half of the twentieth century social structures loosened up, and working and living conditions for everyone improved generation on generation. Somehow Western economies were able to rebound and rebuild from the boom-and-bust model, and the post-war 'baby boomers' were able to ride the wave of capitalism that swept the latter part of the century. Times were good and there seemed to be a decent slice of the pie to go around.

But that's when social mobility seemed to hit a brick wall. In the past 30 years it has regressed at an alarming rate, and although as a country we are wealthier than ever before, income inequality is on the rise, to the point where Generation Y is the first generation that can expect to be worse off than their parents. Because where capitalism is concerned, there is always a downside. New trade links between the US and China were good for Western business and consumers: production was cheap, which meant products were cheap, so consumerism was high. But around the world, work was also cheaper, threatening job security for the working classes and limiting opportunity. Social mobility was the very thing that delivered these years of growth and prosperity – globalization – but now it has also created the reverse. The benefits seem to have eluded the collective taste buds of the majority and we are all left with a very bitter aftertaste.

For decades, income inequality was tolerable, even justified, when it was only access to luxuries that the majority was excluded from.

But now we have a situation where it's the necessities, items considered 'basics' – a place to live, the ability to travel or to save, even the ability to sustain a family – and this is a common theme on both sides of the pond.

Hillary Clinton is quoted as saying: 'The rights of women and girls is the unfinished business of the twenty-first century.' Without question this is true, but if gender equality is the 'unfinished' business of the twenty-first century, then social mobility may be its greatest casualty. It's a growing problem that cuts across all 'other' groups and – if not effectively tackled – could be the economic and social unravelling of the Western world as we know it.

CHAPTER ONE

Poverty

'The test of our progress is not whether we add more to the abundance of those who have much; it is whether we provide enough for those who have too little.'

Franklin D. Roosevelt

One of my earliest memories is of armed militia breaking into my family home in the middle of the night. In the late Seventies, my parents were young and idealistic and wanted to participate in the rebuilding of a new Ghana, so in 1980 – when I was three – we moved from the UK, where I was born, back to Ghana. Their idealism was short-lived: within two years their winter of discontent had been replaced by a summer of terror. As part of the Ghanaian elite, my family was supportive of the previous government. We were wealthy and enjoyed all the trappings that afforded: a large house in the right part of town, maids and servants, posh European cars, private schools, expensive clothes, and a large array of equally glamorous friends. Unfortunately for my parents and their friends that government would be overthrown by a military coup d'état led by Flt Lt Jerry Rawlings. Being part of the elite and also being supporters of the previous government meant that my family belonged to the two least popular groups in the country at the time.

On a balmy, hot summer's night, my family was awoken by armed militia. In a matter of seconds they were ransacking our house, going from room to room, helping themselves to whatever took their fancy. My siblings and I were petrified, my mother hysterical. My father somehow managed to remain stoic and calm until the militia decided that the final item they wished to take was him. My mother begged for mercy for her husband, while we children were too scared to utter a word. Meanwhile my father was quick-thinking enough to ask to speak to the captain of the soldiers in private. They were gone for minutes but it seemed like an eternity. When they returned, the captain was all smiles; he then summoned his troops and they all left. To this day I have no idea exactly what my father said to that captain – all I know is that he promised to go to our family safe and bring out an agreed sum, which the army would return for later. As soon as the soldiers were gone, my family fled with nothing but the shirts on our backs and our passports. We hid overnight at a relative's home and then boarded a flight for London the next morning.

Overnight we went from a charmed life of maids and servants to a council estate in the East End of London, and there started what would become for me a life of straddling the class system as I ricocheted between the haves and have-nots. These pressures would cause irreparable damage to my parents' marriage – they soon divorced and my father moved to California.

Growing up in the East End during the 1980s was an adventure, to say the least. No day was ever the same and there was plenty of mischief to be had. There was always someone you knew who was in a pickle, and usually it was my cousin Reg. If you have seen the TV show *Everybody Hates Chris*, which chronicles comedian Chris Rock's childhood in Brooklyn, mine was the African immigrant version of that, except that my cousin Reg was the calamitous younger Chris Rock character and I was the annoying little sister. My older brother Sam had moved to America with my dad, and my sister Rebecca was much older, so Reg became my de facto sibling and 'roll dog' (partner in mischief).

In my immigrant household, education was valued above all else – anything short of good grades was considered unacceptable. Glowing report cards would be proudly boasted of in front of the 'community' at religious gatherings; feeble excuses would be made for the suspicious absence of not-so-satisfactory report cards, such as, 'Oh, ours hasn't arrived yet,' even though everyone knew what that really meant. Ghanaians of my parents' generation were not a tactile bunch; love was expressed through African food and helping you with your homework, so the words 'I love you' were not something I heard growing up. As far as my parents were concerned, it went without saying. For my parents, like most African immigrants, discipline, hard work, good manners, respect for your elders, and a good education were what mattered. (Oh, and cleanliness. Ghanaians are obsessed with cleanliness. There was an ample supply of Dettol, which was not only used for cleaning dirty surfaces; it was also the Ghanaian answer to bubble bath.)

So I worked hard at school, but my diverse neighbourhood was where I gained a less formal education among people from a range of backgrounds, which in itself meant that I experienced a range of contradictions. I grew up in a single-parent household, but my dad would call constantly from America to check if I had done my homework. My mother worked as a part-time nurse for much of my childhood, but was adamant that I should have a career rather than a job. I had free school dinners and money was tight so our electricity was paid via a box in our home – if we ran out of ten-pence pieces and one-pound coins it meant no electricity. Showers were a luxury and 'bucket baths' were the norm. This meant boiling large pots of water, which was enough to fill one bucket to wash yourself with. Even with all this, I never felt I was less than anyone else. How much money you had or what your parents did didn't make you better than anyone else, and if you thought it did then you would soon stand – or rather fall – corrected.

Where I grew up, your street sense was as important, if not more so, than your book sense. You had to know when to stand up for yourself and when to run. Nobody was rich, but everyone knew someone who knew someone who knew how to save you a quid or make you a quid, and of course there were those who would take that quid off you just because they could. I developed some important core values, which helped me and those around me avoid some of the pitfalls that coincide with living in social housing. And crucially, I was also fortunate to be afforded opportunities within the media when I was young, and then for people to recognize my potential. Growing up connected to people of different backgrounds enabled me to do the same with audiences and celebrity guests. Being aware of the restrictions that background has on those who are different made me socially conscious and determined to create a positive impact, and my African heritage gave me a global perspective and an awareness that talent and opportunity transcend all boundaries.

So, as a black woman from a working-class background, in the context of this book that makes me an 'other' three times over, making my story very unlikely for those who share my demographic (actually it's four times over, but we'll get to that later – see Part Four: The Other Body, pages 183–221). But my journey and my experiences have given me the opportunity to take a 360-degree view and see why my story is far from the norm, what my inclusion adds to society, and how we can all be beneficiaries if we do diversify.

I've often been asked why an entertainment television host would be so passionate about politics. The answer is that my early childhood experiences in Ghana taught me the harsh truth: that leadership matters, politics matter, and, more importantly, policies matter. Ghana is a rare jewel in Africa's crown in that it has never had a civil war and has boasted a mainly peaceful existence since its independence from the British in 1957. The Rawlings coup d'état was an extraordinary period in Ghana's history, and Jerry Rawlings would go on to be democratically elected in 1992, winning 58.3 per cent of the vote, with outside observers declaring the election to be 'free and fair'. So this is not a country where civil unrest is the norm; it's a peace-loving nation. What happened in the late Seventies and early Eighties was a lesson to Ghanaians everywhere: peace and stability is not a given for anyone, and extreme levels of inequality can unravel even the most sophisticated societies.

Wealth inequality

Wealth, or the lack of it, is now the major determiner of the class divide. The British obsession with titles and rank has given way to a more subtle but no less damaging form of discrimination based on material attainment and the education, opportunities, and lifestyle that brings. In recent decades we have bought into the idea of the American Dream: that the wealth gap is something any hard-working or self-believing individual can close, but in both the US and UK, this doesn't seem to be the reality any more.

Education and employment have traditionally been the key active ingredients in effecting the social mobility needed to even out wealth inequality, but if the proof is in the pudding then the recipe needs to change. Journalist and corporate reformer Marjorie Kelly has a really interesting take on this malaise: 'We have words for racism and sexism, but wealth discrimination isn't fully recognized. It is a bias in favour of the wealthy and against labour, the environment and the community.' In other words, economic discrimination is so ingrained that we don't even have a word for it, and it attacks the very heart of our society.

Tackling this issue has been at the forefront of former Labour Health Secretary Alan Milburn's work with the Social Mobility and Child Poverty Commission. Since leaving government Milburn has made it his mission to try to level the playing field and close the ever-growing social mobility gap – he has become the go-to person in the UK, and has been dubbed the 'Social Mobility Tsar' by the British Press. I got the opportunity to question Milburn on his work in this area and why the Commission was founded in the first place.

He was very clear on the purpose of the SMC: 'The Commission was set up because of growing concerns that social mobility was going backwards in Britain. Over decades we have become a wealthier society but we have struggled to become a fairer one. The twentieth-century expectation that each generation would be better off than the preceding one is no longer being met.'

With the traditional methods of social mobility – such as a university education – no longer producing guaranteed results, and the gap between rich and poor becoming greater and greater, we are beginning to see the unpredictable effects that a lack of equality can bring.

38% of 18–34-year-olds name money as their top concern.[*]

It's been said that 'money is the root of all evil', and according to research it's also the root of the most stress, too. The *Observer* newspaper's 'Britain Uncovered' survey cited money worries as the 'greatest source of anxiety for Britons', with 30 per cent of Brits identifying it as their number-one concern, almost as much as the 'next two biggest causes of anxiety – family (16 per cent) and health (16 per cent)' combined. Among young people the figure is even higher.[†] One can't help but wonder if there is a correlation between this and the rise in mental health issues; according to the NHS, between '1993 and 2014 there was a 35 per cent rise in adults reporting severe symptoms of common mental disorders'. Again, this is an area in which young people are worse affected: over the past 25 years depression in young people is up by 70 per cent.[‡] And the pressure

---

[*] *Guardian*: https://www.theguardian.com/society/2015/apr/19/britain-uncovered-survey-attitudes-beliefs-britons-2015

[†] *Guardian*: https://www.theguardian.com/society/2015/apr/19/britain-uncovered-survey-attitudes-beliefs-britons-2015

[‡] *Independent*: http://www.independent.co.uk/life-style/health-and-families/features/teenage-mental-health-crisis-rates-of-depression-have-soared-in-the-past-25-years-a6894676.html

felt by young people in the US is no better. The National College Health Assessment recorded that '33 per cent of students reported feeling so depressed within the previous 12 months that it was difficult to function. Almost 55 per cent reported feeling overwhelming anxiety, while 87 per cent reported feeling overwhelmed by their responsibilities.*'

And sometimes the unforeseen consequences of inequality can be even worse. In Britain, on 14 June 2017, the effects of this ever-growing income divide would test us to our limits when unimaginable tragedy struck. In the Royal Borough of Kensington & Chelsea, where the rich and poor live cheek by jowl, Grenfell Tower, a 24-storey government block of 120 flats, housing 600 people, went up in flames, killing dozens of family members, neighbours, and friends. What made it worse was that this disaster had been preventable. The voracity of the fire was apparently exacerbated by flammable 'cosmetic' cladding from a £10 million facelift that was carried out the previous year. Disbelief, heartbreak, and then anger followed as stories emerged of desperate parents with no hope of escape throwing their children out of windows or jumping themselves, and residents who had become separated from family members while trying to escape searching for them in the hope that they'd also survived the blaze.

It soon became clear to residents that had they lived in a more affluent building, fire prevention technology such as sprinklers, fire alarms, fire extinguishers, fire doors, and emergency lighting would have been installed. This vibrant community had survived the racial tensions of the Seventies; they were the last remaining members of the lower incomes who hadn't been forced out when Notting Hill became desirable and trendy, yet poverty discrimination would prove a force too strong for them to overcome.

---

* National College Health Assessment: http://www.healthline.com/health-news/mental-health-problems-for-college-students-are-increasing-071715

In the aftermath of the fire, suspicion of the establishment grew as news broke that money had been spent on the outside of the block to appease rich locals who did not want to look at this 'eyesore', instead of on vital safety improvements for those inside the block. And worse still, it transpired that residents of Grenfell Tower had campaigned for better fire safety measures, fearing just such a catastrophe, and had been ignored. The divide between the working-class community and the establishment widened still further in the following days, as tensions rose with the daily increase in confirmations of fatalities. Such was the mistrust of the establishment that some would even claim that the fire was allowed to happen because Kensington & Chelsea council placed less value on its poor than its wealthy residents. Tottenham MP David Lammy (who actually lost a friend in the fire – Khadija Saye, a young, aspiring photographer) encapsulated the situation in the title of the Charles Dickens novel *A Tale of Two Cities*.

Days after the Grenfell tragedy, the *Standard* revealed that 68 'social housing' flats in a luxury £2 billion Kensington development had been acquired to permanently house some of the victims. Londoners were aghast when it then transpired that some of the wealthy residents within the luxury block were complaining about the Grenfell residents moving in. One such resident, called Donna, complained to LBC radio host Shelagh Fogarty that her annual service charge was £15,500, and that even though she felt 'sorry' for the victims of Grenfell, if they moved in to her luxury block then she and her husband 'would move'.

Lammy's reference to Dickens is apt. Reactions like Donna's are not too dissimilar to the inequality and disdain for the poor documented by Dickens in his novels. Yet the response of the privileged classes in nineteenth-century Britain to their own poverty crisis was much more decisive. Philanthropists such as the American George Peabody built housing for working-class communities to replace slum housing. Elizabeth Fry campaigned for prison reform, and at the turn of the century the middle-class liberals allied themselves in government with the working-class Labour Party to enact fair labour laws for working people. In these instances, the upper and middle classes saw it as their moral duty to do something for the poor.

I believe this moral duty still exists within the elite, but pressure to reduce public spending and a lack of diversity within the ranks of the establishment means that there is an awkwardness in addressing issues of deprivation and inequality. This was personified by the British Prime Minister Theresa May's response to the tragedy. As the leader of a party promoting austerity (essentially a reduction in public spending on services that less affluent people rely on), she was aware that she might not be warmly received. So when she visited the site of the fire, she decided to speak to the emergency services (quite rightly), but unfortunately failed to speak to and comfort the survivors, who had lost everything. Ironically, it was the Queen who showed her PM how to walk among the people, listening to their experiences and offering sympathy and an alternative narrative that they had not been forgotten by the establishment.

There was a stark contrast, too, with Labour leader Jeremy Corbyn's approach; his own constituency in Islington has also dealt with income inequality issues similar to those in Kensington. I, like many, have not been completely convinced by Corbyn's ability to lead the Labour Party and the UK effectively, but there is no denying that his well-judged response to Grenfell was exactly what the victims and the rest of the country needed. In his Commons speech soon after the tragedy he raged about the injustice of those who had to 'die in a towering inferno – living in poverty while surrounded by a sea of prosperity'.

I agree with Corbyn that inequality has to be addressed, especially as globalization and the changing demography of neighbourhoods will continue to be potential sources of tension in communities. If we are not careful, communities under pressure, who feel that they are experiencing establishment neglect, will lash out in civil unrest, which will cost us all. In fact, we've already seen this happen. In 2011, riots broke out in the historically working-class neighbourhood of Tottenham, and then in other boroughs across London and in other UK cities, in response to the police shooting of Mark Duggan, an unarmed black man. To avoid scenes like that, and tragedies like Grenfell, rather than ignore their plight and anger, it would be far more prudent for the government to invest in policies that include their talents and lead to a fairer society that allows people to transcend their class and not be held hostage by it.

As a way of trying to right the terrible wrongs of Grenfell, party politics should be set aside. We need a united effort by the government, the London Mayor and the leaders of Kensington & Chelsea (K&C) council to provide adequate atonement for those who survived and to honour those who lost their lives. Elizabeth Campbell, the new leader of K&C council, has promised 400 new homes by 2020. However, in the light of what has happened, they cannot and must not be sub-standard homes. They should instead build a state-of-the-art tower at the site of Grenfell and replenish the total 600 units that were destroyed.

This new tower should be a landmark building and a symbol in revolutionary social housing globally. It is the least that can be done. Towers are not the problem – unsafe towers are the problem. As we know, in the luxury property sector high-rise living is the ultimate status symbol and is coveted by the elite. Mayor of London Sadiq Khan has promised 50,000 new social housing units and has also formed a partnership with some of the UK's leading architects. Sir David Adjaye is at the forefront of this initiative. His Sugar Hill development in Harlem, New York, is the future of social housing. The development features a nursery, a rooftop farm, a gallery and a library. This is exactly the sort of development that needs to replace Grenfell, along with a monument to remember those who lost their lives.

Inequality is bad for everyone

Since 1980, the gap between rich and poor has increased exponentially. The broad-based economic prosperity of the post-war years has been replaced by steadfast global competition, diminished unionization, rapid advances in computers and robotics, and government policies shaped by the concentration of political power in the hands of the wealthiest Americans. The vast majority of the benefits of economic growth have gone to the richest 20 per cent of US households, while 60 per cent of American families have found their incomes stagnating or decreasing. This breakdown in the deal between the working classes and the powers that be has led to individuals facing a crisis of identity both in the US and the UK.

It's easy to forget, though, that rising income inequality is not only bad for the poor, it's also seriously harmful for the rich. As Bobby Kennedy reflected in his iconic 1968 speech, a higher GDP does not necessarily mean a better society:

> *Too much and for too long we seem to have surrendered personal excellence and community values in the mere accumulation of material things. Our Gross National Product, now, is over $800 billion dollars a year, but that Gross National Product – if we judge the United States of America by that – that Gross National Product counts air pollution and cigarette advertising, and ambulances to clear our highways of carnage.*
>
> *It counts special locks for our doors and the jails for the people who break them. It counts the destruction of the redwood and the loss of our natural wonder in chaotic sprawl. It counts napalm and counts nuclear warheads and armored cars for the police to fight the riots in our cities. It counts Whitman's rifle and Speck's knife, and the television programmes which glorify violence in order to sell toys to our children.*
>
> *Yet the Gross National Product does not allow for the health of*

our children, the quality of their education or the joy of their play. It does not include the beauty of our poetry or the strength of our marriages, the intelligence of our public debate or the integrity of our public officials. It measures neither our wit nor our courage, neither our wisdom nor our learning, neither our compassion nor our devotion to our country. It measures everything, in short, except that which makes life worthwhile. And it can tell us everything about America except why we are proud that we are Americans.

If this is true here at home, so it is true elsewhere in the world.[*]

The message couldn't be clearer: money isn't everything. And Bobby Kennedy was not alone in identifying a problem with assuming a rich country means a happy one. In his book, *The Spirit Level: Why More Equal Societies Almost Always Do Better*, academic Richard Wilkinson describes the negative societal effects of income inequality and the destruction it has on social mobility. According to Wilkinson, in poorer nations the overall national GDP is a key influence on social and health problems, but for rich, developed nations the key indicator is how wealth is distributed: 'The average well-being of our societies is not dependent any longer on national income and economic growth . . . but the differences between us and where we are in relation to each other now matter very much.'

In part, this could be influenced by the rise in social media usage – there are now 44.9 million smartphone users in the UK, more than double the number in 2011 (21.6 million) and this is set to rise.[†] Smartphones mean greater connectivity to loved ones, but also to a (potentially warped) vision of the lives of the upper classes, where affluence appears to bring instant, Instagram-perfect happiness. Even

---

[*] Bobby Kennedy, GDP Speech, University of Kansas, 18 March 1968: https://www.jfklibrary.org/Research/Research-Aids/Ready-Reference/RFK-Speeches/Remarks-of-Robert-F-Kennedy-at-the-University-of-Kansas-March-18-1968.aspx
[†] https://www.statista.com/statistics/270821/smartphone-user-in-the-united-kingdom-uk

though this is rarely the case, this, in conjunction with a series of other factors, throws the dissatisfaction of those who are struggling to make ends meet into sharp relief.

Higher levels of income inequality also mean higher levels of mental illness, crime and incarceration, overall unhappiness, social instability, and distrust between citizens – and these are issues that affect everyone, not just the poor. The UK and US are two of the most unequal nations in the developed world, and are notably worse than countries such as Japan and Finland, which rank best in terms of income inequality. And if inequality equals an uneasy and unhappy society, then it's in all our best interests – the rich, the poor, and the middling – to reduce that gap.

How does fairness work?

If you're thinking that class fairness is all very good in principle but are wondering how it works in practice, well, in practical terms, firstly it costs. Money should be spent on ensuring that vulnerable working-class communities are protected from market forces, which translates in working-class communities as being 'screwed over because we are poor'. Secondly, if you are sat around a table in an office making decisions that impact on people's lives, and the talent sat around that table are not from diverse class backgrounds, then that is the continuation of the unfair class system that needs to change. If working-class communities are prevented by establishment neglect from speaking at the table then the resentment will turn into rage.

Richard Wilkinson is adamant that there are clear ways to address income inequality, and he's fairly circumspect as to how it's done. Whether it's through fairer taxation like in Scandinavian countries, or through more levelled wages as Japan, he argues that it doesn't matter how you close the income gap as long as you close it.

Labour Peer Baroness Ruth Lister of Burtersett has spent her life campaigning on behalf of the poor, and she also has very clear views about what went wrong with Grenfell Tower in particular, and how the reasons behind it are symbolic of the problems facing society as a whole:

> *For too long people in poverty have been treated with contempt, their lives and their views counting for nothing . . . Had the more powerful listened to their fears about the safety of their homes, this shameful tragedy might have been averted.*

So once again, we see that a key factor in reducing the inequality gap is to listen to and recognize the 'other'. Resentment and anger comes from feeling – or indeed knowing – that your life and experiences are being ignored and undervalued. It's a simple change, it doesn't take much, but in cases like Grenfell, it can save lives.

I was able to discuss these issues in further detail with Baroness Lister on the actual day of the fire when I chaired an LSE panel discussion on inequality between The Baroness, Professor John Powell from USC Berkeley and Liz Sayce from Disability Rights UK. Baroness Lister spoke passionately about the 'hidden injuries of class' and talked more on this issue of 'recognition':

> *The deepest injury of class is lack of or mis-recognition. Recognition has been described by the political philosopher Charles Taylor as 'not just a courtesy we owe people. It is a vital human need' that can only be provided by others. As leading recognition theorist Axel Honneth notes, a striving for recognition rises from 'the experience of humiliation or disrespect'. This experience is all too common for people in poverty, especially in a highly unequal society.*

Recognition and value, then, has to be the jumping-off point for action. And Professor John Powell has an interesting take on how we can do this. He has devised a theory called 'The Circle of Human Concern' – the closer you are to the centre of that circle, the more empathy, value, and reverence society has for you, and the further out you are, the less these positive entitlements are afforded to you. Those on the peripheries or outskirts receive little or none. According to Powell's assessment, there was a time when the centre of the circle was the reserve of elite and privileged white men, but now even they have been replaced, albeit by the profit-making vehicles of their design: corporations. Powell explains that because corporations have smuggled themselves into the centre of the circle, monopolizing society's private space and concentrating wealth and influence there, the most marginalized people in society have been pushed out of the circle – including immigrants, ex-offenders, and those in poverty.[*]

Powell asserts that our job as concerned citizens is to actively expand our 'Circle of Human Concern' to include those who are currently on the outskirts and peripheries, and to change the dynamics of belonging to make sure that all people – and not corporations – are at its centre. By doing this we would not only be recognizing the 'others', we would be reclaiming our moral duty of showing that we care about their plight and intend to change it by creating a fairer, more equal society.

ACTION POINT: Find out if your local supermarket has a food bank collection. If it does, consider adding a couple of items to your next shop – like tinned goods, pasta, or nappies – and dropping them in the collection on your way out.

DISCUSSION POINT: How far from where you are reading this book right now would you need to travel in order to find poverty?

---

[*] http://haasinstitute.berkeley.edu/circle-human-concern

CHAPTER TWO

Power

'As long as poverty, injustice and gross inequality persist in our world, none of us can truly rest.'

Nelson Mandela

In the 2016 EU referendum and presidential election, the working classes in the UK and US decided they'd had enough of 'knowing their place', as the *Frost Report* 'Class Sketch' would have it. And yet this revolt wasn't the usual uprising of the past that involved bloodshed; instead, a simple cross on the ballot paper changed the political status quo overnight and sent the establishment into a tailspin. It is the one way the disenfranchised populace can exert some form of power over their fate.

Ignored voices

Neither country saw this earthquake coming, but if they'd taken more notice of how their voters were feeling, perhaps they would have. In the UK, a gloomy outlook was reflected in a report in February 2016, when the Social Mobility Commission enlisted Ipsos MORI to conduct a poll on intergenerational social mobility. The overall tone of the results were that Britain's best days were behind it: 54 per cent believed that young people's lives would be worse than those of previous generations, and even more worrying was that only one in five believed that better days lay ahead. These findings should have been a warning sign to the Cameron government of the growing dissatisfaction of hardworking Brits, and how this could impact the outcome of the upcoming EU referendum, which would take place four months later. Even though young people themselves voted over-whelmingly to remain in the EU, concerns by their parents and grandparents over their futures may have been partly why 60 per cent of 50–65-year-olds and 65 per cent of over-65s voted Leave.

Though a Remainer himself, Alan Milburn is convinced that these concerns are real and very valid and should have been heeded. He told me:

Britain's deep social mobility problem, for this generation of young people in particular, is getting worse, not better. The barriers to progress are becoming bigger, not smaller. The impact is no longer only felt by the poorest in our society but instead is holding back a whole tranche of low- and middle-income families. The problem they are experiencing is not just social division but a widening geograph-ical divide between our country's great cities, London especially, and those towns and counties that are being left behind economically and hollowed out socially. The divisions we face in Britain impact many more people and places than either the bottom decile in society or the few thousands of youngsters who miss out on a top university.

Whole tracts of Britain feel left behind. Whole communities feel the benefits of globalization have passed them by. Whole sections of society feel they are not getting a fair chance to succeed.

The fact that these communities feel left behind and ignored is why they voted as they did – in a bid to take back some control over their own lives. Famed thinker Noam Chomsky expertly explains how the same thing has happened in the US. In his film and book, *Requiem for the American Dream,* he draws on the history of US economic inequality to show the crucial difference between then and now:

> *During the Great Depression, things were much worse than they are today, but there was an expectation that things were going to get better. There was a real sense of hopefulness. There isn't today . . . Inequality is really unprecedented. In terms of total inequality, it's like the worst periods in American history. But if you refine it more closely, the inequality comes from the extreme wealth in a tiny sector of the population, a fraction of 1 per cent . . . Not only is it extremely unjust in itself, inequality has highly negative consequences on the society as a whole because the very fact of inequality has a corrosive, harmful effect on democracy.*

So there has always been inequality. But in more modern times the disparity between rich and poor has created more than just a class divide: we now have a global wealth divide. According to a pre-Davos (World Economic Forum) 2017 report by Oxfam, eight billionaires control as much wealth as the poorest 50 per cent of the world. Mark Goldring, chief executive of Oxfam GB, was quoted as saying, 'While one in nine people on the planet will go to bed hungry tonight, a small handful of billionaires have so much wealth they would need several lifetimes to spend it.'

25 years: the estimated amount of time before the world sees its first trillionaire.
1 in 10: the number of people who survive on less than $2 a day.*

These unfair consequences of globalization have created a new class, described by economist Guy Standing in his book, *The Precariat:*

* https://www.oxfam.org/en/pressroom/pressreleases/2017-01-16/just-8-men-own-same-wealth-half-world

The New Dangerous Class. Standing explains that the new 'precariat' has 'precarious living standards characterized by low income in insecure employment'.[*]

Standing was one of the first to properly diagnose the rising anger among a sector who had previously been included in the benefits of economic growth, and to identify that their current exclusion was cause for serious concern for everyone: 'The result has been the creation of a global "precariat", consisting of many millions around the world without an anchor of stability. They are becoming a new dangerous class. They are prone to listen to ugly voices, and to use their votes and money to give those voices a political platform of increasing influence.'

However politicians want to label this group – whether it's Ed Miliband's 'Squeezed Middle' or Theresa May's 'JAMs' – Just About Managing' – is not the point. The point is making sure their concerns are addressed. The demographics of the Brexit and Trump votes paint an interesting picture: 70 per cent of those with only GCSEs or less voted to Leave the EU[†] and 67 per cent of non-college-educated white voters ticked for Trump. This data should not be dismissed as xenophobia, racism, or stupidity, but rather as a clear indication that we cannot continue to ignore the concerns of such a sizeable chunk of the population. This demographic is now switched on and politically engaged, because their economic woes no longer allow them to be otherwise.

Politicians are perhaps the worst offenders of the elitism that ignores this group, and recently they have been paying the price. They find themselves frequently stigmatized as being 'out of touch' rather than representatives of the communities they serve. And this provides a problem when you need to connect with people or deliver a narrative that a mass electorate can support and vote for. The

[*] *The Precariat: The New Dangerous Class*, Glasgow Centre for Population Health, Guy Standing Seminar, 22 November, 2011
[†] YouGov: https://yougov.co.uk/news/2016/06/27/how-britain-voted

majority of people in the UK and US do not come from a background of affluence and have come to resent politicians who seek their support but have little understanding of their lives and the issues that concern them. This has led to politicians being described as a 'political class' who are in it for themselves. This growing mistrust of Westminster in the UK and Washington in the US gave a winning boost to both the Brexit and Trump campaigns, illustrating how seismic a change can come from disaffection among the working classes. Whatever you think of Trump, and whether you're a Brexiteer or a Remainer, there is no denying that the consequences in terms of social instability, in both cases, are and will be huge.

Ironically, the lead figures in the Brexit and Trump campaigns were actually part of this elite, and not from the excluded 'other class', but they were able to exploit the anger that exists. This ability to exploit is not the same as empathy, however, so I suspect that ultimately the 'other' class who voted against the political class will be let down, and that the promises of 'winning bigly' and '£350 million a week' for the NHS will not materialize. The challenge will then be to re-engage, rebuild trust, and, yes, diversify. The removal of class barriers and an injection of people from 'other' backgrounds into the political sphere may lead to more effective policies that resonate rather than divide.

A new progressive politics

The rise of populism around the world has made one thing clear: working-class/blue-collar workers no longer want more of the same. I believe there is a real unmet appetite both in the US and the UK for a modern brand of progressive politics – the sort that Emmanuel Macron has come to represent in France and Justin Trudeau in Canada – an evolution of the kind of progressivism of the two Roosevelts and the inclusive capitalism of Lyndon B. Johnson.

Prime Minister Theresa May found this out to her dismay (no pun intended) when she called the snap General Election in June

2017 for reasons that were dubbed by some political pundits as 'self-serving'. She found herself labelled as another 'out of touch' politician when, riding high with a 25-point poll lead, she assumed a historic Tory landslide was all but a given. But as they say, 'a week is a long time in politics', and the final week of the campaign turned out to be disastrous for May. Just like Brexit and Trump, the polls failed to pick up on the rumblings of a working-class revolt.

For the past couple of decades, liberal advocates of globalization have claimed the political centre ground, insisting that this was the only place that elections could be won. Any alternative political offer was subdued or declared unelectable. This view became self-perpetuating as the failure to speak to those on the margins and the lack of focus on combating poverty and inequality caused disillusionment and voter disengagement. It then became permissible to ignore those on the lower economic rungs of society because they didn't vote, as nobody was talking to them.

Then enter stage left Bernie Sanders in the US and Jeremy Corbyn in the UK, both dismissed in the media and political establishment as left-wing class warriors who did not shy away from socialist principles – in fact, they embraced them unashamedly. In return, we saw two old class warriors being embraced by a large unaccounted-for section of the electorate. Bernie Sanders and Jeremy Corbyn hadn't forgotten the poor and disenfranchised and managed to differentiate themselves as the only politicians seeking to challenge a liberal economic model that was leaving behind many of society's most vulnerable. Both Sanders and Corbyn drew support from individuals and celebrities who had previously 'opted out', and pulled in huge crowds. Sanders was unable to secure his party's nomination, while Corbyn on the other hand was selected for the Labour leadership shortlist by Labour MPs, almost in a condescending manner, to demonstrate that his old socialist views would be given a hearing and but eventually dismissed. And yet having Corbyn as an option brought thousands of members of the public (previously ignored) into the Labour Party, who signed up just to elect him. Labour MPs – mainly middle-class Russell Group University educated – were horrified and twice tried to depose Corbyn. They failed due to his appeal with the young and the excluded.

I was very much on the side wishing to challenge Corbyn's leadership. Like many on the centre left of the party, I thought he was not a plausible or viable option to present to the electorate. But Theresa May's snap election meant that Corbyn, unlike Sanders, was given the chance to prove himself with the voters. Again, like most political commentators, I thought Labour would be wiped out by Britain's 'strong and stable' second female prime minister. As a lifelong Labour supporter, I was in complete and utter despair at what I thought spelled the end for the party I so loved. But I, like so many Corbyn doubters, would turn out to be wrong.

He may have been a poor performer in parliamentary questions, but his ability to connect with people and campaign was seriously underestimated. When Corbyn addressed the crowd from the Pyramid Stage at Glastonbury in 2017, he drew in a bigger number than any musical act that year, including Radiohead, Ed Sheeran and the Foo Fighters.[*] As an MP, Corbyn had spent years supporting many of his constituents, who ordinarily were marginalized and ignored. Never a career politician, he was able to demonstrate authentic compassion – as he did in the aftermath of the Grenfell Tower fire – which contrasted with the 'robotic' Theresa May. Corbyn did lose the election, but he managed to wipe out the Conservative government's majority, leaving Theresa May humiliated. His positive manifesto, which promised an end to tuition fees for young people, additional funding for the police, and a higher rate of tax for those earning over £80,000 all deeply resonated with the electorate.

For many, Corbyn's message is one that has resonated from the

---

[*] *NME*: http://www.nme.com/festivals/glastonbury-reacts-jeremy-corbyns-heroic-speech-2093068

outset. My cousin Reg is one such example. Having spent much of his working career as a community organizer, he has met Jeremy Corbyn on multiple occasions and explains the Corbyn appeal:

The first time I met Jeremy Corbyn was when a group of local residents on the Isledon estate had been campaigning for a community centre. The residents had asked Corbyn to speak on their behalf and he came, but he did not try to pressure. He spoke personally about how much effort the residents had put in to this venture in the hope of providing a shared space that could bring together a diverse and deprived community. I was quite struck, as I had never heard a politician speak that way.

The second time I met Corbyn it was unexpected. I was working with one of the mothers on a problematic housing estate to organize a fun day to bring all the residents together. There were no press or photographers but Jeremy Corbyn turned up to support the event because he had been asked by a resident to pop by. He was happy to speak to residents and was troubled by their troubles. In short, he was well thought of.

When people think of Islington they think of the affluent parts such as Upper Street, Canonbury and Highbury, but Corbyn actually represents Finsbury Park, Holloway and Archway, including some of the toughest housing estates, such as the Andover — not too dissimilar from Grenfell Tower. Corbyn lives among these diverse and deprived communities; he doesn't avoid them. He has never toned down his stance in speaking up for their interests to follow the prevailing political mood or presented himself as a smart-suited centrist to gain political office.

For these reasons, Jeremy Corbyn is able to walk among people and empathize during tragedies like Grenfell. If we want a strong and stable society, we need more than just one or two people speaking up for the excluded. We need to diversify who we let in to the debate and who gets to make decisions.

On these occasions, Reg witnessed first-hand a politician who is not 'out of touch' but rather deeply involved and engaged with his constituents. It shows how a new style of politics could indeed manage to listen to, recognize, and respond to those who have too long been ignored. And the lesson here is that the electorate will respond when a more diverse offer is put to them. Political momentum – as well as an organization named Momentum – is certainly on Corbyn's side, but in order to win an election outright he will also need to create a narrative for business and middle-class voters who are fearful of some of his socialist policies.

Demographic changes and the monumental progressive movement that is taking hold in response to modern populism demonstrate that we will need a political system that can find a way to bring together the desire for a decent standard of living and a more inclusive society. We are in a modern era of righteous protest: the 2017 Women's March, with 5 million supporters around the globe, is just the start. Many of those, like myself, who may have voted no to Brexit and do not agree with the views of Donald Trump, still understand the concerns of those who did and agree that the rigged system needs to change, but we do not believe nationalism and protectionism is the way to do it. Rather a reverse approach is needed: a mindful form of internationalism that still enables countries to trade freely but in a balanced manner that factors in a sensible level of national interest.

In a world of social media and increased technological connections, ideas are spread in the simple click of a mouse and swipe of a screen. This requires a new form of leadership that combines the grass roots activism of the Sixties with the power of modern technology-driven movements such as Occupy, the Arab Spring, Black Lives Matter, and the Women's March. It's interesting to note, though, that Occupy and the Arab Spring were short-lived – these 'Leaderless Revolutions', as described by Carne Ross in his book of the same title, were energized by the spirit of collective dissension, but had no central voice or figure, and movements such these can only go so far. It's imperative that impassioned, authentic leaders emerge to create truly long-lasting change. It's these leaders who act as negotiators and inspire people not to give up when it seems that all might be lost.

In the US, both the Tea Party (activists for strict fiscal and social conservatism) and the Birther Movement (which questioned Barack Obama's US citizenship) started out in a leaderless fashion, but once they had a leader and a voice in Donald Trump, they gained unstoppable momentum and were carried all the way to the White House, becoming part of the ideology that is now leading the free world. So I urge anyone reading this book who has been suppressing the leader within to step into that space of fear, to express your opinions and make your voice heard. Don't wait for someone else to be the brave one, because it might actually be your bravery that inspires that someone else to tap into theirs. As the saying goes, 'We are the ones we have been waiting for'. The future won't wait, so take action now.

ACTION POINT: Live below the poverty line for five days with The Hunger Project (http://www.thehungerproject.org.uk/getin-volved/live-below-the-line)

DISCUSSION POINT: Why have Bernie Sanders and Jeremy Corbyn captured the imagination of young people so successfully?

CHAPTER THREE

Opportunity

'We must open the doors of opportunity. But we must also equip our people to walk through those doors.'

Lyndon B. Johnson

We have the ability to break down class barriers. How do I know this? Because I have lived it. All of my life I have understood both sides of the human experience: I was born rich but raised poor, and then went on to achieve success in my own right. I began working in the media at an early age, so benefited from the 'privilege' of being well known, but I'm also a working-class woman of colour and understand the 'prejudice' that elicits too. Many of the talented people I grew up with weren't as fortunate as me. I was no smarter or more talented, I was just lucky enough to have aspirational parents who demanded educational excellence, and state-school teachers who expected the same. This, coupled with a phenomenal early internship programme, set me on a path where I could make something of myself. In short, I was given opportunity, aspiration and encouragement and, in Anansi fashion, all of these factors helped to instill in me a certain level of self-belief.

This formula is not a complex one and can be replicated and scaled. In situations where parental guidance is lacking, we need an educational system robust enough to pick up the slack. It can be done: there are countless examples, such as charter schools like Geoffrey Canada's Harlem Children's Zone, which for over 30 years has had phenomenal educational results working with kids from one of the most deprived communities in Harlem, New York. We know what works – the solutions are in great supply – yet we still choose antiquated educational systems.

The problem is compounded by the fact that those in the most affluent occupations recruit individuals who share their background, and they are supported by those at the most prestigious educational establishments who are doing the same. Throw into the mix the social capital that individuals from affluent backgrounds possess and pass on to their children, such as personal connections, access to cultural activities, and, of course, familiarity with affluence, and the result is that the highest-paying occupations are reserved for young people from the most privileged backgrounds. According to research undertaken by the London School of Economics using Labour Force Survey data, only 4 per cent of doctors, 6 per cent of barristers, 11 per cent of journalists, and 12 per cent of solicitors come from working-class backgrounds.[*] Much of this is down to how those from different backgrounds are perceived.

We can't deny that prejudices exist in relation to how different classes are judged – people are prejudged on their intellect and ability as soon as they open their mouth. Has there ever been a British prime minister with a cockney accent? We've had PMs with southern working-class roots such as Edward Heath and John Major, yet both of these men instinctively knew that in order to progress, the accents of their childhood would need to change. John Major, who proudly celebrated his humble Brixton roots, still adopted a standard English accent along the way. I seem to have done the same without even realizing when and how it happened.

[*] Working Paper – Introducing the Class Ceiling - LSE

The British media is also incredibly London-centric, and not an accurate portrayal of the geographical make-up of the country. I think that's in part why reality entertainment shows such as *The X Factor*, *The Great British Bake Off*, *Gogglebox*, and *Britain's Got Talent* are so successful – they are the rare occasions when we see a balanced representation of the nation on our screens. I would say the same is true for US TV – if we were to go purely by American scripted television we would assume America was only made up of New York and LA. I am no proponent of reality TV – trust me, I've presented enough bad ones to know what I'm talking about! – but it's true that reality formats have enabled communities who have been traditionally excluded by scripted TV to be seen, albeit not always in the best light. They are no longer invisible. The phenomenal success of these shows clearly illustrates the fact that a diverse demographic can build brands, and its power should not be underestimated.

But, if we are to give every young person the opportunity to aspire, to achieve their goals, and to transcend the boundaries of their class, creating a diverse, upwardly mobile workforce that fully reflects every demographic, then we have to begin in the classroom. So far we haven't always been getting it right.

Education opens the door

In March 2017 Theresa May unveiled her plans to set aside £320 million to fund 140 free schools, the majority of which would be grammar schools; a new scheme which would create 70,000 new school places. Within days a cross-party alliance between former Conservative education secretary Nicky Morgan, Liberal Democrat and former deputy prime minister Nick Clegg, and ex-shadow education minister Lucy Powell was set up to oppose Theresa May's plans. This new gang of three presented their argument in a joint op-ed in the *Observer* newspaper:

All the evidence is clear that grammar schools damage social mobility. Those championing selection as the silver bullet for tackling social mobility, or as the panacea for creating good new school places, are misguided. Whilst they can boost attainment for the already highly gifted, they do nothing for the majority of children, who do not attend them. Indeed, in highly selective areas, children not in grammars do worse than their peers in non-selective areas.

As a state-school-educated kid myself, I'm inclined to agree with the 'gang of three'. I understand Theresa May's faith in grammar schools, of course: that style of education set her on the path to leadership, just as it did with Margaret Thatcher and countless other grammar-school-educated success stories, but that was then and this is now. There was a time when grammar schools acted as an effective social mobility pipeline for gifted children from lower-income families to enter white-collar jobs. However, this system of benefiting the top 20 per cent of children in the state-school system worked when we had enough low-skilled manual jobs to go round for the remaining 80 per cent.

As we know, this is no longer the case, so we are going to need an education system that benefits the majority of kids, not just the gifted few. What is the modern answer to grammar schools? Something tells me it isn't more grammar schools . . . We must seek to raise the aspirations and academic attainment levels of a wider range of children – if we fail, this will only worsen our growing income inequality and further entrench our class divides.

I would argue that through our education system we have an opportunity to tackle the issues we have with the 'other' class by creating a class in common – by producing generations of open-minded young people who neither fear nor discriminate against 'others', but instead have an understanding and appreciation of their history, culture, and value. I believe our schools should be a microcosm of society, so educating children selectively and separately based on attainment, background, gender, ethnicity, religion, or any other distinction feels counterproductive to me. In reality, we have schools divided along various lines due to legislative history, tradition, catchment area, income, and of course class. But without too much upheaval we can mitigate these divisions by adding to the national curriculum the opportunity for all students to learn alongside others from different backgrounds, as they would have to do in the workplace. This would be in the form of a national twinning programme between state and private schools, which is underpinned by an annual cross-school project. This would take the form of a diversity module in the curriculum that all students work on every academic year, which increases in difficulty each year but is designed to require a wide range of talents and learning styles and experiences. At present, most of the interaction pupils have with other pupils from different schools usually takes the form of competitions where they are pitted against each other – whether this be through sport, debating or chess tournaments. There is not much room for collaboration with the 'other class'. A state and private school twinning model would encourage social mobility and make schools a true representation of what we need to achieve in our workplaces.

An in-depth exploration into the history of modern-day inequality can be taught with a focus on the emotional and psychological impact that historical moments have had on various groups, not for the purpose of attributing blame or benefit, but more as a way of understanding that we are all collectively living with the legacy and that it can be addressed if the will is there. This can be a vital aid to fostering cross-cultural understanding.

The discussion about inequality, social mobility, and inclusion needs to stop being the sole domain of liberal middle-class university academics. These same academics should be enlisted to develop the diversity module, to go into schools to help teachers disseminate this information. The conversations and the data need to be shared and studied in all schools so that our children interact with some of the smartest minds and brainstorm how best to address some of our most entrenched structural barriers. All this will enable students to see 'other' students as people and potentially friends, rather than demographics or statistics.

To some these discussions may seem too philosophical for our classroom, or not so worthy of time as reading, writing, and arithmetic. I would argue that to create the society we want, we need to make the time and effort. It will require politicians, teachers, and parents to agree that our classrooms should become hubs of debate as well as learning.

In society at large, we tend to exclude the other class from these discussions out of an inherent snobbery that they may lack the sophistication, relevant education, or capacity to understand or be objective. This is something that can be eradicated using the classroom, so that children from all backgrounds can come together and help shape a new tomorrow, the better future that they will be living in as adults.

2.5%: The percentage of kids from poor households in the UK in 2015 (measured by free school meals status) who made it to a Russell Group University, compared to 8.9% of other kids. 13.5%: the percentage of kids from poor homes in the UK who get all A* at GCSEs who make it to Oxbridge.[*]

The training deficit

The key to social mobility and a more inclusive, fair, and successful society is enabling every young person to make the transition from education into a sustainable career that contributes to the economy. The traditional route to a career (as opposed to just a job) – through entrance to a good university and acceptance into a reputable profession via a graduate scheme or internship – is no longer cutting it. Currently young people have to take on large amounts of debt in

[*] From Oxford University's Nuffield College's 2017 Research Project

order to attain a qualification, in the hope that this will gain them entry into a career that will then enable them to repay it. For many, their answer has been 'no deal' – and this at a time when their option of living and working in the rest of the EU will soon no longer be available. So the UK now has very specific challenges that require us to think more broadly about how we ensure that the talents of our young people are utilized and rewarded, against the twin challenges of rising university tuition costs and the implications of Brexit. We will need to look at other options to ensure the upward trajectory of social mobility in the UK.

88%: the percentage of people in the media and creative industries in the UK that have worked for free at some point in their careers.

We need to grow our home talent pool and quickly, to avoid major gaps in our economy. We cannot afford for our young people to be deterred from aspiring to pursue the careers that are needed to maintain our economy for financial reasons. I believe more apprenticeships and work-based learning is a big part of the answer. Apprenticeships provide training, qualifications, and paid employment as a route into a career, as opposed to unpaid internships which, like expensive university fees, have become inaccessible to young people from less affluent backgrounds. We need to increase the types of apprenticeships that are available and ensure that they cover a variety of sectors, including industries where traditionally a degree or higher-level qualification is required. Some universities are offering apprenticeship degrees, but these need to be accessible across a range of universities so that they are recognized as equivalent to those from renowned institutions. Dr Frances Corner OBE, head of the London College of Fashion (LCF), is one leading university head who has publicly committed to diversifying her student population and creating more vocational and flexible learning courses which enable students from poorer backgrounds to study at one of the world's leading fashion institutions. Following her example, we can create a system of higher-education work-based learning with the cost shared between the student and employer.

I'm such a firm advocate of apprenticeship programmes that I co-founded a scheme with the support of the trailblazing entrepreneur Pierre Legrange and his luxury heritage brand Huntsman to help kids from low-income communities like the one I grew up in. Our programme helps young people develop a career in the creative industries, and it's wonderful to see them thriving and starting to believe in themselves. My team and I have been incredibly inspired by Jamie Oliver and the phenomenal work he has done with his Fifteen Foundation, which trains unemployed young people to work in the food industry. In the space of fifteen years his foundation has helped thousands of young people develop successful careers, who might otherwise have fallen by the wayside.

Until we can ensure that the transition from education into employment is as seamless for working-class young people as it is for young people from affluent backgrounds, we will not be able to meet the needs of our economy or our society.

It's not just the UK that needs to worry about this issue. The US is experiencing its own crisis in equipping its young people for the world of work. Professor Stephen Klineberg of the Kinder Institute for Urban Research at Rice University in Houston, Texas, has been studying the changing demographics of America for the past 30 years. Houston is the most ethnically diverse city in America and is seen as a microcosm of the country: what happens in Houston today will happen in the rest of America tomorrow (see my case study on Houston at Diversify.org for more on this). Each year Klineberg produces the Houston Area Survey, a study he has been conducting since 1982. Houstonians eagerly await its annual findings on what their fellow residents think and how their city is changing. I was fortunate enough to interview Professor Klineberg in Houston just days after Trump's election victory. Unlike most liberal progressives, he was unperturbed by Trump's victory but was very clear that America's changing demographics meant that this sort of electoral victory was unlikely to happen again. The bigger question, he felt, was how America was going to deal with the seismic changes that lie ahead.

> *The election of Donald Trump in November 2016 gave powerful testimony to the social and political fissures that divide Americans along the lines of race, class, education, gender, and religion. The most critical division, laid bare in this election, is between those who have found a place in the restructured economy and have benefited from the twin processes of globalization and automation, in contrast to those who have not.*

As we sat talking in a busy hipster café in Harris County, Houston, Professor Klineberg was very clear about how big the challenges were in terms of preparing blue-collar communities for the jobs of the future:

> *According to nationwide figures in 1973, 32 per cent of all the 91 million jobs in America were available to high-school dropouts and another 40 per cent required no more than a high-school diploma. By 2020, however, the Center on Education and the Workforce at Georgetown University predicts that fully 65 per cent of the 164 million jobs that will exist in this country will require some kind of post-secondary credential. And yet of all the eighth graders in Houston area schools in the year 2004, only 68 per cent actually graduated from high school and just 21 per cent had obtained any kind of post-secondary certificate or degree by 2015, 11 years later.*[*]

---

[*] https://kinder.rice.edu/has/

Houston is seen as representative of the country at large and it's very clear that this lack of training presents serious issues in terms of the employability of a very large chunk of the US population. The current system isn't delivering enough citizens who are equipped for the jobs of the future. The ramifications of this are not only problematic for businesses, which will have to source talent from elsewhere, but also for the government. As we know, the knock-on effects of high unemployment rates are catastrophic, from the increased cost in social security right through to higher crime rates.

There are various social initiatives in both the UK and the US to meet these challenges, such as mentoring, internships, and industry outreach across class boundaries. Some industries, such as engineering, have encouraged professionals to go into schools in working-class areas to encourage students to aspire to their sector. Many professionals also volunteer as mentors to pass on experience and knowledge to students from working-class backgrounds to assist them to transcend their class. This needs to be on a much larger scale, though, rather than to cream a few gifted students off the top; we now need leaders brave enough to invest in the types of innovative educational programmes and models that will give all of our young people an education that is fit for the challenges of the twenty-first century.

Equality for the economy

Once young people have made it through the door and into the world of work, opportunity still has a part to play in creating a more equal society. Our industries as well as our societies will benefit from the influx of 'other' workers who were once forgotten by globalization but who, with a little investment, are adequately trained to fill the job vacancies of the future, and they receive a competitive wage for doing so. Given the opportunity, they can maximize their working potential and significantly contribute to the economy. But governments and market leaders have an opportunity here too, if they could only find the moral courage to take it: to curb the worst excesses of big businesses, which drive the wealth gap ever wider.

Let me be clear: the alternative of letting inequality grow and class exclusion continue is unsustainable, especially when this runs alongside economic growth. We've already seen the dire consequences of this. Frances O'Grady – General Secretary of the British Trades Union Congress (TUC), one of the UK's largest trade unions – said: 'Britain is a textbook case of how growing inequality leads to economic crisis. The years before the crash were marked by a sharp rise in remortgaging and the growth of 0 per cent balance transfer credit cards. By 2008 the UK had the highest ratio of household debt to GDP of any major economy.' Discrimination against the 'other' class is therefore not just bad for the workforce in the short-term; it's also bad for the economy in the long-term. But it doesn't have to be this way.

There have been leaders who have realized this and made it their mission to redress the balance. President Theodore Roosevelt was born into one of the wealthiest and most privileged families in New York, but he had an affinity with the poor that had been instilled in him by his philanthropic father. Roosevelt was a fervent capitalist and believed in the power of business to build nations, but he instinctively understood capitalist greed and that, if left to its own devices, big business could run amok, and that would inevitably be detrimental to everyone. Upon entering the White House in 1901, Roosevelt told a reporter: 'These fools on Wall Street think they can go on forever. They can't. I would like to be the buffer between their foolishness and the wrath that is surely to come. Sooner or later, there will be a riotous, wicked, murderous day of atonement.' Roosevelt saw the Oval Office as the 'Steward of the people'; if it needed to be done for the 'common well-being' of the nation, then it must be done.

First up: taking on the titans and power brokers of the day. The Gilded Age had transformed America into a global industrial powerhouse, and this growth was spearheaded by a small group of industrialists who had each monopolized emerging sectors and locked out competition. These industry giants had amassed vast fortunes and were considered to be the men who 'built America' – men such as Carnegie (steel), Rockefeller (oil) and J. P. Morgan (finance). These industrialists may have become incredibly wealthy but their workers had not. Unregulated and free to operate as they saw fit, there was no end to their power. Roosevelt believed something had to be done and he saw himself as just the man to do it. His first target was J. P. Morgan, the most powerful financier in the country. Morgan's unrivalled access to capital meant he was able to dominate multiple industries, one of which was the railways that he controlled through his Northern Securities trust. Roosevelt embarked on an anti-trust expedition, which earned him the nickname of the 'Trust Buster'.

He was further bolstered by the Muckrakers, a new breed of rockstar investigative journalist, who would embark on lengthy, well-researched reporting that exposed many of the unfair practices of the business titans Roosevelt was after. Articles in popular periodicals such as *McClure's* would help shape public opinion and pave the way for Roosevelt to make change. He also took his message directly to the people and embarked on a whistle-stop tour of the country in what he termed the 'Bully Pulpit', enthusiastically meeting everyday Americans and engaging them in the debate. All of this led him to a landslide victory in 1904, making him the first 'President to win a term in his own right after having ascended to the Presidency upon the death of his predecessor'.*

Now he had his own mandate he could really get to work. He initiated an investigation into Standard Oil and the oil industry in general, and in 1906 his administration filed an anti-trust lawsuit against Standard Oil. The case would last for three years and a Circuit

* https://millercenter.org/president/roosevelt/campaigns-and-elections

Court of four judges would eventually rule in the government's favour in April 1909, a month after Roosevelt left office. Standard Oil appealed to the Supreme Court and lost in May 1911, forcing the dismantling of the company and marking the end of the trust era, which in turn opened the market, allowing more entrepreneurs to compete.

This kind of progressive approach to try to address inequality is something we can learn from even now, over 100 years later. Roosevelt's fears would prove to be justified with the great Wall Street Crash of 1929, and we are still recovering from our own nearly 10 years after it happened. How many more financial crashes will it take before we've learnt our lesson – that equality is good for everyone?

Globally, our economic challenges are complex, but I believe that embracing the 'other' is an important part of the solution. This is especially true when it comes to class, since there is a direct link between class and workforce. On one side, we have a decline in industries, which previously provided working-class occupations but are now being replaced by technology, plus competition from emerging economies with lower wages. On the other side, we have the increasing demand for infrastructure professionals and the specialist jobs that robots can't do. These occupations need to attract talent from diverse backgrounds in order to effectively meet our needs for increased transport, connectivity, and housing for our growing diverse populations.

We'll need to be as ready to invest in humanity as in infrastructure. We'll need enough people who are well trained and well paid to keep us physically and mentally healthy for the duration of our lives (which are getting longer and requiring more specialist care). We'll need to plug the hole of shortages in the NHS, teaching, and social work. We'll also need educators, employment specialists, and social infra-structure professionals who will help reduce class and cultural barriers to ensure that we continue to diversify to meet our future needs. We accept that the future needs to be built and so, as we put a premium on the innovators who will bring this about, we must also place an equal value on how and from where we are going to train and source this talent. The jobs of the future must be filled with the diverse talent of the future.

ACTION POINT: Speak to your manager or HR department about what work experience, internship or apprenticeship opportunities there are in your business. How are they advertised? What are the qualification requirements? And how are candidates remunerated?

DISCUSSION POINT: Should more be done to prevent nepotism? Or is it fair enough that parents should help their kids get ahead?

The Other Way

'Either we all live in a decent world, or nobody does.'

George Orwell

Our societies are changing at such a rapid pace that it can be hard to keep up and remain focused on how we can influence that change. But, ultimately, as artificial intelligence surpasses human intelligence and virtual reality becomes the new reality, we will have to place a higher premium on the things that make us human – the things that robots can't emulate, such as real creativity and genuine compassion. Society will be forced to look again at what and who we value and how we measure the success of our nations. I am reminded of Robert F. Kennedy's words: '[GDP] measures everything, in short, except that which makes life worthwhile.'

Robert Kennedy realized even back in the Sixties that we were more than the sum of the money our nations generate, more than who has what. GDP takes into account the bottom line, the unedifying part of the economy: the weapons we make, the prisons we build, and the poisons we create to pollute our bodies and the environment. Using GDP as the primary measure of a nation's success fails to adequately value charity workers, volunteers, low-paid care workers, and the things that cannot be drilled down to a metric, such as empathy and happiness. In failing to recognize this, we will continue to perpetuate the divisions of a high-wealth, low-value society.

RFK reminds us to celebrate a more inclusive economic approach, but also reminds us that we should never become complacent in pressing for all of the elements that make a balanced and prosperous nation. If we fail to understand that we need a healthy society as much as a healthy economy, we will lose both. Just as we are starting to recognize that mental and spiritual health can impact our physical health, we need to realize that a nation's spiritual and moral health invariably impacts its financial health. Until we fix those elements, our financial health will continue to remain out of balance.

The Numbers

Social mobility in the UK – having a high-class background almost doubles your chances of making it to the professional class[*]

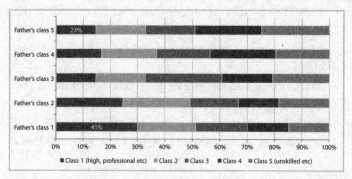

Social mobility in the US – having a high-class background more than doubles your chances of making it into the professional class[†]

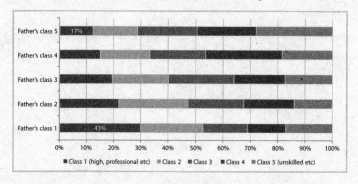

---

[*] Centre for Social Investigation using UK Household Longitudinal Study
[†] Centre for Social Investigation using General Social Survey

Need-to-know facts and figures:

- **4%:** the percentage of doctors that come from working class backgrounds in the UK. For barristers, it is **6%** and journalists **11%**
- **88%:** the percentage of people in the media and creative industries in the UK that have worked for free at some point in their careers
- **2.5%:** The percentage of kids from poor households in the UK (measured by Free school meals status) who made it to a Russell Group University, compared to 8.9% of other kids. (UK)
- **13.5%:** the percentage of kids from poor homes in the UK who get <u>all</u> A* at GCSE who make it to Oxbridge
- **21%:** the percentage of smart poor kids in the US who complete college, compared to **41%** of mediocre rich kids

THE THIRD DEGREE OF INTEGRATION

Connect with the Other

'We are like islands in the sea, separate on the surface but connected in the deep.'

William James

Thanks to Stanley Milgram's 1967 'small world experiment' (see page xx), we say that everyone in the world is connected by 'six degrees of separation' – an oxymoron, as how can we be connected if we are separated? The question 50 years later is how would this experiment work today if we had to post a package across racial, religious, or class boundaries rather than regional or state lines? Where we see a lack of social interaction across these boundaries it might well take a lot more than six degrees. Our social circles reflect what we find familiar and safe (see Degree 2: Check Your Circle, xx), which is fine until we need the talents and cooperation of 'others' outside of our comfort zones. And in the twenty-first century we will need to utilize these talents to meet the challenges of creating sustainable prosperity. A model where the usual suspects do well and growth comes at the cost of marginalization and a lack of opportunity is unsustainable – particularly in a democracy.

On the surface, it may seem that there is little or nothing that we as individuals can do about these issues, but we can challenge ourselves to make a start by changing the trends in our own personal spheres, which, when compounded, will ultimately affect humanity as a whole.

The 'one in six' equation

Having challenged our isms in Degree 1 by looking inwards and asking ourselves some difficult questions, are we reinforcing existing barriers and divisions or are we involved in dissolving them through our own example? Are we reflecting and including the diversity around us?

Through Degree 2 we have checked our circle, most of which will reflect who we are and what we think, comprising those we feel we have things in common with. If you do already have a diverse circle, then you have an excellent platform from which to encourage diversity by connecting people across boundaries within your circle. However, if our circle doesn't include any deviation from our own identity, beliefs, and background then our understanding of society and the people we share it with will be limited. This would be something to note and possibly address – which leads us to Degree 3: connecting with the 'other'.

The cornerstone of Degree 3 is the 'one in six' equation: out of every six new people that you are able to 'choose' to connect with, make one of them an 'other' – someone different from yourself. It's through genuine interpersonal relationships that the magic happens and the barriers come down – it's then that hearts and minds are opened.

If Milgram's theory is based on connecting to people you already know, then the Six Degrees of Integration principle is based on connecting with 'others' that you don't know or could get to know better. This may sound a little prescribed and perhaps even contrived, but we have to start somewhere.

Engaging with people outside of our comfort zone will be difficult, especially in scenarios not set up for social interaction. However, the more frequently we challenge ourselves, the more we learn about our surroundings and where a conversation might be possible. Work and family/social commitments can limit our circle, but it can also expand it as well. It is, after all, most likely that we will connect with an 'other' at work or at a social function. Admittedly, it's unlikely that we will make a best friend in one encounter, but it is possible to leave a positive impression that will encourage future interaction. Human beings are diverse but incredibly similar, so there will always be some common points of reference, which is a good place to start connecting.

If you are a decision maker or influencer in the workplace or in your social group, then take responsibility to impart change and advocate for the inclusion of 'others'. Your experience and awareness through the previous steps will put you in a position to confidently champion change or challenge excluding practices. Excluding practices can be found within all groups, and the more experience and connection you have within an 'other' group, the better your ability to champion their cause for inclusion and challenge behaviours or practices that exclude them.

Above all, when seeking to form connections with others outside your circle, remember that kindness is key.[*]

---

[*] This reminds me of a lovely poem by my best friend of 20 years, songwriter Gerry DeVeaux, who believes it is 'cool to be nice' and he should know – the *Sunday Times Style* magazine once dubbed him the 'King of cool': *Be cool be nice / Not just once not just twice / With everything you do or say / Kindness takes you all the way.* You can read the full poem on www.Diversify.org

PART FOUR

THE OTHER BODY

'Disability is the inability to see ability.'

Vikas Khanna

The Old Way

People with mental and physical disabilities have been condemned, alienated, even feared, perhaps more than any other group throughout history – their disability explained away, overtly or subconsciously, as a punishment from God, inferior genetics, bad karma, dishonour on the family, or simply being backwards. Their options have been severely limited and they've had to live and work in conditions that could accommodate their disability – unless of course their disability could be used as a reason to bar them from employment in the first place. Obviously, this is made worse if they are from a poor background, resulting in destitution or a reliance on charity – not least because, in the UK, life costs £550 more on average a month if you're disabled.* And it's not just here: unfortunately 80 per cent of the global disabled population currently lives in the world's poorest countries.

Prejudice against people with disabilities is often more subtle than against certain 'others', but it is nonetheless still there. At the height of the popularity of the sci-fi TV series *The X-Files*, there was an episode titled 'Quagmire' in which Agent Mulder tells Agent Scully that he would have liked to have been born disabled, so he wouldn't be expected to work as hard and would be considered 'courageous'

---

* Scope, 'Priced Out', 2014

for even holding down a job, let alone thriving in one. An article by the National Collaborative Workforce and Disability (NCWD) describes the ignorant tone of this episode and its reflection of wider societal attitudes:

> *The fact that a respected character on one of America's most popular television shows expressed this viewpoint exemplifies the rampant attitudinal barriers hindering people with disabilities in or trying to enter the workforce. People with disabilities face many barriers every day – from physical obstacles in buildings to systemic barriers in employment and civic programs. Yet, often, the most difficult barriers to overcome are attitudes other people carry regarding people with disabilities. Whether born from ignorance, fear, misunderstanding or hate, these attitudes keep people from appreciating – and experiencing – the full potential a person with a disability can achieve.* [*]

The article goes on to explain the complexities of attitude change, and how it is not possible to legislate for this. It states that the best way to change the way that those with disabilities are viewed is to increase their visibility and familiarity – in the workplace, socially, in education, and at home. By addressing these issues head-on, we open up greater opportunities not only for those directly affected by disability, but for everyone.

[*] http://www.ncwd-youth.info/attitudinal-barriers-for-people-with-disabilities

CHAPTER ONE

Pigeonholing

'There is no greater disability in society, than the inability to see a person as more.'

Robert Hensel

On a rainy autumn morning in 1992, the events of a split second would interrupt my life for the next four years and completely change the trajectory of it from that moment onwards. The day started like any other. I was 15 years old and needed to get to school. I performed my usual routine on autopilot: I woke up at 7 a.m., got dressed in my navy-blue girls' school uniform, scoffed down a quick, unhealthy breakfast and ran out to catch my 8 a.m. bus. It was an incredibly wet morning even by London standards, but in an effort to look cool I had selected a stylish yet inappropriate jacket that was not adequate for the weather. I had also forgotten my umbrella, so already things were not going too well. I was completely drenched as I stepped onto the zebra crossing. Luckily I eyed my bus in the distance, so at least I wouldn't have to endure the rain for much longer. Then suddenly I heard the screeching sound of a car hitting its brakes, the thumping sound of a car hitting a body and the thundering sound of that body hitting concrete. It was only when I came to and saw the crowd of people gathered around me that I realized it was me the car had hit.

As I lay helpless and motionless on the ground, a teacher from a nearby school who had witnessed the incident rushed over to help. In true teacher fashion, she completely took over the situation and brought some semblance of order to all the chaos. She collected the coats of the bystanders and covered me up, as by that point the shock was starting to wear off and I was shivering uncontrollably, which soon turned into floods of tears as the excruciating pain of the impact began to set in. This teacher remained calm and started to crack jokes, which managed to distract me enough to enable me to tell her my name and address. Her main message to me was to remain still and she stood guard to make sure no one moved me until the ambulance came. I could see from the corner of my eye a shock-ridden man helplessly looking on from a distance – I would later learn he was the driver of the vehicle.

My injuries were serious. I had suffered dislocated and fractured C5 and C6 bones (part of the spinal segment at the back of the neck). A few centimetres were the deciding factor between me being able to make a full recovery or spending the rest of my life as a quadriplegic. I would be bed-bound for almost a year with head and skeletal traction, which involved metal rods screwed into my skull, pulling my spinal cord into place. This meant I was unable to move from the neck down. I would need help bathing, brushing my teeth, going to the toilet, eating, reading, writing, and doing all of the things I had taken for granted as a happy-go-lucky precocious teenager. The doctors had originally hoped that my injuries would heal naturally, but when after almost a year this didn't happen, they decided that the only option was to operate. The next three years would involve delicate spinal operations and bone grafts, hours of gruelling physiotherapy, mobility only through wheelchairs, and then wearing a neck brace 24 hours a day. I was eventually able to make a full recovery physically, but mentally and emotionally I was forever changed.

In hindsight I consider my 'accident' as a gift. The year I spent in hospital, unable to move, meant that I had to focus on my internal life as my physical life was beyond my control. As a way of coping I started meditating. Even though at 15 I had no concept of mindfulness or contemplative thinking, I knew I needed a process of endurance that would help me to stay calm, positive, and, most of all, hopeful – this meant that I didn't feel sorry for myself and focused on my recovery, regardless of my prognosis. I also developed an ability to enjoy my own company, as I spent many hours alone while my parents were at work and my siblings and friends were at school. I was able to experience first-hand the kindness and compassion of people, from the teacher who came to my aid when the accident first happened, to the phenomenal NHS nurses and doctors who took care of me, right through to my school friends, who created a rota system of daily visits.

But the thing for which I am most grateful is the resilience the accident gave me. Don't get me wrong – it wasn't all peaches and cream. To this day I still have lingering trauma and face constant reminders of what happened to me. I am super-cautious when crossing the road, fast cars terrify me, I can never go bungee jumping, and, after having to sleep on my back for over four years, I can now only fall asleep on my side. But my four years as a physically disabled person taught me so much about life and made me see how limiting society is towards those who don't fit the mould of the physical or mental 'norm'. The indignity of trying to fit into a world that sees you as abnormal can be demoralizing and demeaning. While I wore my neck brace, I was the butt of offensive jokes (though I must admit some were funny), I was constantly stared at in public, and it was incredibly frustrating having to recount at every new encounter how and why I was wearing this large contraption – it was all that anyone saw of me. For those people who were too polite to ask 'What happened?', it was the elephant in the room and I would feel compelled to volunteer the information to diffuse the air of discomfort.

Only 17% of disabled people were born with their disabilities.[*]

I am one of many, many people who will have experienced these indignities at some point in their lives, whether they were born with a disability or, like me, found themselves suddenly disabled in the space of a split second. In the UK there are 11.9 million disabled people – that's almost 1 in 5 (19 per cent) of the population.[†] Globally, there are over 650 million people living with some form of disability: approximately 10 per cent of the world's population.[‡] As my story shows, injury or illness can befall anyone at any time. The disabled are also the most diverse of our 'other' groups, covering all ages, genders, orientations, ethnic groups, religious backgrounds, and social classes. Disability itself covers a multitude of physical and mental conditions limiting people's senses and abilities. These conditions may or may not be visible and some may be hidden due to the various stigmas that have been attributed to disability. Mental illness, for example, is still often deemed a taboo in our society, and yet it's something that affects such a large percentage of the population. According to the National Alliance of Mental Illness (NAMI) in the US: '1 in 5 adults in the US – 43.8 million, or 18.5 per cent – experiences mental illness in a given year.'[§] The picture is similar in the UK. The mental health charity Mind reports that '1 in 4 people in the UK will experience a mental health problem each year.'[¶] Of all of our 'other' groups it is the disabled that are the most discriminated

---

[*] Papworth Trust Report - Disability in the United Kingdom 2016 Facts and Figures: http://www.papworthtrust.org.uk/sites/default/files/Disability%20Facts%20and%20 Figures%202016.pdf

[†] Papworth Trust Report – Disability in the United Kingdom 2016 Facts and Figures: http://www.papworthtrust.org.uk/campaigns/disability-facts-and-figures

[‡] https://www.disabled-world.com/disability/statistics/

[§] Disability in the United Kingdom 2016 Facts and Figures:

[¶] https://www.mind.org.uk/information-support/types-of-mental-health-problems/ statistics-and-facts-about-mental-health/how-common-are-mental-health-problems/ #.WYbjmIXoDB8

against and ignored in society, and yet it's the one 'other' group that you are almost bound to be part of at some point in your life.

> 67%: the proportion of people with mental health problems who receive benefits but say they either want to work or are looking for work.[*]

So why, with all this diversity within the disabled community, do we insist on pigeonholing disabled people? Obviously, classification of some kind is necessary when it comes to ensuring that people can access the help they need and obtain the appropriate benefits, but our current position is that we allow disabled people to fit into just two categories: firstly, the inspirations – bionic human beings who have succeeded in their chosen fields. And secondly, the segregated – the people who face a world that does not meet their needs, and the stigmas associated with their disability, such as suspicion of abusing the welfare state and the incredulity that comes with an invisible disability. Only by evolving beyond the inspiration or segregation model and giving people with disabilities the ability to function as an individual, free from the associations of their condition, will we enable a true and fair sense of self to develop.

Challenging the tags

For people with disabilities – especially visible ones – their sense of self is compromised from the very beginning as a direct result of how other people view them. But there are several notable figures out there who have proved that their disability doesn't define who they are. A few years ago, I had the good fortune to spend a little time with American athlete and model Aimee Mullins when she agreed to speak on a WIE panel about resilience. You can't help but

* Rethink Mental Illness

be engulfed by Aimee's confidence and unapologetic zest for life. Having been born with a missing fibula, both of her legs were amputated when she was just a year old, but Aimee would go on to achieve athletic success and showcase her multiple prosthetic legs as a symbol of innovative design. And as a spokesmodel for L'Oréal, she, like British TV presenter Sophie Morgan, would also help to redefine our standards of beauty and desirability.

I was enthralled and speechless as Aimee shared the thesaurus synonyms for 'disabled': 'crippled, helpless, useless, wrecked, stalled, maimed, wounded, mangled, lame, mutilated, run-down, worn-out, weakened, impotent, castrated, paralyzed, handicapped, senile, decrepit, laid-up, done-up, done-for, done-in, cracked-up, counted-out; see also hurt, useless and weak'. The antonyms were equally offensive: 'healthy, strong, capable'. Aimee could have easily absorbed these limiting tags had her childhood doctor not instilled a belief in her that her 'disability' need not define her as less. I have been using the term 'disabled' as a common reference point throughout this section, but my hope is that we all refrain from believing the negative connotations that are currently associated with the word. Together we can give the word new meaning and diversify our view of what 'able bodied' means.

Another woman who challenged how disabled people are seen and defined was the effervescent Australian comedian, writer, and disability rights activist Stella Young. Now, as it happens I am heterosexual, but if there was a woman who could have changed that it would have been her. She was born with a severe form of osteogenesis imperfecta (OI), a genetic disorder that affects the bones, causing them to easily break. Stella's OI meant she was wheelchair-bound for most of her life, but her fiercely sharp intellect, dry wit, and sardonic sense of humour made it almost impossible for people to focus on her restricted mobility. Sadly, she passed away in 2014 at the young age of 32, but in her short time on this planet she made great strides in challenging the way we see disability by encouraging people to ask uncomfortable questions and engage in difficult conversations.

Stella was also an active proponent of disability employment rights and candid about her own career woes and the discrimination she faced in the workplace, which led to a long-winded detour of becoming a teacher and then eventually achieving her dream of becoming a journalist. She also served as the editor of *Ramp Up*, an online digital platform aimed at Australia's disabled community. In a 2012 *Ramp Up* editorial she dissected society's fascination with objectifying disabled people into what she dubbed as 'inspiration porn', where wider society uses people with disabilities as a tool or 'inspiration' for overcoming adversity, the subtext being 'it could be worse, you could be like this disabled person'. I would highly recommend her hilarious TEDx talk entitled 'I'm not your inspiration, thank you very much'. In this talk she describes a moment when she started teaching and one of the children in the class asked when she was going to give her 'inspiration' talk. At first baffled by the question, Stella pressed the child further. It turned out that this was the only capacity in which that child had experienced a disabled adult in the context of a classroom.

It's true that children seldom see their teachers as someone with a disability or vulnerability, and when they do see an adult with a disability in the classroom, it's usually in the form of a 'motivational speaker'. This is why the hiring of Cerrie Burnell as the host of British children's television channel CBeebies in 2009 was so important. Cerrie was born without a right forearm and proudly displays it on screen, normalizing physical disability for young children all over the country. Cerrie has also spoken at WIE, and is someone who is defying the 'norm' in all areas of her life – a few years ago, as a single mother, she adopted a mixed-race daughter, who in turn inspired her to write her first children's book, *Snowflakes*.

Citing a lack of inspiring disabled characters in the books she read as a dyslexic child, her second book, *Mermaid*, features a young protagonist who is an excellent swimmer, but also happens to be a wheelchair user. This effectively achieves two things in one: familiarizing young children with disability and therefore dispelling any fear or discomfort they may have around it, but also representing it as incidental, rather than the defining feature of that character. Undoubtedly, this approach has been informed by Cerrie's own experiences: 'Writing inclusively comes naturally to me,' she says, 'perhaps because I have multiple diversities, each of which I'm proud of, but none of which singly define me.'* With any luck, the children who have watched Cerrie on TV and read her books will carry these unconscious lessons through into adulthood, resulting in a generation that are less likely to pigeonhole disabled people – the ones they meet, and the ones they may one day become.

Pigeonholing those with disabilities either as 'motivation' or as a segregated 'other' who cannot contribute to society leads us down a very narrow path of understanding. The latter is of course outwardly damaging, to the disabled person in question but also to society as a whole, as we'll see in the following chapters, but the former is also needlessly limiting. Adults as well as children expect to be inspired by those who have 'overcome' the adversity of their disability, and this form of objectification further 'otherizes' those with disabilities and somehow makes them extraordinary and not normal. The reality is far more complex and nuanced, the experience different for every individual. Stella Young argued that we need to completely revise how we view disability, and she summarized her TEDx talk with this powerful statement, of which we should all take note: 'Disability doesn't make you exceptional, but questioning what you think you know about it does.'

---

* *Guardian*: https://www.theguardian.com/childrens-books-site/2015/may/11/cerrie-burnell-diversity-in-childrens-books-disability

CHAPTER TWO

Invisibility

'The disability is not the problem, the accessibility is the problem.'
Mohamed Jemni

Throughout this book I have discussed the power of perception and how it can shape reality for better or worse. For those of us who can see, the major impact of visual images can alter our perceptions in an instant or seep into our subconscious subliminally and change our thinking over time. Recently, for example, the mainstream success of the London and Rio Paralympics, along with Prince Harry's Invictus Games for wounded servicemen and women, completely turned society's idea of an 'able body' on its head in a way that one would think should improve things for people with disabilities. As Tim Hollingsworth, Chief Executive of the British Paralympic Association, explained to me: *'The strength and excitement of the sporting competition, aligned with a very real and public presentation of impairment, has done much to shift the narrative and undoubtedly put the focus more on what people are able to do rather than what they are not.'*

Sporting events such as these are not only a showcase of the talent and resilience of people around the world who have overcome a disability; they show an image of our best self – the one we want to live up to – and the world supporting their exceptional achievements, accrediting them with the awe and dignity their heroism and athleticism deserves. However, the real test is not in the stadium, it's when the fanfare is over. The real question is: do we live up to the promise of inclusion that is the essence of events like the Paralympics? Sadly, it's in these moments that we routinely fall short. We allow disabled people to be an inspiration on the public stage, but these same people, who have been hailed as heroes in the press, will often face a daily battle when they are out of the public eye, living their everyday lives. These failures would normally remain unreported by the media, but irony and celebrity will always help to grab a headline. This was the case when a celebrated British Paralympian was made to feel 'disabled'.

Anne Wafula Strike, a Paralympian and wheelchair-user, was prevented from using the bathroom on a three-hour cross-country train journey because the disabled toilet was unavailable. The well-meaning staff on the train were sympathetic and wanted to help, but they were unable to put the facility back in working order. With no other option available, Anne ended up wetting herself. In true Paralympian style, she refused to feel humiliated and beaten by this and instead took her story to the media to raise awareness of the routine exclusion and indignities that disabled people have to face. We must all take responsibility for incidents like this. Something as simple as complaining when a facility does not have wheelchair access, or no longer shrugging our shoulders when we see an out-of-order toilet or facility for a disabled person as 'not a problem for us' is an important part of addressing our perceptions around the disabled. Anne Wafula Strike may well have felt humiliated in that moment, but it's the rest of us who should feel embarrassed for ignoring, and therefore condoning, the failure to include her needs. Even being a national treasure doesn't protect you from the dangers of discrimination, and sometimes this can turn violent, as was the case for *Silent Witness* star Liz Carr who was reportedly injured in an unprovoked attack by a man armed with pairs of scissors. Carr, who is wheelchair bound, was set upon as she crossed a road near Euston in Central London. Fortunately, she was accompanied by a carer who managed to ward off the attacker, and got away with non-life threatening head injuries. Safety and security can be even more precarious as a disabled person in an 'able' bodied world*.

When we can actually see what disabled people are capable of achieving we can move beyond the pity and discomfort we feel when faced with somebody we see as less fortunate than ourselves. Once we recognize and acknowledge the potential that is currently being untapped, perhaps then we can really start to involve all disabled people as valued contributors to society. But before we can do that, we need to really *see* them and meet their needs accordingly.

Improving visibility

As is so often the case, increased visibility – and therefore familiarization – begins with the media, and we can definitely see positive changes happening in popular culture. The hit HBO show *Game of Thrones*, for example, has an interesting take on disability, and attributes special qualities or abilities to characters who are disabled. There are two sibling characters in the show who become disabled: Bran loses the ability to walk and his sister Arya loses her sight. As a result of his restricted mobility, Bran develops a clairvoyant ability to see into the past and the future, and when Arya loses her sight she is able to defeat a fully-sighted attacker due to her other enhanced senses. And Tyrion, who played by actor Peter Dinklage and is one of the major characters in the show, was born a dwarf and suffers prejudice even within his own family. His small size in a very martial world has seen him develop a keen understanding of people, shrewd strategic thinking, and the ability to talk his way out of many deadly situations.

---

* http://www.telegraph.co.uk/news/2017/08/16/silentwitness-star-liz-carr-stabbed-head-edward-scissorhands/

But we need not only look to the world of fantasy to see the potential within our disabled community. Both Stephen Hawking and John Nash are examples of human genius, men recognized both within and beyond their respective fields of physics and mathematics. John Nash was a world-renowned mathematician who also suffered from paranoid schizophrenia – he was depicted by Russell Crowe in the 2001 movie *A Beautiful Mind*. Stephen Hawking was studying at Cambridge when he was diagnosed with motor neurone disease, a degenerative condition that caused him to become paralyzed, relying on technology to move and communicate. Hawking has been at the forefront of many scientific breakthroughs and is regarded as one of the most brilliant thinkers of our time, but he was already on his way to becoming an exceptional theoretical physicist when his illness struck. I can't help but wonder, if his physical disability had developed from birth, would there have been both the educational and societal infrastructure to allow his extraordinary mental ability to thrive? Over time, how many potential change agents have we missed, talked down to and relegated to antiquated teaching techniques, who have been unable to foster the genius that lay within them as a result? I also believe that Hawking's brilliance and resilience in the face of his disability has actually enhanced his contribution to humanity beyond what it would have been without it.

Fortunately for both Hawking and Nash (and us), their disabilities were not seen as something that detracted from their ability to contribute to society. It's worth noting, however, that both Stephen Hawking and John Nash were white privileged men who could access the best university education in their respective countries: Oxford and Cambridge in the UK and Princeton in the US. Had their background, gender, or ethnicity been different, it's quite possible their potential for brilliance might have been missed and, along with that, their priceless contribution to society.

19.2% of working-age disabled people do not hold any formal qualification, compared to 6.5% of working-age non-disabled people.*

Indeed, it may seem that wealth and privilege can be a cushion against any discriminatory blow. This was certainly the case with two former US presidents whose disabilities certainly didn't hinder their careers. Both Franklin D. Roosevelt, who couldn't walk unaided, and John F. Kennedy, who suffered from an endocrine disorder called Addison's disease, managed to hide their disability from public view and became successful, handsome, charismatic leaders. It could well be argued that they were successful presidents because of their disabilities, not despite them, as their personal battles gave them an extra level of resilience and empathy. FDR in particular had an understanding of human suffering that his privileged background would have otherwise shielded him from. But ironically, because both men felt the need to hide their disability, as their position was perceived to require them to be able-bodied, their successes could not be said to have changed public perceptions.

It has taken centuries for society to recognize the additional qualities that a person with a disability may have to offer and the collective benefits of inclusivity. There are campaigns for gender equality, racial equality, and LGBTQ rights, but seldom do you see the same political conversations being had around disability representation at the highest levels of the corporate world. The same is true in the corridors of power. Although they haven't hidden their disabilities like FDR and JFK, their UK counterparts are still few and far between. To date David Blunkett has been the first and only blind cabinet minister in the UK, with few aware that former prime minister Gordon Brown is blind in one eye, and currently there are only five MPs in Parliament with disabilities – that is less than 1 per cent. Given that

* Disability Facts and Figures, DWP. Published 16 January 2014

one in five people in the UK has a disability, such a lack of disabled representatives in our Parliament is completely unacceptable.

In 2000, George W. Bush gave a speech at the National Association for Advancement of Colored People (NAACP) convention, in which he spoke of the 'soft bigotry of low expectations'. Although President Bush was speaking about the plight of African-American children and the US education system, the same can be said about how we perceive those living with disabilities. We make little room for variations in the functionalities of the human body or mind and expect less from those who are deemed atypical.

In reality, every individual has their struggles. But whatever our challenges, they do not detract from our skills or talents. In some cases our ability to overcome these challenges may enhance a skill or talent. This logic could be applied to any of our 'other' groups, but is probably most applicable to disabled people. In the way that a deaf Beethoven was able to create timeless music, or Ray Charles or Stevie Wonder could perform without seeing their audience, we can never know what their abilities would have been without their disabilities, but we do know that their disabilities in no way diminished their abilities – and most probably enhanced them.

Start early

So how do we make it easier for disabled people to overcome these challenges and realize their potential? If we want inclusion to become the norm, where we have an understanding that a positive response to diversity produces tangible benefits for us all, then undoubtedly we need to start in our schools. The playground and classroom are where we first experience diversity, or the lack of it, and this is when we are first starting to form views and opinions. The manner in which schools in the UK and US address diversity will be crucial in determining how future generations view inclusion.

If disability and neurodiversity is absent from their school experience, children may be ignorant of how to be inclusive of these – and those with disabilities are likely to be forced to 'get used to' segregation and missed opportunities at a formative age. If there are disabled students but the school does not have the adequate systems in place to actively include them in learning with able-bodied students, then educational segregation is seen as not only normal but also necessary, and easier for both parties. Unfortunately this empowers the view that these students should be separated or put in institutions, so as not to make them feel inadequate or to hold others back. The worst-case scenario is when disabled and neurodiverse students are treated negatively or as deviants, as was the case with Daniel Ten, a-year-old Canadian autistic boy who was restrained and handcuffed by police while on school premises. This type of approach in a school is likely to leave other children with the impression that disability and neurodiversity is a problem, a nuisance, or even a danger to 'the rest of us'.

56%: the percentage of disabled people who say they have experienced hostility, aggression, or violence from a stranger because of their condition.[*]

90%: the number of people with learning difficulties who have been a victim of hate crime or bullying.[†]

It is this type of thinking that made the US Individuals with Disabilities Education Act (IDEA) of 1975 controversial in its day. IDEA was signed by President Ford and required all states that accepted money from the federal government to provide equal access to education for children with disabilities, in addition to providing them with one free meal per day. Although a step in the right direc-

[*] Mencap: https://www.mencap.org.uk/get-involved/campaigning/hear-my-voice/hear-my-voice-hate-crime

[†] Disability Hate Crimes: Does Anyone Really Hate Disabled People? By Mark Sherry, Routledge, 2016

tion, IDEA still only took disabled children from being excluded to the point of being tolerated and accommodated. It took almost three more decades to get to a place where disabled and neurodiverse children would be seen as an asset – and that inclusion improved the attainment levels of all students.

The one-size-fits-all approach to learning favours the few over the many. If education is simply seen as a means of selection, the result will be inequality. But if we can allow for diverse learning styles, we could have an educational experience tailored to bring out the best in each student. Universal Design Learning (UDL) is such a framework, providing a more flexible approach that accommodates both the range of neurodiverse students as well as those without specialist needs. What UDL's creator, David H. Rose, Ed.D. of the Harvard Graduate School of Education and the Centre for Applied Special Technology (CAST), had in mind when he came up with the idea in the Nineties was offering students various means of acquiring knowledge and skills, and using their interests and strengths to motivate learning. For example, if you have a child who thrives on physical activity and being outside, then being sat in a classroom may not be the best way of teaching that child about angles, shapes, and how to measure area. Alternatively, writing argumentative prose or essays could be taught using model blocks or pictures, if that is where the student's strengths lie. The logical outcome would be to continue this into the workplace, providing a truly tailored approach to managing staff and client/ customer relationships to ensure the best outcomes. This makes total sense and surely must be the way forward.

Our journey towards inclusion is by no means complete, but where we've made progress we have not only produced disabled and neuro- diverse students able to actively participate in our workforce and economy, we have also produced more emotionally intelligent able- bodied students who can understand and communicate effectively with customers, colleagues, and clients across all the spectrums of physical capacity and neurodiversity. And this, of course, benefits all of us in terms of what we are able to produce, sell, and create for people across the globe.

The tangible benefits

The other vital way in which we must recognize and meet the needs of our disabled community is in the nitty-gritty, everyday details of how our world actually works. As my story showed, injury or illness can make anyone 'disabled' (temporarily or permanently) at any time, so it's in all our interests to design a world that fits all, and at the moment the way that our world has been designed completely excludes the disabled in a myriad of ways. Historically this has been, in part, due to financial reasons, technological limitations, societal stigmas, and the fact that the designers and decision makers themselves were less likely to be disabled. And sadly, most us who fit the 'norm' don't even notice simple things like ramps without handrails, drains near dropped kerbs, or everyday consumer products unavailable with braille. But given that it's estimated that citizens of countries with a life expectancy of 70 and over will spend 'on average about 8 years, or 11.5 per cent of their lifespan, living with disabilities',[*] it's something we really should all notice and think about.

47%: the percentage of disabled people who say they are withdrawing from society because the services they receive do not enable them to take part in community life.[†]

Throughout this book I've been making the case for inclusion as more than just the buzzword of progressives, but as something from

[*] Disabled World According to the UN Development Program (UNDP): https://www.disabled-world.com/disability/statistics
[†] Taylor and Francis, http://www.tandfonline.com/doi/abs/10.1080/09687599.2016.1152952?scroll=top&needAccess=true&journalCode=cdso20

which we derive tangible benefits as a society. One of the clearest non-economic examples of this by far is 'universal design'. This term was coined by architect Ronald L. Mace to describe the revolutionary style of 'inclusive design', creating buildings, spaces, products, and devices that were made to be inclusive of a broad spectrum of physical needs from the outset (rather than as an add-on, which is usually the case). Another great breakthrough in this area was by Selwyn Goldsmith, author of *Designing for the Disabled*, who is regarded as the pioneer of free access. He is the inventor of the dropped kerb, now a design feature we all take for granted.

These products, services, and facilities, designed to be as accessible as possible to people of differing physical abilities and ages, obviously benefit the able-bodied, too. Anyone travelling with heavy luggage or children in pushchairs will have benefited from dropped curbs and buildings with wider access points and automatic doors; and many without a disability have happily enjoyed a good audiobook and used an electric toothbrush. Subtitles on TV and video content is another example. In fact, more people with full hearing use these than those who are non-hearing. They have even been used to help tackle adult illiteracy. So next time you're enjoying a foreign-language film or are at the gym, airport lounge, or bar reading the subtitles on a muted screen, remember where the idea came from.

Initially, some of these changes were considered controversial – they seemed too costly, and arguments were made that the benefits to a minority versus the cost to businesses or taxpayers did not weigh up. Time has proved otherwise, with the benefits to all of us far outweighing the costs. Many of these innovations came about only because designers of products, services and facilities were required to consider a minority group, and thereby delivered results to consumers that were far better than they otherwise would have been.

It just goes to show what we can achieve when we take the time and effort to see, recognize, and address the needs of those with disabilities. If we stop treating disabled people at best as an inconvenience and at worst as invisible, the benefits for all of us will be manifold – and sometimes even unexpected.

ACTION POINT: If you don't know it already, learn the alphabet and/or some basic phrases – 'hello'; 'how are you' – in sign language. www.british–sign.co.uk can help.

DISCUSSION POINT: If a person in a wheelchair started in your place of work tomorrow, would your workplace be able to accommodate them?

CHAPTER THREE

The Lost Workforce

'There is a plan and a purpose, a value to every life, no matter what its location, age, gender or disability.'

Sharron Angle

60%: the percentage of people with learning disabilities who are able to work and would like a job.
6%: the percentage who have one.[*]

In the past, our approach to disabled people in the workplace has been one of half-hearted accommodation, rather than true integration. This has a direct impact on our economy. Equal opportunities and protection from discrimination for disabled people came on the back of legislation primarily aimed at tackling discrimination against women and ethnic minorities in the 1960s and 1970s. It was at the end of the twentieth century that we began to see in the US the Americans with Disabilities Act of 1990, and in the UK the Disability Discrimination Act of 1995. Both of these acts required amendments made to them (2010's Equality Act in the UK) to better meet the

[*] Mencap: https://www.mencap.org.uk/get-involved/learning-disability-work-experience-week

needs of disabled people. The onus on both countries was around preventing discrimination and requiring employers to make 'reasonable' adjustments to accommodate disabled workers. But collectively we need to go further than this, from tolerance and accommodation to understanding and valuing. Once we comprehend the unique contribution that a so-called disabled person can bring to a role, we will incentivize them, boost our businesses, and ultimately strengthen our economy against the diverse challenges of the future.

Progressive hiring

In the UK, only 46.3% of working-age disabled people are in employment, compared to 76.4% of working-age non-disabled people.[*] This compares to just 17.5% in employment in the US.[†] These startling statistics indicate that in both countries the majority of disabled people are not in employment, and many of those who can work are not being properly utilized and are being supported by the welfare state.

The annual UK disability benefit budget is £60 billion, and disabilities minister Penny Mordaunt recently faced harsh criticism when, as part of a £3.7 billion cost-cutting exercise, she tried to revoke Personal Independence Payment (PIP) benefits for more than 160,000 people living with disabilities. The backlash was made worse when George Freeman, a Tory MP and senior adviser to Theresa May, argued that disability benefits should 'only go to really disabled people' and not to those 'taking pills at home, who suffer from anxiety'. Freeman addressed his comments via Trump's favourite platform of communication, Twitter. Unlike Trump, he apologized, tweeting: 'Having experienced myself traumatic anxiety as a child carer living w alcohol [sic] I know all too well the pain anxiety + depression causes . . . Which is why as a former Health Minister and

---

[*] Department for Work and Pensions
[†] Bureau of Labor Statistics

Policy Adviser I am passionate about supporting Mental Health and Disability, and hugely regret if my comment about the need to prioritize the most "serious disabilities" inadvertently caused any offence which was not intended.'

I think the government has missed a trick here. The underlying assumption of this cost-cutting is that a large proportion of people living on disability benefits are cheats and system abusers. We all accept the need for a balanced budget, but I would argue that it's much more cost-effective and beneficial long-term to deal with the causes rather than the effects. We need to focus on the bigger issue of how we better integrate the hundreds of thousands of unemployed disabled people who want to work but find it difficult to access opportunities in a society that has not fully factored in their needs.

I am not alone in my thinking. My views are also shared by Liz Sayce, CEO of Disability Rights UK:

> *After a successful period of campaigns by the disability movement for equal participation across society, the financial crash ushered in an erosion of rights. Eligibility for social care and benefits support were restricted to those considered 'vulnerable', leaving many supposedly 'undeserving' disabled people without support to participate in community life, education or employment. Being considered 'vulnerable' or 'undeserving' is no choice at all. We need investment in disabled people's potential and full participation. With one in five of the population living with a long-term health condition or disability, a commitment to full participation could transform our society. An inclusive society would maximize everyone's contributions, gain from the experience that living with disability brings (often problem-solving, creativity, empathy) and achieve a world where everyone belongs.*

With this in mind, because disability is so broad and wide-ranging in terms of the impact it has on the individuals who are affected, surely we need an overall talent or skills audit of our disabled population to better identify the areas and careers to which they are best suited, particularly those with more intellectual-based difficulties such as Down's syndrome or autism. The tech community has been very astute in identifying the benefits of hiring people with autism to perform their more complicated coding and programming. Salesforce, Bankwest, Microsoft and Hewlett Packard have actively begun seeking out people on the autistic spectrum to join their teams. In the case of Hewlett Packard, a member of their cybersecurity team had been flipping burgers in McDonald's for two years before joining them. Until then his inability to communicate had always worked against him in interviews and prevented him from being hired in accordance to his ability. A key aspect of Asperger's is single-minded focus; this trait can be seen as disruptive in the wider world, but is an extraordinary asset in the tech world and start-up community. In his book *Zero to One*, PayPal co-founder and Facebook investor Peter Thiel advocates hiring staff with autism and Asperger's to avoid 'herd-like thinking and behavior' in companies;[*] instead, you end up with individuals who have a different method of processing information and solving scientific conundrums,[†] who may well come up with solutions no one else has thought of.

Such progressive hiring practices are not an altruistic move by these corporations – they're a smart business move, based on Judy Singer's 'neurodiversity' theory, which doesn't look at autism as an illness or a disorder but rather as a natural variation in the human brain. Singer, herself autistic, states that 'the "Neurologically Different" represent a new addition to the familiar political categories of class/gender/race and will augment the insights of the social model of disability'.[‡]

---

[*] *Zero to One* by Peter Thiel (Crown Business, 2014): http://zerotoonebook.com/
[†] *Guardian*: https://www.theguardian.com/world/2013/may/22/german-it-firm-sap-seeks-autistic-workers
[‡] http://www.institute4learning.com/resources/articles/neurodiversity/

The skills rush

In the face of global competition, the twenty-first century is about to see a 'Skills Rush' – a mind and innovation grab where the companies and countries that succeed will be able to identify and refine the required skills wherever they find them. And in the case of our disabled populations, we need to rethink how we view their potential, otherwise we will be missing out. Some companies are already way ahead of the pack. In 2016 Angela Merkel, the German Chancellor, had the foresight in the face of much controversy to admit refugees from Syria at the start of the conflict. On the face of it this appeared a benign liberal gesture that would cause a strain on German resources. However, this early wave of refugees comprised the well-educated professionals with skills that the German economy needs for the future. Indeed, Germany as a country seems to be particularly pragmatic on the issue of skills. The BBC reported in 2013 that the German software giant SAP has gone as far as setting itself a target of people with autism spectrum disorder (ASD) accounting for 1 per cent of its global workforce by 2020. One of their executives, Luisa Delgado, was quoted as saying: 'Only by employing people who think differently and spark innovation will SAP be prepared to handle the challenges of the twenty-first century.'[*]

Now, for the first time, the West (North America and Europe) is facing challenges from economies around the world. Eastern economies (such as China and India) as well as the South (Brazil, Nigeria, South Africa, Egypt) boast countries with young and growing populations. For the UK and the US to compete we will need to utilize our entire pool of talent and accept that disabled doesn't mean not able.

A 10% rise in the employment rate among disabled adults would contribute an extra £12 billion to the Exchequer by 2030.[†]

[*] BBC: http://www.bbc.co.uk/news/business-22621829
[†] Scope, 'Enabling Work', 2015

It feels to me that we have reached a crossroads in the UK and the US. Do we do away with the vestiges of so-called political correctness, like diversity and inclusion, so we can go back to an education system and a workforce that churn out people with a very narrow view of what society is and who we need to accommodate? Or do we push on for a future where the case for inclusion becomes the mantra of the pragmatist as well as the liberal?

ACTION POINT: Ask a person with disabilities if you can spend a day shadowing them.

DISCUSSION POINT: What if we made it easier to work, not harder to claim benefits?

The Other Way

'My disability exists not because I use a wheelchair, but because the broader environment isn't accessible.'

Stella Young

The number-one hope of most expectant parents is that their child is born 'healthy' and not in any way disabled. For many parents, finding out that their child is not 'normal' and that all the dreams they had planned may no longer come to pass is a pain that cuts to the core. But there are also so many joys to be had from appreciating people as they are, for their uniqueness and personality, if only we can remember to do so. In her widely celebrated poem 'Welcome to Holland', Emily Perl Kingsley poignantly articulates the complexities of giving birth to a disabled child in an able-bodied world. Sometimes, she explains, we may have planned for a trip to Italy and life detours us to Holland, but by pining for Italy we miss all that Holland has to offer. Sometimes we have to wake up and smell the tulips! You can read the full piece at www.Diversify.org

One of my dearest friends, the Australian author Kathy Lette, knows this very well. We've been friends for over 15 years and have shared many of life's' highs and lows. Her son, Julian (Jules), was diagnosed with Asperger's (a developmental disorder at the milder end of the autism spectrum) at three years old and Kathy has spoken publicly about the struggles of mothering a child who doesn't fit into society's norm. For many years Jules suffered intense bullying, which ranged from being locked in a dog kennel to having a note stuck on his back that read: 'I'm a retard – kick me'. Now aged 25, he has a photographic memory and a computer-like capacity for consuming knowledge – gifts that serve him well for learning scripts in his new-found fame as an actor on the cast of the BBC One series *Holby City*. Knowing how tough Jules's journey has been has made his success all the sweeter for those of us who love and adore him, but no one is more proud than Kathy: 'Jules joining the cast of *Holby* is the best thing that could have happened. His confidence, morale, and self-esteem is up, which is incredible because so many people with autism are made to feel so inadequate.'

The producers of *Holby City* were discerning in casting someone who actually had autism to play an autistic character, and we need to see more of this kind of decision making. After all, gone are the days when it was seen as acceptable for someone of a different race to play a known person of colour – the same must become commonplace where disabled roles are concerned.

Actress Sally Phillips is also parent to a child with a disability. Her documentary, *A World Without Down's Syndrome?*, provides a refreshing angle on the question of whether or not we would eradicate such forms of disability if we could, given that *in utero* NHS screening for Down's syndrome is now available. She focuses on the benefits of difference and diversity of the mind. Sally's eldest child Olly, who has Down's syndrome, stars in this moving, smart, funny film, which shows all that he has added to their family and how much they have all evolved as a result.

So, what if the new normal was that there wasn't a 'normal', but rather an acceptance and celebration of uniqueness and individuality – a diversity of mind and body? We are all constrained by social hierarchies and criteria of value, and perhaps the disabled are most affected by this. Their discrimination is one that is so ubiquitous that it is seldom acknowledged, discussed, or challenged, and maybe it's high time we start. With the influence and prejudice of wider society taken out of the loop, individuals – disabled and non-disabled – could connect on an equal footing, without the labels that society awards us.

How refreshing and healing it might be for all of us to connect with individuals with a different way of looking at the world. Maybe then we would all ultimately recognize that those with an intellectual or developmental disability have as much, if not more, to offer the world as the world has to offer them.

The Numbers

Rates of employment and representation in higher occupations in Britain by disability status.[*]

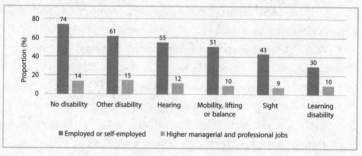

Monthly labour earnings and income by disability status in Britain.[†]

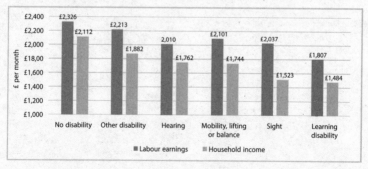

[*] Understanding Society
[†] Understanding Society

Need-to-know facts and figures:

- **30%:** the proportion of people with a long-term physical health problem who also have a mental health problem (*Source*: The King's Fund)
- **67%:** the proportion of people with mental health problems who were receiving benefits but said they either wanted to work or were looking for work (*Source*: Rethink Mental Illness)
- **40%:** the proportion of people with a mental health problem or learning disability in England who were employed in 2015, and **8%:** the proportion who were unemployed (*Source*: NHS Confederation)
- **48%:** the proportion of people in England receiving Employment Support Allowance in August 2015 who had a mental or behavioural disorder (*Source*: NHS Confederation)
- **27%:** the proportion of working-age people with disabilities in the US who were employed in 2015, and **72%:** the proportion of people without disabilities who were employed (*Source*: Bureau of Labor Statistics)

Change Your Mind

'Progress is impossible without change, and those who cannot change their minds cannot change anything.'

George Bernard Shaw

We are born into the world absorbing information through all our senses — data that filters through our environment and shapes our minds as we grow. As we are exposed to different experiences and ideas, our beliefs take form and we begin to make judgements based upon those beliefs. However, once these viewpoints have taken root in our adult minds, they can become extremely difficult to change or transcend. The seventeenth-century Jesuit missionary St Francis Xavier said, 'Give me the child until he is seven and I'll give you the man.' Unfortunately, most of us are adults and have therefore already been conditioned, so we must try to modify ideas that have already formed.

In order to do this, it helps to understand a little of how our beliefs are created in the first place. Michael Shermer, founder of the Skeptics Society and editor-in-chief of its magazine *Skeptic*, has spent a lifetime studying where beliefs come from. In his *New York Times* bestseller, *The Believing Brain*, he explores the brain's process in forming a belief. It begins with 'patternicity: the tendency to find meaningful patterns in both meaningful and meaningless data'; the second process he calls 'agenticity: the tendency to infuse patterns with meaning, intention, and agency'. In other words, our brains have evolved to connect the dots of our world into meaningful patterns to explain why things happen. These patterns become beliefs, and the brain then begins to look for confirmatory evidence to support those beliefs, which, once found, serves to reinforce them. And round and round the process goes, in a feedback loop of belief confirmation.

But this is only the individual story. Carl Jung, in his theory of the 'collective unconscious', describes how ideas and beliefs held by individuals can then form parts of a latent mob mentality within a group – something that has been a particularly potent force in terms of shaping our world. Religious and political leaders throughout history have sought to manipulate the collective thinking of popula-tions to bring about their desired ends, and Jung warns how dangerous this can be. During the Second World War alone we saw the devas-tating consequences of tapping into shared feelings of fear, pain, anger, and loss.

And these shared feelings don't just spring from the here and now. Their origins go back centuries, even millennia. This primal, age-old fear of the 'other' has been exploited time and time again, and this is where 'other' people lose their individual humanity and become reduced to symbols, metaphors, and stereotypes – nothing more than the defining attribute of their collective group.

We know the story off by heart. We've seen the movie and read the history book. And yet it seems that this collective thinking rules us. So how do we change this? Is it even possible to change not only what we've always been taught to believe, but also the unconscious negativity hat we've inherited from our ancestors?

All of these ills are within the mind and therefore this is where we must target the problem. This is not an immediate thing, of course – it takes time and practice to train our brains to respond differently – but that doesn't mean it can't be done. We first need to move from being collectively unconscious to being individually conscious of how and why we feel and respond the way we do. As we've seen, we have been hardwired to fear what is unfamiliar and different as part of our primal survival mechanism, but times change, and to survive and prosper in this age we need to work collaboratively with the 'other', rather than fight or flee from them.

Once we accept how we feel and why, without letting blame or guilt distract us, we can begin the process of upgrading our thinking by applying logic to the problem: 'I want the best people around me with the skills and qualities I need because that benefits me. To find the best people I need to search the widest possible pool'. However, the thought process that occurs when our fear of the 'other' kicks in is: 'I am comfortable with a smaller pool that I am familiar with and I feel that the skills and qualities I need are in my pool'. This collective unconscious response may have kept our ancestors safe, but it is now limiting our ability to attract the best people. Therefore, we must intervene when our brain senses difference and reroute our thinking to see opportunity rather than fear. This process needs to be repeated and reinforced by continually challenging ourselves to explore the opportunities within diversity. Once that piece of code is accepted and we work on removing the outdated process, we make progress. That's not to say we won't still default to the previous setting now and then, but our new understanding will recognize the error and auto-correct.

The media has usually been the laboratory where experiments with diversity have been either tested successfully or denied access. Indeed, it's now so ubiquitous that it rivals religion and the state in its ability to shape people's thinking. As an industry there have always been competing interests within it, though. In times of racial segregation, black artists and sports stars were promoted through the media, which helped to break down barriers. But on the flipside, the media has also fostered taboos such as inter-racial relationships and a lack of inclusion for disabled, LGBTQ, and women in the industry.

Naturally, all of this influences us. The power of the mass media is immense, and it does have the choice to either challenge or reinforce the 'collective unconscious'. A balanced news media could present stories that challenge, for example, the association of Muslims and terror. Representations of women could be more reflective of how they actually look, with the focus on attributes other than their appearance. Unfortunately, both the UK and US media industries have repeatedly been accused of lacking diversity at a time when society is becoming more diverse but also witnessing a growing intolerance of difference. This is another area where we, as consumers, need to apply our neuro-reprogramming. It's important to remember that the media's power over our brains is secondary to our own. As we start to change our thinking, we are better able to filter and challenge the images and ideas we are fed, enabling us to make informed decisions on the content and providers we support and to put pressure on those within the industry to better reflect the diverse population. Once we start to change our own minds, we can help change other minds, and then – and only then – will we be able to change our actions.

PART FIVE

THE OTHER SEX

'I am the love that dare not speak its name.'

Lord Alfred Douglas

The Old Way

The LGBTQ community has been socially and economically excluded, just like any 'other' group, yet they are the only group to have been persecuted for the very thing that makes us human: our feelings and emotions. Like those with a disability, LGBTQ people rarely share their 'otherness' with loved ones, and whereas a family may feel a desire to support and protect the diversity that a disabled member adds, this is not always the case if they are gay, lesbian, bisexual, or transgender, often leaving them even more isolated.

Perhaps the most famous case of a member of the LGBTQ community being persecuted for their sexuality in the UK is the notorious trial of Oscar Wilde. The author and playwright was drawn into an unjust 'gross indecency' trial in 1895 – dubbed 'the trial of the century' – and was sentenced to two years' hard labour for homosexuality, which at the time was still illegal in Britain. The real reason behind the trial was Wilde's relationship with his younger lover, Lord Alfred Douglas, the son of Wilde's nemesis, the Marquess of Queensberry. 'Two Loves', Douglas's poem to Wilde, was used as evidence by the prosecution, and its epic line, 'I am the love that dare not speak its name', would help to seal Wilde's fate, as it seemed to speak unequivocally of their forbidden relationship. Time in prison would be the undoing of Wilde, and he died three years after his release while exiled in Paris.

Wilde's story is certainly not a one-off. LGBTQ figures were still being persecuted long into the twentieth century. The British mathematician and Second World War code-breaker Alan Turing – now recognized as one of the major pioneers of modern-day computing – was convicted of 'gross indecency' in 1952. He lost his job at GCHQ and was subjected to experimental 'chemical castration' in an attempt to 'cure' him of his homosexuality, which he was offered as an alternative to a prison sentence. The effects it had on him physically and mentally were devastating and he committed suicide in 1954. His vast contribution to the war effort in breaking the Enigma Code and aiding the Allied victory was swept under the carpet until very recently, when he was given a posthumous royal pardon in 2013.

In the US, as recently as the 1970s, Harvey Milk became the first openly gay person to reach public office when he was elected to the San Francisco Board of Supervisors – a triumphant moment in the struggle for gay rights in the country – only to be murdered 11 months later, in 1978, by one of his colleagues.

These are extreme cases but they're indicative of the fear and hostility that the LGBTQ community has historically met with. For centuries many simply had to suppress and hide it, pretend they were not 'other', and the emotional and mental cost of this is unimaginable. Others have had to endure a sliding scale of such treatment, in ways that don't always make the headlines, on a daily basis for their entire lives.

Today, things have progressed hugely – in the last 20 years especially social attitudes have, for the most part, changed dramatically; gay rights have been fought for and won, and thousands now take to the streets in cities across the world each year to celebrate Pride. Indeed, Gay Pride had a heightened significance in 2017 as we celebrated the 50th anniversary of the part decriminalization of homosexuality in the UK. There were raucous events up and down the country, with institutions, businesses, and museums all participating in the activities. The British media also showed its support – Channel 4 and BBC Two both ran seasons showcasing stories of fact and fiction featuring gay characters, and I was lucky enough to chair a panel with some of Britain's leading gay and trans actors and writers.

The ubiquitous nature of the celebrations shows us how far we have come, but the fact that it's taken almost half a century to get from decriminalization to marriage equality for same-sex couples shows how long change can take. For some, this change may have come too fast, for others it probably feels like a lifetime. As much as we applaud the progress that has been made, we also have to acknowledge that we're not there yet. As always, there is much more work to be done.

CHAPTER ONE

Old Views

'It comes to this then: there always have been people like me and always will be, and generally they have been persecuted.'

E. M. Forster

A brief history of homosexuality

The earliest documents concerning same-sex relationships come from Ancient Greece – and yet society has always had a tumultuous relationship with sexuality, leading, in turn, to social and cultural tensions. In ancient and classical times, curiosity and diversity were the drivers of civilization and human development, so many of our modern 'isms' would have been viewed as counterproductive. It was considered normal and useful for an accomplished male philosopher, political leader, or scientist to take another younger male as an apprentice/lover, to form a bond, pass on learning and, of course, to satisfy desire. During these ancient times of diverse influences, the development of ideas and technological advancements mattered most – the ability to contribute outweighed whatever pleasure was indulged in or whatever feelings were held.

In Ancient Greece and Phrygia, and later in the Roman Republic, the Goddess Cybele was worshipped by a cult of men who castrated themselves, and thereafter took female dress and referred to themselves as female, representing early examples of transsexual figures. Soon, though, the rise of the Abrahamic faiths saw the decline of the classical era and the sexual exploration, curiosity, and diversity of thought which had produced it. The incorporation of the Catholic Church as the official religion of the Roman Empire gave rise to a new negative attitude towards homosexuality, and the rapid spread of Islam across the Middle East and North Africa further standardized these new beliefs. In this context, those with alternative lifestyles were now seen as dangerous heretics and were persecuted accordingly. Following the decline of the Roman Empire, learning and advancement slowed and Europe entered the 'Dark Ages'. During this era, religion replaced philosophy, and expansionist warlord rulers used it to underpin intolerance and persecution of gay people or anyone suspected as such. Barbaric punishments such as torture, mutilation, castration, and death were commonplace.

Ironically, during this same period and beyond into the later Middle Ages and the Renaissance, gay individuals prevailed within the hierarchy of religious institutions, among the aristocratic elites, and even within the monarchies of many countries. Both Islam and Christianity at this time discouraged male–female socialization outside of appropriate courtship and marriage, but monks and nuns were sequestered away in remote locations, where same-sex relationships frequently developed. The power of the aristocracy exempted this level of society from persecution for the most part, but they were still subject to rumour and ridicule if suspected of being gay. Queen Christina, the seventeenth-century Swedish monarch, shocked her court by dressing as a man and taking part in typically masculine activities such as hunting, equestrian sports, and swordplay. She adamantly refused to marry, even abdicating her throne as a result. Historians believe that her long-time lady-in-waiting, Ebba Sparre, was likely her lover. And in English history, too, there have been plenty of kings (such as

William II, Edward II, and James I) who were rumoured to have 'preferred the company of men'.

During the Renaissance you also find gay individuals such as Leonardo da Vinci being protected and sponsored by rulers and powerful individuals, not because of their social status but because of their skills and talents. This has been a common theme throughout history – that as we seek to advance as a civilization, we overlook prejudices in favour of the skills and attributes an individual has to offer. But we need not kid ourselves that Europe's advancement led to freedoms for the gay community in general – those not of use to a patron or a person of power were left to face popular disdain and the wrath of the state.

It was not until the Enlightenment of the eighteenth century that some progress was made in Europe. It was the Napoleonic Code, introduced during the French Revolution, that decriminalized 'victimless crimes' such as sodomy in French-occupied countries, made possible by the resentment of some liberal sectors towards the Church in Catholic countries. In Protestant countries such as the UK, however, where the Church was less austere, there was little general reaction against statutes that were religious in origin, and as a result many of those countries retained their statutes on sodomy until late into the twentieth century.

The last known execution for homosexuality in Great Britain happened in 1835 with the hanging of James Pratt and John Smith at Newgate Prison after being caught together in private lodgings. By the latter part of the nineteenth century, however, change was in the air in Protestant countries. Gay men of privilege – usually from the arts – began secretly campaigning through their art forms (and it had to be secret due to the strict mainstream Victorian opinions on morality) to change the minds of those in power and the reading classes. In 1861 the punishment for sodomy in England and Wales was reduced from the death penalty to life imprisonment, and in 1885 the law changed again to punish the broader felony of 'gross indecency', referring to 'homosexual acts', with a standard sentence of two years' hard labour – the very law that Oscar Wilde and Alan Turing fell foul of.

Fast-forward to the twentieth century – a revolutionary century in every sense – with 'other' groups all over the world beginning to reason that freedom and equality should have a wider remit. Africans and those of African descent objected to being excluded from the democracy and self-determination that their European masters enjoyed, while women were no longer willing to be denied the same freedoms and rights as men: the right to choose their political leaders, to choose whether they wanted to give birth, and to choose how to dress. So perhaps it was inevitable that in a world where every 'other' group was fighting to access or maintain their inalienable rights, gay individuals would also take up the fight for the right to love whomsoever they pleased – a right afforded to everybody else, whatever their ethnicity, social background, gender, or faith, as long as they were heterosexual.

Progress interrupted

The breakthrough came in 1967 when homosexual acts between two men in private were finally decriminalized for those over 21 (the law had never applied to women because lesbianism simply wasn't recognized), but the battle was far from over. Stoked by the hysteria surrounding the AIDS epidemic during the 1980s, Section 28 of the 1988 Local Government Act was implemented by Margaret Thatcher's Conservative government and stipulated that local authorities 'shall not intentionally promote homosexuality or publish material with the intention of promoting homosexuality' or 'promote the teaching in any maintained school of the acceptability of homosexuality as a pretended family relationship'. This was a severe blow to the progression of gay rights, and proved just how much work there was still to be done to change mainstream society's attitudes.

For many families wedded to religious dogma and traditional roles, LGBTQ issues were at worst an abomination of something sacred, and at best ignored, which allowed ignorance to flourish. Indeed, thanks to Section 28 prohibiting any information about homosexuality being taught in schools, ignorance was encouraged, even enforced.

It is doubtful whether the majority of the British population understood why Section 28 was so significant. Many of those who supported it believed they were making a stand to protect the innocence of ('straight') children. But what about the children who were not straight or did not identify with a particular gender? What about their sense of belonging? Unfortunately, during this period there were still many parents who were ill equipped to suitably educate their children about LGBTQ issues, and so it was vital for schools to fill this gap – but of course they couldn't.

This discriminatory legislation galvanized the LGBTQ community to fight against it, and although it would take over a decade and a change of government, equality and justice did eventually win the day. Section 28 was repealed by the Scottish Parliament in 2000 and the rest of the country followed in 2003. This repeal couldn't have happened without the relentless and strategic campaigning of Stonewall, the gay rights group (named after the Stonewall riots in New York in 1969 following a police raid on a gay club) that was founded in 1989 in response to Section 28, helping to change the media narrative from hostility to one of sympathy for LGBTQ rights. Without this rise in awareness, politicians may not have felt the public was ready for the much-needed policy changes to better integrate the LGBTQ community into wider society.

45% of LGBTQ young people have been bullied at school for their sexuality.[*]

* The School Report, 2017, Cambridge University/Stonewall: http://www.stone wall.org.uk/sites/default/files/the_school_report_2017.pdf

With Section 28 a thing of the past, schools are now free to support and nurture their LGBTQ students – and it's imperative that they do. A 2017 study by Cambridge University for Stonewall found that 40 per cent of LGBTQ young people are not taught anything about LGBTQ issues at school,[*] and only 17 per cent of secondary school teachers have been trained to deal with homophobic bullying.[†] Being educated about homosexuality in school provides a new narrative for pubescent children who are discovering their sexual identity: that they are not alone, that they are not 'abnormal', that to be 'other' than heterosexual is a natural occurrence. And, just as importantly, it teaches those kids who are not LGBTQ to respect their classmates' sexuality. To renounce this responsibility in the past, and to leave explanations of homosexuality to conservative religious and cultural elements, or playground cruelty, was negligent and deeply damaging to those growing up in fear and confusion, and we must now embrace a different path for the sake of *all* young people.

27% of young trans people have attempted suicide.[‡]

The battle for family acceptance

The need for sexual equality in the classroom is particularly important given that there is often a parallel, more personal struggle going on to achieve it in the home. I've seen for myself what a challenge this can be. Growing up in a working-class community and as part of an African immigrant family showed me two different sets of values regarding sexuality – both 'traditional' and not entirely comfortable with any 'other' kind of sex. So neither my Christian African background nor my playground experiences taught me anything positive about homosexuality. Combine this with the British

[*] The School Report, 2017, Cambridge University/Stonewall
[†] The Teachers' Report 2014, YouGov/Stonewall
[‡] METRO Youth Chances Survey, 2014

tradition of keeping a stiff upper lip, or in many cases remaining tight-lipped, and you create an environment of denial and incomprehension.

In my neighbourhood there was little discussion about LGBTQ issues, apart from the odd derisory insult in the playground or on the street: both 'gay' and 'lezza' were slurs for those who failed to meet the stereotypical expectations of their gender. To be called 'gay' implied that a boy was a sissy and liked playing with girls and wasn't tough enough to be a 'real boy', and a 'lezza' was a girl who wasn't conventionally attractive or who liked doing things that were not considered feminine – in both cases they were children who just didn't fit in: 'others'. So there was little support that I was aware of for anyone experiencing any confusion around their gender or sexuality.

At home the issue was never discussed; it was assumed that I was straight and would not engage in the unmentionable activity until I reached a respectable age, or – even better – was married. Thank goodness I didn't wait for the latter option. But I couldn't imagine facing the daunting prospect of having a conversation with my parents about any of this – and if I'd needed to explain to them that the sexual activity would be non-conventional and might not lead to grandchildren.

For LGBTQ individuals living in families where these things aren't open for discussion, the courage needed to start that conversation is immense, and the risk of being hurt and rejected by those you love extremely high. So their sexuality already makes them an 'other' in the eyes of society, but they can often become an 'other' in the eyes of their own family, too. The family has always been the primary unit of identification for an individual: a unit of shared beliefs and values, a unit that gives us a sense of belonging long before wider society gives us a sense of being either part of the community or an 'other'. It's supposed to be a source of unconditional love, but children who are born gay can find themselves excluded from this love, all because their feelings and sense of self are different to what has been ascribed to them by their nearest and dearest. Nowhere is sexual orientation and gender more important. In traditional conservative – often religious – families, your gender denotes your role and status, and there is only one possible sexual orientation for the preservation of that institution – one that results in procreation. Any deviation is considered perverse, dangerous, and ultimately devastating for the continuation of the family line. At best, the response of traditional families might be wilful ignorance or encouraged secrecy; at worst the result may be exclusion from the family home altogether.

25% of homeless young people are LGBT.[*]
69% of homeless LGBTQ young people said that mental, emotional, or sexual abuse from a family member played a part in their leaving home.[†]

This rejection can cause painful family breakdown and internal conflict, with a serious impact on the mental health of children and young people, which is already a serious issue globally. A 2014 survey by LGBTQ support group METRO found that 42 per cent of young LGBTQ people have sought medical help for depression or anxiety, compared to 29 per cent of heterosexual, non-trans respondents; 52 per cent had self-harmed (compared to 35 per cent of heterosexual, non-trans respondents); and 44 per cent had considered suicide (compared to 26 per cent of heterosexual, non-trans respondents). Again, this is why it is so important that schools educate our children about difference. We must be honest: we are not yet at the place where the majority of families are able or willing to provide the support and positive self-image that LGBTQ children desperately

[*] Albert Kennedy Trust Survey, 2015: http://www.dazeddigital.com/artsandculture/article/23865/1/a-quarter-of-the-uks-homeless-youth-are-lgbt
[†] Albert Kennedy Trust Survey, 2015

need. Failure to do this leaves us with these unacceptable mental health stats among our young LGBTQ community.

If we succeed in educating all children about LGBTQ, we can create a more tolerant and inclusive environment, which will enable children to thrive and develop their talents without fear of ridicule or victimization. By investing in education, we avoid the cost to our health service of having to cope with the mental health implications for LGBTQ young people, and we would gain the knock-on effects where those same young people carry these values of tolerance and inclusion into their workplace and into their families as adults – meaning that young people of the future needn't suffer in the way that they clearly are today.

ACTION POINT: Search for 'coming out stories' online for a glimpse into the sometimes heartbreaking, sometimes heart-warming world of coming out.

DISCUSSION POINT: What do you think the objective of Section 28 was?

CHAPTER TWO

New Opportunities

'Sexuality is as wide as the sea.'

Derek Jarman

The struggle for equality for the LGBTQ community over the last 30 years has been twofold. They had to get the government onside, so that legislation such as Section 28 was repealed and same-sex marriage brought in, and they had to change the hearts and minds of the general public, too. In order to achieve this, the media would prove a powerful ally.

The power of the media

My first experience of homophobia happened aged nine via the medium of television. Colin Russell (played by actor Michael Cashman) joining *EastEnders* in 1986 was a revolutionary moment in British popular culture and it was how I learnt what being gay was. Having grown up in a family where sexuality was not discussed, Michael Cashman's character normalized for me something I had no experience or concept of, and showed me the ignorance of homophobia – in particular from Dot Cotton, the iconic character on the show, who upon discovering that Colin and his partner Barry shared a bed began to fear that they had AIDS and that she would catch it from doing their washing in the laundrette. The storyline focused on the relationship between the gay couple and their neighbours rather than the stereotypes of gay men leading lives of debauchery. I could appreciate that these were two ordinary people who were part of a community (one based on the community I lived in), who were being bullied for no reason other than the fact that they were in love and shared a bed – just like any other couple.

As a nine-year-old girl, the significance of Colin and Barry sharing a bed hadn't occurred to me, but I knew they were different and were made to feel wrong because of it. The British are fond of the phrase 'live and let live', which speaks to our values of tolerance and inclusivity, and this touching storyline embodied this sentiment. Dot Cotton was an openly Christian character representing the older generation, who eventually sees the contradiction of her Christian values and her persecution of two people she had previously been friendly with. The moment when Dot apologized to Colin, saying, 'I've missed having you as a friend,' was a pivotal one for me and, I imagine, for a huge part of the population.

This, along with the storyline of another (heterosexual) man who was the first mainstream television character to be HIV-positive, helped debunk the pervasive ignorance and fear of AIDS during the 1980s that linked homosexuality unequivocally with the disease. I spoke to Michael Cashman about the impact Colin had on helping to reshape the nation's thinking. It certainly wasn't all plain sailing. He described the painful homophobic tabloid reporting of the day, including a *Sun* newspaper headline that read 'Eastbenders'. Some of the viewers were just as outraged, as of course was conservative social campaigner Mary Whitehouse. The storyline even prompted questions in the House of Commons. However, for every voice of condemnation there were a dozen voices of support, such as one viewer who wrote to describe how she had explained Colin kissing

Barry to her young child as 'Colin loves Barry the way Mummy loves Daddy'.

Cashman was full of praise for the show's producers, Julia Smith and the legendary late Tony Holland. Holland was openly gay himself and helped to masterfully craft the ordinariness of Colin and Barry's relationship for the small screen. And once again, it demonstrates how vital it is that, when it comes to the important decision-making processes in our society, we ask, 'Is everyone in the room?' A soap opera with such mass appeal as *EastEnders* is a powerful platform, so it was a brave and influential move to air this storyline at all, but it also had a heavy duty to treat the story and its characters with respect, responsibility, and realism. By having a diverse team in the room, including people like Holland, to shape this representation of gay people brought an authenticity and a level of understanding that wouldn't have been achieved otherwise.

Michael Cashman would go on to take his activism from the screen to the political arena. For 30 years he has been at the forefront of LGBTQ rights in the UK and, in particular, the battle to rid the nation of Section 28. He was one of the original co-founders of Stonewall in 1989, and later became a leading MEP (Member of the European Parliament) and is now a member of the House of Lords.

It's clear that the media has a vital and powerful role to play in breaking down people's prejudices and normalizing the 'other' sex. Television especially, with its central role within almost every household, speaks intimately to its viewers on a daily basis. The BBC had certainly done its bit to raise awareness and help normalize homosexuality, and soon the UK's Channel 4 followed suit in 1994, when its soap *Brookside* gave us the first pre-watershed lesbian kiss between Beth Jordache and Margaret Clemence (played by Anna Friel and Nicola Stephenson respectively). At the time, showing on-screen affection between a lesbian couple was controversial and of course invited complaints, particularly from parents on behalf of their 'impressionable children'. And they were right – children were impacted by television's inclusion of LGBTQ relationships: the attitudes of the young people of Britain – namely my generation, Generation X – were to be much more open-minded than their parents. The older generations had witnessed the first ever (postwatershed) televised lesbian kiss 20 years previously in 1974 in the BBC drama *Girl*, which starred Alison Steadman and Myra Frances, but by the mid-1990s teens and young adults were devouring cult classic shows such as *Queer As Folk* and *This Life*, which dealt openly, frankly, and explicitly with gay sex and relationships. These shows, each controversial and ground-breaking in their time, set the scene for many of the progressive changes of the following decades and broke down barriers, allowing each generation to overcome their prejudices a little bit more than the last. They also paved the way for the concerted effort that is now being made in the UK and the US to improve the representation of LGBTQ characters on primetime TV.

4.8%: the percentage of regular characters on scripted primetime US programmes that are LGBTQ in 2016.[*]
16: the number of transgender characters across broadcast, cable, and streaming programmes in the US in 2016.[†]

A creative outlet

One of the earliest mediums to give a sympathetic outing to the LGBTQ community was the literary world. Some of the most talented poets and writers fell outside the then conventions of sexuality but, as with Oscar Wilde, they were constrained by the repressive laws condemning and persecuting expressions of alternative love. History

[*] GLAAD report 'Where We Are on TV' 2016–2017. This is the highest percentage GLAAD has ever found: https://www.glaad.org/whereweareontv16
[†] GLAAD report 'Where We Are on TV' 2016–2017. This number is more than double that of the previous year

is littered with such creatives and artists who have either had their voice suppressed or were persecuted for their sexuality. E. M. Forster, for example, wrote the first draft of his pioneering novel *Maurice*, about a love affair between two men, as early as 1914, but he wrote to a friend that it was 'unpublishable until my death and England's'. He did at least live to see homosexuality decriminalized, but indeed the novel wasn't published until after his death, in 1971.

It is widely accepted that the creative, cultural, and media industries have traditionally led the way in valuing the diversity that the LGBTQ community brings. Literature, theatre, fashion, art, music, and television have probably been the most progressive, helping to bring the LGBTQ community out of closeted exile by portraying them as part of society, rather than ignoring them. By making it possible for a Jean-Paul Gaultier, a Gianni Versace, an Alexander McQueen, an Elton John, or a Keith Haring to excel in their careers, we have all benefited. Music is perhaps the sector that has had the most success in encouraging society to acknowledge and recognize the LGBTQ community, allowing musicians to reflect themselves through their art form much more than their counterparts on the big screen. In the 1970s, the disco era, followed by the new romantic movement, saw musicians experiment with sexuality and gender. Androgynous or openly effeminate musicians such as David Bowie's Ziggy Stardust, Boy George, Elton John, Freddie Mercury, and then, eventually, George Michael, successfully introduced people to the idea that alternative sexual preference and gender identities could be accommodated within society without destroying it – in fact, they could enhance and expand it. Songs about love, desire, and loss could be equally applicable to traditional relationships and alternative ones. When those creating this art are in the public eye, society benefits in more ways than one: they challenge traditional views on what is normal, and they help to establish a new and more diverse image of 'normal'.

Despite these pioneering figures in our pop culture, many others in the public eye have had to hide their true selves for fear of ruining their public image. Even today, it is still considered a 'brave' step for a cisgender performer (a person whose sense of personal identity and gender corresponds with their birth sex) to 'come out' – even more so in macho cultures such as hip hop, where musician Frank Ocean's openness in 2012 was seen as an incredibly bold move. Celebrities from the world of music and film cultivate an image to connect with their fans, usually based on sex and attraction, which raises the fear that 'coming out' may suddenly make them appear unattainable to their fans and cause their popularity to suffer. Using this argument, married stars with kids should all be in the closet, as surely a spouse and kids should make one unattainable too, but the last time I checked, people were still buying Beyoncé's music despite her marital status.

It's pretty shocking that we still hold our breath when somebody in the public eye comes out, wondering how society will respond to them. Hollywood is certainly yet to reconcile its complicated relationship with sexuality. The day when we can have gay action heroes or superheroes and it not be controversial feels a long way off. And since the beginnings of the industry, and still to this day, many of its biggest onscreen stars and those behind the camera have never felt that they could be openly gay or bisexual without compromising their careers – Rock Hudson, Tab Hunter, Anthony Perkins, Marlene Dietrich, to name a few.

TV talk show host Ellen DeGeneres initially had an extremely negative experience coming out as a lesbian in 1997 in both her comedy show and in real life to Oprah. Fortunately she was eventually able to use her TV platform to appeal to the US public, who (like their counterparts in the UK) have become considerably more progressive in their thinking on LGBTQ issues over the last 20 years. In Hollywood, women have been the ones to lead the way on this – A-listers such as Jodie Foster, Ellen Page, and Kristen Stewart have all 'come out' in recent years – but it has required some courage to do so. The atmosphere is still not one of open and immediate accept-ance, particularly for gay male stars, who still feel a reluctance to be themselves with the public.

The sooner we remedy this the better, because all of our creative arts – our music, TV, film, and fashion – are at their richest and most diverse when we allow people to be themselves, unfettered and without judgement.

A political force

Imagine if we were to take this same inclusive approach to LGBTQ individuals in other sectors, too, such as politics, public service, sport, construction, education, or banking. Would we not further enrich these areas by utilizing the talents and skills currently missed? If we allowed diversity without expectations of gender or sexuality, we could see everyone from the LGBTQ community as able to use their innate skills and qualities – skills and qualities that we have tended to label or categorize as feminine or masculine. For example, society judges compassion, organization, and nurture as feminine traits, so roles in HR administration, care work, and teaching are assumed to be suited more to females, with an unwitting bias that excludes men or women who have perceived male characteristics. On the other hand, manual or physical labour, leadership, and strategic roles are thought better suited to males, so in these areas we see a bias against women and men displaying characteristics perceived as effeminate. As we've already seen, we lose out when we attribute skills and qualities by gender, and we do exactly the same when we judge based on sexuality.

The world of politics is an interesting case in point. There are a few prominent gay politicians in the UK, but only a few. After all, in decades gone by, if a politician was discovered to be gay, it usually meant the end of their career, and that shadow still hangs over the Houses of Parliament. It's fair to say that Lord Peter Mandelson has been a polarizing figure in British politics, but whether you love him or loathe him, his ease with his homosexuality should be celebrated. Here is an example of an openly gay senior politician who has held a number of high-profile positions within the previous Labour government and the European Union, whose sexuality has not been seen as an issue or a hindrance. Another politician who has forged ahead on LGBTQ issues is Lord Waheed Alli, Britain's only openly gay Muslim politician. Lord Alli was instrumental in spearheading LGBTQ equality legislation such as the Civil Partnerships Act of 2004 and the legalization of same-sex marriage in 2014, convincing two straight prime ministers – Tony Blair and David Cameron – that this was the right thing to do (in Cameron's case, against the wishes of many Conservative politicians and party activists). As yet, though, we have never had an openly gay political leader, and certainly the UK has never had a gay leader who has campaigned on LGBTQ issues. Perhaps popular Scottish Conservative politician Ruth Davidson might buck this trend. The LGBTQ community would certainly benefit from strong role models, confident in their orientation, who are able to inspire other LGBTQ individuals to pursue a political path.

45 (out of 650): the number of openly LGBTQ MPs currently in the UK Parliament.[*]

The situation is complicated further by gay politicians who support discrimination against LGBTQ individuals – or at least don't oppose it. Former UK politician Michael Portillo, who admitted to 'homosexual experiences' but felt the need to relegate them to his distant past, resigned from politics soon after losing support from sections of his party. Portillo, while Secretary of State for Defence in a Conservative government, originally supported Section 28 and

[*] http://www.bbc.co.uk/news/election-2017-40232272

endorsed the ban on homosexuals fighting in the military. He was accused by gay rights activist Peter Tatchell of hypocrisy.

Peter Tatchell, on the other hand, is probably the closest the UK has come to a gay activist-turned-politician in the vein of Harvey Milk. In 1978, Tatchell joined the Labour Party and moved to Bermondsey, a working-class neighbourhood in South-east London. He became a leading member of a left-wing faction planning to depose the right-wing councillors controlling the Bermondsey Constituency Labour Party. They won, and Tatchell went on to be selected to succeed the sitting MP on retirement. He was thought too 'radical' by sections of his party, but the doubters eventually caved and subsequently allowed him to stand in the Bermondsey by-election, held in February 1983.

However, internal Labour Party divisions, plus his presumed homosexuality (which he refused to confirm or deny), were used against him. In an infamous and shameful election campaign, Tatchell was assaulted, received death threats, had his property broken into, and a live bullet posted through his letterbox. The safe Labour seat went to the Liberal candidate, Simon Hughes, amid allegations of xenophobia (Tatchell was born in Australia) and homophobia on the campaign trail (one Liberal campaign leaflet talked of a 'straight choice' between Liberal and Labour). Hughes subsequently apologized for the wording, and ironically later came out as bisexual himself.

No 'other' group has been perceived as such a moral threat to society as the LGBTQ community. In the UK many gay politicians on the right and left have preferred to keep their sexuality private and have resisted being too vocal on LGBTQ issues. Elected politicians often hail from affluent family backgrounds, which tend to be socially conservative, with traditional expectations of what constitutes 'respectability' (a stable marriage with children), which up until recently did not accommodate same-sex couples. Politicians from these types of background are therefore less likely to perceive the voting public as any more open-minded, so are less likely to 'come out'. In these more liberal times, fewer gay politicians engage in sham marriages or relationships, but, faced with media intrusion and potential blackmail situations, some still feel the need to do so.

Sadly, those who have 'come out' may choose not to associate themselves with gay issues outside of the general consensus to limit further scrutiny. But there is hope. Europe is leading the way in elevating openly gay individuals into positions of political leadership. Luxembourg currently has its first openly gay prime minister, Xavier Bettel – the third openly gay head of government following Iceland's prime minister, Jóhanna Sigurðardóttir, and Belgium's prime minister Elio Di Rupo. As of October 2014, Bettel is the only openly gay world leader. His policies have included reforms on same-sex marriage and replacing religious instruction in schools with general ethics classes. We also see further progress in Ireland, a country formerly defined by its strict Catholic views on sexuality; it has now chosen an openly gay, half-Indian prime minister, Leo Varadkar. His 'improbable journey' is something we should all be inspired by.

ACTION POINT: Have a conversation with your friends or family about sexuality.

DISCUSSION POINT: Should baby clothes and toys be gender neutral? Or are girls biologically predisposed to prefer dolls, and boys naturally more interested in machines and guns?

The Cost of the Closet

'It takes no compromise to give people their rights . . . it takes no money to respect the individual.'

Harvey Milk

Fear and intolerance of LGBTQ figures robbed us of the genius of men like Oscar Wilde and Alan Turing – classic examples of excluding the best talent because they were 'other' – and it might also have robbed us of one of the most significant economic theories of recent times if things had gone a little differently.

John Maynard Keynes was an eminent economist, who was part of the eccentric, bohemian world of the Bloomsbury Set in the early twentieth century. In his younger years he was actively homosexual, conducting numerous affairs with men at a time when it was still illegal, and the Bloomsbury Set provided a safe space for him to live his truth. But by 1925 he had fallen in love with and married a woman – a Russian ballerina named Lydia Lopokova. The love was genuine, but it was also useful for Keynes's career that he now conformed to society's standard of a happily married man. He would go on to develop one of the major economic theories of the last 100 years: Keynesian economics, which is arguably one of the few economic approaches that has saved and improved the lives of many, as opposed to the alternative models by economists such as Friedrich Hayek and Milton Friedman, which have benefited the few. His idea of stimulating economic activity through government-sponsored infrastructure was able to lift the US out of the Great Depression, fund Britain's Second World War efforts and rebuild the UK economy after the war.

Had Keynes been excluded for the attributes that made him an outsider, the economic fallout for the West could have been disastrous, but as chance would have it, he wasn't. In particular, he was welcomed into Winston Churchill's exclusive dining club, 'The Other Club', which he set up in 1911 in response to Churchill himself being excluded from 'The Club' – the leading London society of the day for notable thinkers and artists. Unfortunately, members were still exclusively those from elite backgrounds, but in Churchill's defence, he was at least savvy enough to widen his pool to include many within the elite who, like himself, were outside insiders. Eton and Cambridge educated, but also bohemian, Keynes fitted the bill and his inclusion in 1927 strengthened and sustained the credibility of The Other Club, whereas the exclusion of Churchill went on to weaken the standing of The (original) Club. The Other Club soon eclipsed The Club. We've seen the same thing happen more recently, when those initially excluded, such as Oprah Winfrey, Mark Zuckerberg, and Jeremy Corbyn, have gone on to eclipse those who originally excluded them.

There's a message for all elite groups here who operate via such exclusivity: failing to see the importance of diversity as the world changes around you means you can lose relevance and standing, endangering the very elite status you seek to maintain.

Money talks

As all these examples show, the workplace is where the benefits of inclusion go beyond social and mental wellbeing to reach our economy. We all thrive when people of talent are allowed to pursue success – it benefits everyone through the tax regime – so where potential is stunted and talent lost, it's at the expense of us all. A 2013 report entitled 'The Cost of the Closet' by the Human Rights Foundation Campaign in the US states that 'despite a changing social and legal landscape for LGBTQ people, still over half (53 per cent) of LGBTQ workers nationwide hide who they are at work'.* The report goes on to talk about workplace support practices that have fallen short because they haven't been able to change a culture that has led to LGBTQ staff members feeling uncomfortable at work. This costs businesses in terms of talent drain and subsequent recruitment.

Organizations such as Stonewall are making great strides to help more workplaces become environments in which LGBTQ staff can thrive as their authentic selves, but there is still some way to go. The problem is self-perpetuating: nobody wants to come out because of the fear of prejudice, and hence there are not enough role models to encourage people to come out. Take the example of Apple chief Tim Cook, who came out in 2014. Prior to this, there were no openly gay Fortune 500 CEOs, and given that broad estimates suggest that between 5 and 10 per cent of people are LGBT, this is a significant under-representation in the world of big business. So yes, businesses are making progress, but this does tend to vary according to the industry sector.

Considering how much impact the tech industry has in shaping consumer behaviour, the lack of diversity in terms of sexuality, gender, and race is a real issue for this macho community. I would argue that this harsh landscape can be off-putting for those who do not thrive in that sort of environment. PayPal co-founder and Trump

---

* http://www.hrc.org/resources/the-cost-of-the-closet-and-the-rewards-of-inclusion

adviser Peter Thiel is one of the few openly gay men to make it into the tech 'rock star' class. Thiel is a triple anomaly: he is a gay man in tech, an open Republican in tech, and an openly gay Republican. This is the man who announced at the 2016 Republican convention that he was 'proud to be gay' and, politics aside, his honesty is exactly the kind of bravery we need to see more of in business, leadership, and within the workplace.

Outside the home, many sectors – especially those considered the preserve of the alpha male – have been hostile to the inclusion of gay and lesbian people, such as the military (the most recent case at the time of writing being President Trump's proposed transgender ban in the military), the police, the fire service, and sports, plus, of course, professions of trust and influence such as education and politics. Even though homosexuality has been legal since 1967 in the UK, until more recently exposure as an LGBTQ person in any of these professions would likely be the end of your career, either forcibly or through public pressure. The arguments against the inclusion of LGBTQ individuals are woefully shaky, stemming from the kind of ignorance and stereotypes that present gay men as effeminate and thus ineffective in professions requiring physical strength, or as predatory and incapable of sexual self-control when in close quarters with straight men. The same was said of straight men when women started entering the workplace in large numbers, and, as we've seen, that didn't turn out too badly . . .

ACTION POINT: If you wouldn't ordinarily, consider going to the next Pride event that takes place near you.

DISCUSSION POINT: Was your own sexuality assumed by others before you recognized it yourself? Has this limited your experiences?

The Other Way

'The only love worthy of a name is unconditional.'

John Powell

When we allow people to be themselves and refrain from forcing them into poorly fitting boxes, their contribution can be amazing and life-changing for millions. But we can only free others from their constraints when we free ourselves from our limiting beliefs – our collective ignorance when it comes to understanding what may seem unnatural and perverse. Why would a woman have intense feelings for another woman? Why would someone born as male feel they are really a woman? How can someone be both gay and straight? We don't have to know the answers to these questions to free ourselves. We only need to show compassion, empathy, and, most of all, acceptance.

Perhaps the religious community has the most work to do in this area. I was raised Christian and as an adult I still find comfort and solace in the Bible. I am not ashamed to admit that I try to read a passage from the 'good book' daily. However, I know and love far too many LGBTQ people to believe they are destined 'for hell'. The Abrahamic faiths have yet to reconcile their reluctance to accept homosexuality. Pope Francis's apology to the gay community in 2016 was certainly a step in the right direction – his outspokenness on the need for the church to welcome LGBTQ people has done much to heal this fractured relationship: 'When a person (who is gay) arrives before Jesus, Jesus certainly will not say, "Go away because you are homosexual."' I personally believe the argument surrounding the ordination of gay bishops or the rights of gay couples to be married in church is something that needs to be settled by the Church, but those of us who are of faith, who believe in inclusivity, need to be bold and outspoken.

LGBTQ rights have come a long way but there is still a considerable distance to go. There are 74 countries in the world where homosexuality remains illegal and 10 where it is still punishable by death. This is absolutely unacceptable and we in the West must be the moral compass for the world. This means dealing with any of our own lingering prejudices and misgivings by becoming advocates for all forms of love 'other' than our own. Imagine a world in which no one is persecuted for who they love. In which no gay or transgender child grows up wanting to harm themselves because it's less painful than enduring the bullying at school. In which every same-sex couple who want to spend their lives together can enjoy the same legal rights as every other couple. In which every LGBTQ person is able to fully be themselves at work, in private or public, and embrace their natural skills to maximize their potential. In which every LGBTQ person sees themselves fairly reflected in the cinema, on TV, in books, and on stage. We need to reach this place, and we are on our way there – but we need to keep travelling.

THE OTHER SEX:

The Numbers

Differences in employment outcomes between heterosexual and LGBT groups in Britain[*]

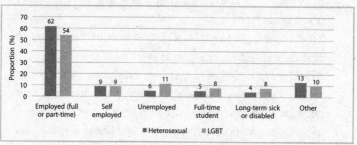

Monthly differences in earnings and incomes between heterosexual and LGBT groups in Britain[†]

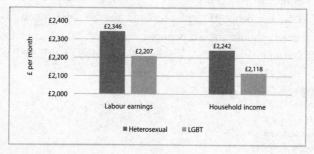

* Understanding Society, 2009
† Understanding Society, 2009

Need-to-know facts and figures

- **1 in 10**: the proportion of gay and bisexual men aged 16-19 who had attempted to take their own life in the past year, and **1 in 16**: the proportion of 16-24 year-old gay and bisexual men who reported doing so[*]

- **63%**: The proportion of LGB respondents who agreed that senior leaders were visibly committed to sexual orientation equality in 2016, and **53%**: the proportion reporting this in 2015[†]

- **17%**: the proportion of LGB people reported experiencing homophobic crime or incidents in the previous three years; **78%**: the proportion of victims who did not report anything to the police, and **67%**: the proportion who did not report it to anyone[‡]

- **27**: the number of out LGBTI Members of Parliament in Britain, the highest in the world[§]

- **36%**: the proportion of transgender individuals who reported feeling comfortable disclosing their sexual orientation to their colleagues and **56%**: the proportion of LGB staff reporting this[¶]

- **19%**: the proportion of lesbian, gay and bisexual employees who reported experiencing verbal bullying from colleagues, customers or service users because of their sexual orientation in the last five years[**]

- **33%**: the proportion of people in the US who stated that society should not accept homosexuality in 2013, higher than that in Canada (**14%**), Britain, and Australia (both **18%**)[††]

[*] Stonewall, 2012
[†] Stonewall, 2016
[‡] ILGA-Europe
[§] *Gay Star News*
[¶] Stonewall, 2016
[**] Stonewall, 2013
[††] Pew Research Center

Celebrate Difference

'I will, from this day, strive to forge togetherness out of our differences.'

Josefa Iloilo

Wouldn't it be great if everyone not only felt comfortable with difference, but actually celebrated it, while also remembering all that we have in common?

Exposure breeds familiarity and familiarity dispels fear, so why not routinely put yourself in a different environment, somewhere outside of your comfort zone, for part of your day, week, or month? This could be mentoring at a school where students are predominantly from a different background to your own, or you might consider volunteering at a charity that supports a vulnerable group such as refugees, disabled people, or the LGBTQ community. Or you could start simply by changing where you choose to shop or your means of travel. Any of these options will challenge your comfort levels and give you an opportunity to engage with someone who has a different worldview to yours – they might even get you thinking about a topic you'd never considered before. These types of actions will empower you, giving you the knowledge and experience to make different choices, whether that's how you choose to recruit for a job, where you advertise to customers, or how you choose to improve your working or home environment.

Decide that you will go out and seek difference and find the best it has to offer. Act out of generosity as well as self-interest, and offer opportunities and guidance if you are in a position to do so. Going to awareness events or doing your own research (reading a book on diversity, perhaps . . .) will give you some context to the experiences of 'others', but it will also give you generalizations, so take the initiative to understand not just the shared experiences of 'other' groups, but also the personal journey of an individual from a section of society that you may be unfamiliar with.

'And the time I take to do this helps me how?' I hear you ask. Well, I'm glad you asked. Marketers and advertisers have many imaginative ways of collecting data on our history, preferences, and attributes, because they want to better understand what makes humanity tick in order to ascertain what the market needs and wants. But nothing can replace real human contact. Getting to know someone and their environment gives you a truer picture than any market research can of what service or product you can offer that they might value. You can identify common interests and common points of reference that run across social groups, and you will also be able to better evaluate the attributes of individuals and the part their 'otherness' may contribute, whether it be their resilience, their ability to multitask, their facility to adapt to change, their creative capacity, or their willingness to share, lead or be part of a team and resolve conflict. They will all likely have their own views on diversity and how to utilize it to common advantage. Ultimately, by connecting to and understanding people who are different, you will have a diverse portfolio of talent to support you. If you only have people around you who share your experiences and worldview, you are limiting yourself. That 'other' may just have the solution to a dilemma you face, whether it be personal or professional. And they may see your perceived issue as an opportunity.

Acknowledging and accepting diversity as a blessing rather than a problem enables us to take a different perspective on any challenge we face, leaving us better equipped to address the complex issues of today. The diversity of London and New York, for example, has seen both cities benefit from some of the best engineers, artists, entrepreneurs, and financial experts from across the world (see the case study at Diversify.org for a detailed analysis of London's diversity boom). The results are evident in the buildings, culture, businesses, and financial success of both cities. If we could encourage even more diversity into the mix, it could make both cities world leaders in integration and social justice: the first cities to show how all of the talents of their citizens can be utilized. Two cities that could become engines of prosperity and social development for an entire country, and a beacon to the rest of the world – that would definitely be something worth celebrating.

This model doesn't just apply to those two cities, however – the benefits of diversity can be practised and enjoyed in any community anywhere. So, to start making this a reality in your community, the next time you encounter the 'other', don't just notice the difference – look for ways to celebrate it.

PART SIX

THE OTHER AGE

'Youth is the gift of nature, but age is a work of art.'
Stanislaw Jerzy Lec

The Old Way

Since the advent of industrialization, the most valuable human beings have been those of working age, as they generate the income that fuels economic growth. And, because of our emphasis on economic status in the West, we have begun to marginalize and ignore those who are too young or too old to make a financial contribution.

Ageism is a damning form of exclusion because it subverts the very mechanism that enabled us to endure as a species. Early humans thrived because their young people were their most valuable asset as the future hunters and gatherers, and the elders who were no longer active were still esteemed for their wisdom and moral guidance.

But somewhere along the way we've lost this framework. Children have been ignored and suffered extreme exploitation from the agrarian revolution up until the campaigns to end child labour during the Industrial Revolution, and one could argue that they are exploited even to this day due to their naivety: advertisers have mercilessly marketed products to children and teenagers that at best are trivial distractions and at worst are a health hazard – such a sugar-laden food and drink. Meanwhile the older generation tends to look back wistfully at the 'good old days', lamenting the loss of homogenous communities formed of people from similar backgrounds, often connected by extended family ties or friendships that have lasted generations. In this environment, older people were still treated as elders within their communities by the younger members, and were afforded a level of care and respect unknown today.

However, de-industrialization and the deregulation of banking and migration in the latter decades of the last century saw the end of these harmonized communities. In tune with the mantra of 1980s individualism, earners moved away from their traditional neighbourhoods and the focus became the nuclear family, with grandparents often not considered part of the immediate family. The result was separation, with many young people growing up without regular contact with their grandparents, so that wisdom was no longer being passed down from the older generation, and their natural place within the extended family was gone, leaving many at risk of isolation and loneliness. And with that age became an 'other' group, with major detrimental consequences for its members.

This separation of the younger and older generations in the UK and US created both a social and political divide, and fast-moving social changes would grow this generational gap even further. Voting behaviour tells us that grandparents tend towards socially conservative views, with their grandchildren on the liberal side, and with younger people taking longer to enter the job and property markets than previous generations, the divide has got wider still.

The result has been the negative stereotyping of each generation by the other: younger people are of course noisy, lazy, fickle, disengaged, disrespectful of authority, and lacking in morals and commitment, while older people are cantankerous, slow, out of touch, feeble, boring, backwards-looking, and intolerant. These negative stereotypes have seeped into society and become established. Socially, we've become less willing to embrace and learn from the 'other' age, with both old and young being subject to neglect, condescension, and, in the worst cases, abuse by the systems that are meant to care for them.

Even if we discount empathy and social justice, we should all be invested in addressing these imbalances in society, since age is one of life's universal truths. For most of us, our lives will be bookended by a lack of independence – when we are too young, too frail, or otherwise too challenged to care for ourselves. Wouldn't we all agree that to be independent and treated with respect is a state we would hope to enjoy for as much of our lives as possible?

CHAPTER ONE

Generation Y

'Our youth are not failing the system; the system is failing our youth.'

Rachel Jackson

Ironically, despite the many parallels in the dismissive way that younger and older people are treated, it hasn't helped them to see a common purpose, divided as they are by their different responses to exclusion. Older people tend to withdraw inwards and exercise their frustration through civic participation or creating an exclusive space reserved for those who think and feel as they do. Their approach creates less urgency but is strategic and quietly effective. Young people, on the other hand, prefer to respond more directly and emotively, which of course draws little empathy from the older generation. Marching, riots, civil disobedience, and, in some cases, criminality do draw attention to young people, but it can also label them without fully addressing their needs. Both the media and politicians do a fine job of showing young people attention without really listening to them – we all hear the noise, but we don't hear what they are saying. If we listen, we will often find gems. I was struck by young activists Swarz Macaly and Reece Yeboah, who were such a credit to their generation when they were interviewed on Channel

4 News by Krishnan Guru-Murthy about the Grenfell relief effort. Speaking about a horror we all struggle to articulate and make sense of, both these exemplary young people spoke with such passion and eloquence about what policy makers needed to do to rectify the Grenfell crisis.

On balance, older people have always been afforded slightly more respect by society than young people. Today, the reality of a wealthier and healthier older population – mainly due to improved living and healthcare standards after the Second World War, the decline in infant mortality, and more opportunities for women – has already registered with governments and businesses. Members of the baby boomer generation have mostly retired on good pensions and remain active consumers, wielding the power of the 'grey pound' and proving a key demographic in terms of their voting power. As a result, they've become a focal constituency of right-of-centre parties in both the UK and the US, who have often favoured older, more consistent voters over the young in political decisions. And with both countries sending its electorate to the polls for several life-changing votes in the last two years alone, this has left a generation of millennials feeling politically disenfranchised.

The alienated electorate

By and large, young and old people find themselves on opposing sides of most arguments, with each side played off against the other. Pensioners often become useful supporters for politicians positioning themselves as 'law and order' candidates, just as young people are valuable allies for those who want to implement radical change or challenge the status quo. However, this model was turned on its head during the EU referendum vote in 2016. Yes, young and older people were on opposite sides of the argument, but it was the younger generation who supported the status quo and older people who most wanted a radical change. And yet, in this case, the 'radical change' argument was framed around a glorious past (pre-EU) that could be brought back to the UK along with jobs, money, and 'control'; a reversal of globalization, immigration, and most of the social changes of the past 40 years imposed by 'Europe' would then occur, with a cool £350 million a week thrown in for the National Health Service!

Young people are always the future, but on this occasion many of them were not allowed to be present. Over 1.5 million 16–18-year-olds were excluded from voting in the EU referendum, even though this group of young people in Scotland had been granted a vote in the independence referendum two years earlier. Had they all been given a voice on their future this time, the result might well have been different.

The Conservative-led coalition government had no time for the youth vote and sought to restrict it rather than court it, through a series of actions that have dramatically reduced youth voter registration levels. As a result of the introduction of Individual Electoral Registration (IER) it is estimated that 800,000 people have dropped off the electoral register, which is approximately 1.8 per cent of the UK electorate, and the areas worst hit are those with large student populations, such as Canterbury, with a 13 per cent drop, and Cambridge and Dundee West, both down by 11 per cent.[*]

The previous voting registration system allowed universities to block register their students and also for heads of households to register every eligible voter living in their home, but the new system requires that all voters register individually. The referendum was held when universities were on recess, which meant all students would have needed to re-register at home in order to vote. During the referendum campaign, this change in legislation would come back to haunt the Cameron government – a panic rush ensued to get UK youngsters registered when it was realized that they needed a high

---

[*] *Guardian*: https://www.theguardian.com/politics/2016/jan/31/electoral-register-loses-estimated-800000-people-since-changes-to-system

turnout of the youth vote in order for Remain to win. It was too little, too late.

The Remain campaign, like most previous elections, unfortunately didn't pay enough attention to young people, preferring to court the middle-class, middle-aged vote instead. As a board member of the campaign I hold my hands up and accept part of the blame. We could have done more and given extra support to the fantastic team over-seeing youth outreach (the same can also be said of the working-class and BAME vote). The tactic was to speak to people who already had a stake in the economy and warn them how disruptive it would be to economic stability if we were to leave. There was no hope of radical change to offer to young people, so admittedly it would have been a tough sell: that by maintaining the status quo we could do better and maybe even address some of the injustices they had faced after the various broken promises from politicians. Despite all of this, the young people who did vote voted overwhelmingly in favour of staying in the EU – and were left feeling robbed and cheated by both politicians and the older generation, who had voted overwhelmingly to leave.

Broken promises

Young people had every reason to feel they had been 'screwed over' by politicians in the UK even before the EU referendum. Disillusionment set in, especially after the 2010 election when the Liberal Democrat Party, at that time the third largest political party, completely reneged on a pre-election promise to abolish student tuition fees, which would spare young people the burden of being saddled with crippling debt before embarking on their careers. As the junior party in the resulting coalition, the Liberal Democrats had to abandon some of their policies, of which the abolition of tuition fees was one. It was blow to all those young people who had turned out to vote for a party that was addressing their concerns, only to find themselves jettisoned for political expediency.

David Cameron's government had also led the decision to stop housing benefit payments to those between the ages of 18 and 21, the same group for whom home ownership was becoming increasingly inaccessible. These young people were now stuck at home with parents who would perhaps rather they were gone, and finding that employers were judging them more on their lack of experience than their enthusiasm and potential. The housing benefit cut was thought by some to be ideological, as the money raised from it was minimal, affecting as it did only 11,000 people. Its primary function seemed to be to send a message that young people should not aspire to a life on benefits. With a record such as this, by the time the EU referendum came around, Cameron – an establishment figure who had restricted their voting rights and presided over public sector cuts directed right at them – was never likely to have the Pied Piper effect on the youth vote.

Cameron's government had grossly underestimated the importance of supporting the younger generation. There are plenty of young people who for whatever reason can't live at home and so need help to live independently until they can support themselves. I was fortunate enough to meet just such an individual at the 2015 WIE awards. Poppy Noor, an East Londoner like myself, was a deserving winner of our inspirational young person's award. Poppy is now a freelance journalist but was previously homeless and living in a hostel, but housing benefit allowed her to cover her rent and continue with her studies, which led her all the way to Cambridge. Now she makes her contribution by writing for newspapers like the *Guardian*, providing an honest youth perspective on issues around class, politics, inequality, and education. Her unique story provides an authentic voice for her generation that would otherwise not be heard without the safety net of support from the state. And governments would do well to keep people like Poppy on side.

In search of hope

This parallel disillusionment among British and American millennials has led to a disdain for centrist politicians on both sides of the Atlantic, which has split the vote on the left, allowing the populism of the right to claim two stunning victories. But these same young voters would exact their revenge in the 2017 UK election. Dubbed the 'battle of the ages', it would see the Conservative government and the Prime Minister Theresa May lose the generation game and their parliamentary majority along with it, leaving us with another hung parliament. The Conservatives were relying on their reliable older voters, and yet, possibly due to her overwhelming lead in the polls, Theresa May decided she could afford to advocate policies in their 2017 manifesto that addressed public spending but disadvantaged older voters needing care for dementia. The established wisdom was to protect the interests of older voters, but Theresa May expected that older, socially conservative, patriotic voters who wanted to leave the EU would never vote for the Labour leader Jeremy Corbyn – a pro-immigration republican with a pacifist leaning. It backfired dramatically. Not just because Theresa May found she was not as popular among voters as the polls had indicated, but because young voters, who were traditionally assumed to be apathetic and unreliable, turned out in droves to vote for Corbyn.

Even though they didn't receive the leadership from him that was required during the EU referendum, in 2017 many young people now found in him a leader whose principles matched their own ideas of economic justice – something that had been absent from the political discourse. Corbyn – characterized as weak and inept by both the mainstream media and his political opponents – was speaking to large crowds of inspired, passionate young people who had been largely ignored for years. They admired his stance on social inequality, nuclear weapons, and taxation, especially when he was ridiculed by the establishment for his views but stuck to them. Corbyn appeared to have a genuine concern for the marginalized and an understanding of their plight. His idealistic and benign message was full of hope and optimism, and that is the strength of young people that most mainstream politicians have failed to appreciate. The young are endowed with optimism and high ideals that are unhampered by the sometimes harsh reality of life. The first estimates of the youth turnout for the election was 72 per cent. That figure was later adjusted by YouGov to 58 per cent, but even so it was a substantial increase from 43 per cent in 2015. The 'youthquake', as it was dubbed by the British press, played a substantial role in Corbyn's 10-point surge in Labour's share of the vote – even improving on Blair's nine-point gain in the 1997 landslide – and shaking up the political landscape of Britain.[*]

What the Corbyn-inspired 'youthquake' demonstrated was that the youth vote was a sleeping giant that needed the right stimulant to awaken it. It showed us the power young people can have when they mobilize and organize, but more importantly it showed that politicians who continue to ignore the needs and concerns of the young do so at their own peril. As Corbyn shadow cabinet member and Labour MP for Brent Dawn Butler schooled me, 'There was a submarine campaign happening among the younger generation that those of you in your elite bubbles were unaware of. They wanted change and Jeremy represented that change.'

In the US, someone who also spoke the language of young people around social justice and taking on the establishment that had routinely sold them out was Bernie Sanders. The 75-year-old senator and veteran of the civil rights era became a hero for millennials during the 2016 Democratic primaries. Bernie went off the usual script and talked about injustices that were not being discussed by more mainstream politicians. Even though his opponent Hillary Clinton went on to win the Democratic nomination, she was unable

[*] *Guardian* https://www.theguardian.com/politics/2017/jun/09/corbyn-may-young-voters-labour-surge

to attract sizeable support from 'Bernie supporters', even after she received Sanders' endorsement. The failure to bring in Sanders as a running mate along with some of his more progressive policies may have been fatal. Donald Trump was able to position himself as the radical anti-establishment candidate instead, and the rest, as they say, is history.

We will never know what might have happened if different choices had been made by establishment figures during the EU referendum and the US election, but I think it's safe to say that in both cases the losing sides failed to listen, engage, and inspire enough of our young people. As a society, we have collectively taken a 'we know best' approach, and in doing so we have ignored the very people whose futures are being decided.

ACTION POINT: Ask a realtive under the age of 18 how they would vote if they could.

DISCUSSION POINT: Are you in favour of lowering the voting age to 16?

CHAPTER TWO

Agents of Change

'If we are to reach real peace in this world . . . we shall have to begin with children.'

Mahatma Gandhi

The real cost of sidelining the voice of Generation Y is that when their passion and energy is harnessed, it is fearless, defiant, and breaks convention, making them powerful agents of change. You only have to look at the roles that students have played in some of the most defining moments of the twentieth century to see this in action, from ending the Vietnam War and fighting for civil rights, to the independence campaigns of colonial India, Africa, and the Caribbean. Students stood fearless in the face of brutal massacres such as Sharpeville in the struggle against Apartheid, and the Tiananmen Square protest in Communist China, where they took on one of the oldest and most powerful countries in the world. The image of a single student standing defiantly in front of a huge army tank will live on into infinity.

The younger generation often lacks the fear and hesitation that comes from experience, and so may be quick to question, dare to be different, and challenge the tried and tested. This behaviour can upset the established order and introduce uncertainty and sometimes chaos, but it also brings change that was previously impossible, along with the fresh new ideas that we need in order to adapt the way we do things in an ever-changing world.

It starts with trust

When I started my career as a young television presenter barely out of my teens, my bosses understood that they were not part of the age group they were tasked with reaching, so they wisely recruited presenters from that age bracket and also gave us a degree of creative freedom on our shows. Our MTV bosses allowed me and Richard Blackwood to pair up and present the *MTV Select* show in our own style – a move seen by some as controversial for having two young black presenters catering to a mainstream audience. The show went on to become one of MTVs top-rated shows. For a young person making that call, it would have been a no-brainer, as they would have been engaged with the rise in popularity of black culture during the Noughties. Richard and I, being closer to our target audience, were well aware of this and were able to deliver the show in a manner that celebrated elements of black culture in an authentic and light-hearted manner, making it accessible to a mainstream audience. We also understood that our generation was much more open-minded than previous generations.

When moving on to T4, Channel 4's youth entertainment show, I and my team of presenters, all in our early twenties, were again given creative input into the show and worked with a young production team. This was perfect, as we had young people making content for other young people. As interviewers, my co-presenters (Vernon Kay, Dermot O'Leary, Steve Jones, Margherita Taylor, Miquita Oliver, Alexa Chung) and I asked the questions we knew our audience would want to ask if they were with whichever celebrity guest we happened to be interviewing. We had the same irreverence and wit that young people had with their peers and we spoke their language. I honestly feel blessed to have been part of both of these shows, not only because of what they did for me in terms of my career at a relatively young age, but because I was able to witness first-hand what happens when you allow young people to have opportunity and responsibility. I am a product of that opportunity myself, but what has never escaped me is the fact that so many more young people of talent never get those same chances. At least now the opportunities that I was given have enabled me to speak on behalf of those whose voices are not heard.

Giving young people responsibility for making decisions is an integral part of their development – something we all need to be aware of. Schools, youth groups, and sporting and cultural organizations all offer adolescents the opportunity of some form of leadership over other youngsters as a prefect, junior coach, or youth leader. The Duke of Edinburgh's Award (DofE) rewards young people aged from 14–25 who complete some form of measurable self-improvement. Available in 144 nations, the scheme is one of the world's leading youth achievement awards and a great example of the fact that exams should not be the only barometer for youth attainment. Of course academic exams are vital, but they can also be limiting and don't always access the full array of talents that a young person may have.

Initiatives like the 'Youth Parliament' and 'Young Mayor' are also fantastic schemes that allow young people the chance to experience responsibility. We need more opportunities like this, but with real decisions to make and also the chance to make mistakes, to learn how to deal with the consequences and how to find solutions. The experience that adults have means they are afforded the opportunity to make decisions, but that experience does not necessarily make them better decision makers. It simply allows them to take an informed guess of what will happen, based on past experience and what they have been told or read. Young people need experience of taking decisions and making mistakes and then dealing with the consequences and resolving a situation early on so that they aren't afraid of risks in the future. Success and failure are both facts of life, which is why we must allow young people to experience both to be better prepared as adults. This will only come with opportunity and responsibility. I am reminded of a line from the coming-of-age poem 'If' by Rudyard Kipling: 'If you can meet with triumph and disaster and treat those two imposters just the same . . .'

Young entrepreneurs

We have not yet had the courage to invest our young people with the opportunities and responsibilities they need to effectively take on the mantle of leadership. We cherish them as children, but want to keep them safe and excluded from reality as long as possible. The old adage still rings true that we wish them to be seen but not heard. The British education system, and to some degree that of the US, works on a nineteenth-century model that produces either compliant low-skilled workers among the lower classes, or leaders and administrators of commercial interests, government agencies, or overseas territories among the more affluent. Our twenty-first-century young people don't fit the nineteenth-century moulds we created. Essentially, we are trying to fit round pegs into square holes, and calling them failures when they don't fit.

This is not the story for everyone who follows their own path, however. Mark Zuckerberg is probably the world's best-known college dropout, leaving Harvard to set up Facebook without completing his degree. Evan Spiegel, the co-founder of Snapchat, was also someone who deviated from the path set out for him. He took an unpaid internship within the sales division at Red Bull drinks company and parlayed that into one of the biggest tech businesses in the world. This trend was set by Steve Jobs and Bill Gates, who also stepped away from the paths assigned to them, preferring to become entrepreneurs rather than simply working towards becoming executives within existing companies. Of course, these were all young white males of privilege who had the confidence and social capital to challenge the status quo and eventually become part of the technology establishment, but even so, they changed the game and signalled to other young people that you could choose another path and achieve a greater success than was originally intended for you.

On this side of the Atlantic we have our own high-profile dropout, Sir Richard Branson, who grew the Virgin empire from a one-man teenage brand into one of the most recognizable brands in the world. Like Gates and Jobs, his story inspired a new generation of young entrepreneurs, such as Nick D'Aloisio, founder of the new aggregation app Summly. Founding the business when he was just 15 years old, D'Aloisio become the youngest person ever to raise venture capital funding. His investors included the likes of Stephen Fry, Yoko Ono, and Ashton Kutcher. At the tender age of 17, D'Aloisio sold Summly to Yahoo for a reported $30 million. Never one to follow the expected path, he has hung up his start-up boots for now and is currently a student at Oxford University.

Another impressive young entrepreneur is Jamal Edwards MBE of SB.TV Global LTD, who started his business as a teenager. Unlike his stateside equivalents, Edwards is a young black man who grew up in council housing as opposed to affluence. His parents may not have been able to afford an expensive education that would result in him studying at Harvard or Oxford, but he was given a camera for his birthday and the creative space to pursue his passion for music and media. Jamal filmed the budding young artists that he grew up around, creating videos of them on YouTube and generating a huge following. SB.TV is the go-to channel for youth content and many creative talents have passed through the SB.TV pipeline, including global music sensation and former busker Ed Sheeran.

When young people, especially those from excluded groups, create their own subcultures like this, complete with norms, values, and consumer and brand preferences, it creates an opportunity for those who understand the codes of these subcultures to launch businesses that provide services that mainstream businesses simply cannot comprehend. And when mainstream businesses do have the foresight to invest in or recruit these young people, they are able to create a bridge between mainstream society and the subculture. But even in doing so, many companies still only invest in a limited number of young people, usually from a particular social class, curbing them once again with the voice of experience. This results in lost opportunities, both to harness the creativity and enthusiasm of young people, and to provide services that meet their needs. These persistent young entrepreneurs all prove that when we provide the right environment and circumstances, young people can defy and supersede our expectations.

Young people certainly have time on their side, but in the current circumstances that appears to be all they do have. They leave university laden down with debt, they have the lowest employment levels of any group, and they are under-represented politically. Mhairi Black (from Scotland – it seems to be a theme here), elected in May 2015, was 20 years and 237 days old, making her the youngest MP elected to the House of Commons of the United Kingdom since 1832. She defeated the standing MP Douglas Alexander, an experienced establishment politician who had been a minister in the Labour governments under Tony Blair and Gordon Brown. At present there are only four members of the UK Parliament under 30. In the US it seems you have to be at least 30 to make entry level for Congress, with Elise Marie Stefanik being the youngest member of the US Congress at 32. In the aftermath of Donald Trump's victory and the Brexit vote, young people who voted the opposite way see older people as a reactionary conservative block to progressive policies. Perhaps if they saw themselves more proportionately represented in the world of politics, they might be less disillusioned and more motivated to engage in the decisions that will determine their future. They can make great change happen, if they're just given the chance.

> **ACTION POINT:** Channel your inner young entrepreneur. What app or service would improve your life? The more blue-sky the idea, the better!
>
> **DISCUSSION POINT:** Should there be an *upper* age limit on the right to vote?

CHAPTER THREE

Intergenerational Living

'Age is an issue of mind over matter. If you don't mind, it doesn't matter.'

Mark Twain

46% of adults questioned in 2016 were not confident that their retirement income would give them the standard of living they hope for.[*]

Today, the vast majority of contact between older and younger sections of the community tends to be through family, although, as I've stated previously, even this is on the decline. This has to change, though, because both generations will require each other in the challenges to come. Younger people need the wisdom of their elders to show them how to achieve their goals and to guide them patiently through life's trials, but parents who are concerned with putting enough food on the table may not have the time to impart this wisdom. Therefore the relationship kids have with their grandparents or the equivalent is integral in helping them gain an understanding of their place in the world from a reflective, experienced viewpoint. In turn,

[*] Office for National Statistics

the older generation need young people to help them adapt and remain informed about the changing world, to encourage them to be independent while still able, and to support them with friendship and respect once they are no longer self-sufficient. They can also remind them that they still have an important purpose in society, guiding the generation to become future leaders, instead of a marginalized, exploited group without a voice.

In African, Asian, and Latin cultures, where extended family ties are maintained and valued, grandparents and elders in the community have a much more significant role in raising children than they do in the UK and US. Older family members tend not to retire to a secluded place, to be cared for by strangers in their final years; they remain active members of the community, assisting with childcare, providing general advice and guidance, helping to resolve family and intergenerational disputes, and officiating over rites-of-passage ceremonies. They are valued and respected for these contributions, which reinforce the customs and practices of society as it transitions from one generation to the next, protecting its essence and stability. In our own society, older people will have to play a larger role as retirement age increases in order to take account of the ageing population with fewer younger people to support it. For this reason, we rely on migration, mostly from those same areas of the world that are still producing enough children and still maintain links with elder relatives. From a Western perspective, our ageing population, combined with the fact that our young people have fewer opportunities to acquire the employment and housing necessary to sustain a family, are two of the greatest long-term challenges our politicians will have to resolve in the future. It's without doubt a ticking timebomb.

Learning from the 'other'

In other cultures this issue might present an opportunity for communities to seize rather than a problem for politicians: an ageing and relatively affluent population would mean more senior and experienced members of society to teach and care for younger members, and vice versa. But Western societies are not completely alien to the concept of intergenerational living. Humanitas in the Netherlands is a retirement home with a difference. Their scheme promotes intergenerational living with local students, who are given modest rent-free accommodation in return for spending at least 30 hours each month with Humanitas's elderly residents, acting as 'good neighbours'. Being a 'good neighbour' involves the students performing duties such as watching sports, celebrating birthdays, and spending quality time with incapacitated senior residents. Gea Sijpkes, the CEO of Humanitas, is confident about the positive results of intergenerational living: 'The students bring the outside world in. There is lots of warmth in the contact. "A smile a day keeps the doctor away."' The students are expected to adhere to just one rule, which is not to be a 'nuisance' to the older residents, though Sijpkes isn't too worried about this: '. . . since most of the older people living at the home are hard of hearing'.

Aaron Lewis, a video reporter for Dateline Australia, profiled Humanitas and was surprised by the influence the residents were having on each other. He wasn't sure who was leading who astray: drinking games, parties, and talk about one topic in particular – 'sex'. Lewis said:

> It would be easy to dismiss this sort of thing as libidinous gossip, and it certainly was, but the truth is that the friendships that have evolved at Humanitas do seem to awaken something in both the young and the old who live there. The young move slowly and more attentively through their bustling world as a result, and the elder residents have fresh stories to share and an endless barrage of questions about the changing world outside the old medieval walls.*

---

* http://www.sbs.com.au/news/dateline/story/my-93-year-old-flatmate

Humanitas's intergenerational living model tackles two serious problems facing many Western societies, including the UK: rising accommodation costs for young people, and cuts in social care for the elderly. According to Sijpkes: 'Amsterdam was short of 9,000 student rooms in 2014 alone, while two years earlier, the Dutch government cut care funding for people over 80.' Humanitas was able to fill in these gaps and the benefits are clearly not just financial.

10%: the proportion of people aged 65 and over who reported meeting socially with friends, relatives, or colleagues less than once a week or never.[*]

Two more nursing homes in the Netherlands have adopted the Humanitas model, and there are also similar schemes in Lyons, France and Cleveland, Ohio. A similar programme that started in Barcelona has been scaled up and is now available in more than 20 Spanish cities.

This is a model that should be replicated in university towns throughout the UK and US to tackle isolation and loneliness among the elderly and help reduce student debt. The loneliness and exclusion that the older generation face as they begin to lose long-term friends and family members is a problem for which we should all take collective responsibility. In these twilight years, many older people find that it's their relationships with young people that sustain them and give them that sense of purpose as a wise counsellor.

This symbiotic relationship between the old and the young is nowhere more evident than in the Ashanti royal culture of Ghana, where the elder noblewomen elect the next Ashanti Hene (Ashanti king) from a selection of potential male royal heirs. This arrangement encourages intergenerational relationships, as the young

* European Social Survey, 2014

hopefuls are conscious that their chances of ascending to the throne depend on gaining the approval of these wise women. However, the elders also have to invest their time and wisdom in the younger members of the royal family to ensure that whoever the future king is, they are able to uphold the Ashanti traditions and make good decisions. This method of raising children with the help of elders is spread throughout Ashanti culture and most of Africa. Children are so integral to the survival of the older generation that families who have more children than their incomes can afford will donate their children to elders in the community. These children become surrogate grandchildren, helping to maintain the home and providing care for the elders as they become infirm. In return the elders provide shelter, sustenance, and guidance from their life experience.

Wise elders

Occasionally, even in Western culture, this kind of cross-generational connection happens completely organically, without the need for a scheme or tradition to kick-start it, and there really is nothing better than the beauty of a spontaneous genuine friendship. I read a lovely story in the *Independent* newspaper about Ellie Walker, a friendly 22-year-old shop assistant, who took matters into her own hands when she discovered that one of her elderly customers, Edwin Holmes, was suffering from loneliness. Holmes was a widower living in an old people's home in Leeds and he often enjoyed visiting the supermarket where Ellie worked for a nice chat as he did his shopping. During one of their conversations, Ellie asked Edwin how he was spending Christmas and it transpired that his daughter and grand-daughter had emigrated to Australia, so he would be spending the holiday alone. Saddened to hear this, Ellie decided to treat him to a Christmas dinner at the supermarket café. Edwin was so overjoyed he turned up in his best suit with a well-deserved bunch of flowers for Ellie. Ellie's act of kindness no doubt showed Edwin that he still mattered, and Ellie realized after her experience with Edwin that when in future a gentleman (albeit slightly younger) agrees to meet for lunch or dinner she should expect him to arrive in a 'smart suit with flowers' for her!*

In my twenties, I had my own experience of an intergenerational friendship when I moved into a house in Pimlico, a fairly well-to-do part of London. It was only a 45-minute Tube journey from the council estate in Walthamstow where I grew up, but the distance between my experiences and those of my neighbours could not have been further apart. My immediate neighbour in Pimlico was Piers Dixon, an elderly former Conservative MP, so I wasn't expecting to have much in common with him. How wrong I was. I found him to be such a joy to spend time with, completely charming and full of the most fanciful stories and experiences. He would delight in telling me about his clandestine meetings with Jacqueline Kennedy Onassis, life as Winston Churchill's son-in-law, and dinners with leading members of previous Tory governments.

I sensed that he enjoyed having someone to relive his intriguing life with, and I found that I'd outgrown the small talk of the showbiz parties that I was expected to attend as a media personality. I actually welcomed the opportunity to talk with someone who had lived through and been an active decision-maker during much of the history I had studied at school. His idiosyncrasies and traditional views were endearing and I valued having him as my neighbour and friend. The prevailing view from the outside looking in might have been that we would have been a disastrous pairing as next door neighbours – me with my background in the music industry and hailing from a very different time and culture, and him from a world of affluence and influence, raised when women and people of colour were anything

---

* https://www.indy100.com/article/supermarket-worker-elderly-widower-date-friends-family-sainsburys-leeds-7609611

but equal. But no, we made the conscious decision to connect and were both enriched as a result.

Sadly, Piers passed away in early 2017. His funeral was a wonderful celebration of his glorious life and was attended by his family, friends, neighbours (past and present), and leading figures from the world of politics, including Foreign Secretary Boris Johnson.

The unexpected joy I experienced as a result of my friendship with Piers has led me to actively seek out other friendships with wise elders. Mrs Irene Sinclair is the sixtieth oldest living person in Britain; at 108 she is in complete charge of all of her faculties, wears lipstick every day, and is as sharp as any teenager. She is funny, engaging, and full of priceless pearls of wisdom. I met Irene a couple of years ago after we honoured her with the WIE Lifetime Achievement Award. Irene has led no ordinary life – she was a respected history teacher in her country of birth, Guyana, at a time when women were expected to stay at home and raise the kids. Teaching and raising the aspirations of her nation's children has been a life-long calling for her, so after moving to the UK when she was in her late forties, she continued this passion by educating countless children in her local Stoke Newington community in London.

Then, at 96, she experienced a career change with a difference. Having been retired for three decades, she made history when she was cast as the global face of Dove, making her one of the oldest models in the world. A stunning image shot by famed fashion photographer Rankin was plastered on billboards all over the world, which resulted in Irene travelling on numerous international promotional tours and conducting interviews with glamorous fashion magazines. Her secret to a long, happy, and healthy life? 'Spread love everywhere you go and you can't go wrong.' And her advice to any young person with a dream? 'Never give up. If I can become an international model at 96, then anything is possible.' Irene has no intention of slowing down and is already planning her 109th birthday party to top the large bash she threw for her 100th, which had more than that number of attendees.

While I was living in New York I was also fortunate enough to develop an intergenerational friendship with Amir Dossal and his wife Tas. Amir is a veteran at the UN and has spent the past four decades in public service, fighting for the world's poor and also championing public/private sector partnerships through his Global Partnerships Forum. Originally from India, Amir and Tas have been such great role models for me in exemplifying the tenets of diversity and inclusion. They are two of the least prejudicial people I have ever met and really do treat people based on the 'content of their character'. In 2017 Amir was deservedly awarded the International Ellis Island Gold Medal of Honor, and his speech on the night not only reflects how he and Tas view the world, it is also a clarion call for us all:

The world is in turmoil, and the only way we can be successful is by collaboration. We really need to be colour blind and without borders, and think of others and how we can make a difference for them.

Many novels and films have been written about these kinds of friendships that can develop between individuals whose ages, experiences, and points of reference would normally preclude them from forming any type of bond. In the majority, the individuals have an initial disconnect but then discover that they have something to offer each other, and manage to heal a hidden pain in the other or fill a familial void, possibly the role of a grandparent, parent, or child. The lesson usually is that, regardless of who you are or your status in society, the knowledge, experience, and patience from someone older can be like water in a desert. And to me this feels particularly pertinent in our society today, where knowledge is everywhere but wisdom is scarce, and experiences that can't be shared on social media are quickly forgotten. The mutual benefits of connecting with the 'other age' are priceless. Yes, the stories are great, but you can't beat experiencing these kinds of friendships for real in your own life.

ACTION POINT: Find out about Good Gyms in your area – a scheme which combines volunteering with keeping fit: www.goodgym.org

DISCUSSION POINT: Do you feel optimistic about your own old age?

The Other Way

'It takes a village to raise a child.'

African proverb

I'd like to end on another personal story which illustrates how inter-generational living can benefit everyone. You might think that the son of an African immigrant single mother on benefits would grow up to be a drain on society and unlikely to make a positive contribution, but I know for a fact that this story has a different ending, thanks to a bond that grew across the generations.

This boy's mother was befriended by an older white working-class couple from East London in a climate where there was potential for fear and hostility on both sides. In this instance, though, love prevailed and the African child – born into a culture different to his mother's – gained surrogate grandparents who cherished him and at times even helped bridge the gap between him and his mother. They provided the patience and time that a struggling single mother in a foreign land couldn't; the mother and her child provided a childless couple with the unconditional love and reverence that was due to them in their twilight years.

The child came to understand intimately both his African heritage and English culture, celebrating the best of both and understanding their challenges, too. As an adult, he has gone on to dedicate his working life to helping others in need, always going that extra mile. This was the example he learned as a child from the white working-class Englishman and his wife whom his mother called her guardian angels. African culture celebrates its elders by naming children in honour of older relatives. And so his mother, perhaps hoping her son would always be influenced by the spirit of the kind Englishman who worked in the factory that she cleaned, chose to name her first son in his honour – Reg. That child is my cousin, Reg.

Reg senior (known as 'Uncle Reg') sadly passed away just as my cousin (known as 'Little Reg') turned 16 and left secondary school. And Auntie Maud, Uncle Reg's widow, found herself without the life partner she had known since the age of 14, and alone in a neighbourhood where many of her friends were also passing away. Even though Reg and his mum began to grow apart, they both remained close to Auntie Maud, who often interceded between them. The values that Auntie Maud and Uncle Reg had instilled in 'Little Reg' kept him on the straight and narrow, even after he'd left home and was experiencing the freedom, excitement, and danger of London's street culture. And his exposure to older people, along with his Ghanaian roots, has gifted him with a respect and reverence for older people of all ethnicities that he carries with him wherever he goes.

Reg's relationship with Auntie Maud lasted well into his thirties, when she began suffering from dementia. Fortunately Reg and his mum were still local and able to visit her at the sheltered home where she spent her last years. Sadly, Auntie Maud's dementia meant that she began to forget many of the people in the photos around the room and her lifetime experiences, but Reg recalled many of the stories of Maud and Uncle Reg's younger days, which he loved to relay back to her during his visits.

When Auntie Maud finally passed, Reg delivered a moving eulogy at her funeral, and there wasn't a dry eye in the house:

I didn't grow up with my grandparents but I never had to be envious of kids at school who got doted on by their grandparents, because I was just as cherished. I was taken to parks in summer holidays, taken to museums. You cooked me all my favourite foods and bought all the treats that I wasn't supposed to eat too often. And of course, the best thing about grandparents is they're the only ones that get to tell your parents not to be so hard on you. Auntie Maud, you always stuck up for me, even when I was naughty. You never forgot me and never made me feel like I was different.

Both you and Uncle Reg taught me things all the time. You used to help me with my school work and you also taught me things without saying a word – things that I understand more now. You were never one to talk about love, feelings, or religion, but the way you took care of my mum and our whole family taught me more about love and helping people than I could have learnt anywhere else . . .

Both you and Uncle Reg passed down to me experiences that many people of my generation unfortunately have no connection with. I grew up hearing about rationing and air raids and families and communities pulling together. I saw you live in a street where neighbours stopped and talked to you on a sunny day or handed you a cake or a sandwich over the garden fence. Everything and everyone was part of the community, because that's how people treated one another and where every adult was uncle and auntie and I was Little Reg . . .

. . . I couldn't imagine my life without you both in it. I still can't. But my life has definitely been richer with you in it. I'm happy that you passed on your experiences to me so I was able to give them back to you over the last couple of years . . .

My cousin Reg remembers the bond he had with elders growing up because he is a product of their influence. He recognizes that his story is perhaps unique, even improbable to some, but the beauty of bridging the generational gap in this way is that it gives younger people patient and reflective guidance, which lives on well after the elders have passed, and enriches the lives of the elders in return.

For a richer, more complete life we need to value all stages of it, from the cradle to the grave. The modern world is built on the wisdom of the old, and the dynamism of the young, and the greatest reward for all of us is to connect the two, so that the exchange of ideas, wisdom, compassion, and care can enrich both generations. We know that our young are the future, so let's make sure they understand what has gone before and can access that knowledge to help propel them forward.

The Numbers

Political engagement, by age group[*]

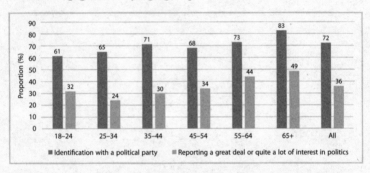

Voter turnout in the 2015 General Election, by age group[†]

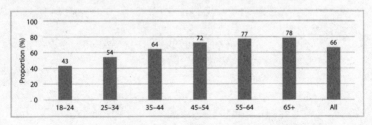

[*] British Social Attitudes Survey 2013
[†] Ipsos MORI

Relationships with people under 30 and over 70 by respondent's age, UK, 2008[*]

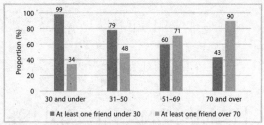

Need-to-know facts and figures

- **50%:** the proportion of 18-29 year olds in Britain who reported feeling confident that they would have an adequate standard of living in old age; **62%:** the proportion of people aged 50 and over reporting this. There was no equivalent age gap in the US (*Source*: Pew Research Center)
- **3%:** the proportion of people aged 17-24 who reported meeting socially with friends, relatives or colleagues, less than once a week or never; **10%:** the proportion of people aged 65 and over saying this (*Source*: 2014 European Social Survey)
- **26%:** the proportion of people aged 17-24 who reported that in the last year they have never felt lack of respect because of their age; **88%:** the proportion of people aged 65 and over saying this (*Source*: 2008 European Social Survey)
- **50%:** the proportion of people aged 17-24 who reported high levels of worry about the levels of crime committed by people in their 20s; **67%:** the proportion of people aged 65 and over saying this (*Source*: 2008 European Social Survey)
- **53%:** the proportion of people aged 17-24 who reported that in the last year they have never been treated badly because of their age; **83%:** the proportion of people aged 65 and over saying this (*Source*: 2008 European Social Survey)

[*] European Social Survey

THE SIXTH DEGREE OF INTEGRATION

CHAMPION THE CAUSE

'There is more power in unity than division.'

Emanuel Cleaver

In the words of TED: 'ideas worth spreading'. Pass the message on. Collective change begins with individuals influencing other individuals. In the age of social networking, when much of our communication happens online, for the final Degree I urge you to also foster your connections offline.

You can do this in an evening or once a month, in a single moment or over a lifetime. But I'd encourage you to feel empowered to challenge others as well as yourself. Nothing changes if we do nothing or do what we've always done. All of us who want a better environment inside and outside our homes are going to have to work for it if we want to see progress. Tutting and shaking our heads at the TV just won't cut it any more, and those of us with privilege no longer have the luxury of ignorance. Changing society is not a spectator sport – you have to be in the game to shape the game. No more sitting in an ivory tower like Rapunzel waiting for a political Prince Charming to bring about a fairer and more inclusive society. Martin Luther King said, 'The arc of the moral universe is long, but it bends toward justice.' But it doesn't bend by itself, and when we realize that it can twist just as easily in the direction away from justice depending on who is pushing, our ivory towers don't seem so high any more.

We've all known individuals who had the potential to contribute more had they been better understood or helped to overcome barriers. If you are in a position of leadership or support within business, education, or any setting where a diverse range of people interact, then this approach may be something that you can implement. However, if you are in a setting where there is not a diverse range of people interacting, then this is where social networks and travel can play an important role. Work with 'others' in your local community and achieve a win-win buy-in for positive change. We are not expected to get this right overnight, but we start with dialogue and empathy, and from there we can move on together.

So what else can be done in practical terms if you want to champion the change you wish to see?

IF you have one evening:

- If you're time-poor, or prefer something a little more intimate, then breaking bread can be a very powerful way to do this. Host a 'Diversify Dinner' as a way to share and connect with strangers, which allows for open and honest dialogue. Our website, Diversify.org, offers tips on how to go about hosting one. Choose a restaurant with a diverse menu and select a list of discussion topics to accompany each course (our 'Diversify' discussion cards or discussion points can help you select your topics). There is no expectation to see your dinner companions again, although this sharing experience can perhaps create meaningful new 'other' friendships. You could also host a dinner at home, asking your friends to each bring an 'other' guest – there are many diverse recipes to choose from on our website.

- We should be active in our own neighbourhoods, challenging exclusion, intolerance, and injustice through engagement and dialogue. If we think our local councillors or elected officials are not acting in an inclusive way, then we should get a conversation started with them and with others. Write, call, or join a political party and turn up at your local representative's regular constituency meetings. Form or find a campaign interest group with other like-minded people or, better still, run for office yourself – public office should not be an exclusive domain for career politicians.

- Question policies and procedures in your local sphere, officialdom, or at work when you think they may not be working in the best interests of everyone. A good example would be the recruitment and progression policies and procedures of your workplace. If they do not deliver proportional diversity at all levels then this could be a good place to start a conversation. Perhaps just start by asking 'why not?' Find a few colleagues who will work with you, as there is power in numbers. UK professions such as accountancy and law began asking those same questions and we now have the fantastic 'Prime Commitment' and 'Access to Accountancy' schemes, offering work experience opportunities to students from non-affluent backgrounds, helping to diversify the talent pools in both of those industries.

- When socializing with friends or colleagues, feel comfortable questioning ideas or activities and offer an alternative if you feel that the action or activity is not inclusive. This may be as simple as where to go for a drink – something that broadens the contact you and your circle have with many different people in our society.

- Donate to charities that promote causes you are passionate about, and consider taking this a step further by allowing your activism to influence your spending in general. As a consumer, become mindful of where you spend your money. Champion the companies and brands whose practices and principles are in alignment with your own and reach out to company CEOs via social media to question them on their diversity policies. Companies only survive because of their customers, so as a consumer you have immense power.

- Sign the petition on the Diversify website calling to institute National Unity Day – a new UK bank holiday that would be about bringing communities together. To find out more, go to www.Diversify.org.

IF you have one evening a month:

- Create your own 'Diversify' group, where people can speak openly and confidentially. Think of it like a book club, a community that should have the ability to influence change. Create a safe space for honest and open discussion about all of the issues covered in this book, where everyone is able to share their pain, their fears, their ignorance, and their confusion. Our 'Diversify' discussion cards can help set the tone and provide a framework for your debates, or you can use the discussion points included in this book – or indeed create your own – if you prefer. It should be facilitated by someone who works to increase their own awareness and that of others, someone with the authority, responsibility, and desire to implement improvements linked to input from the group. Among the leadership and at all levels there should be an understanding of how championing diversity benefits everybody. Lastly, consistency and authenticity are key. The desire to champion diversity must be sincere rather than a passing fad or topic of the moment.

- Most of us have difficulty making our voices heard or discussing uncomfortable topics, which is why I would suggest you start with a 'Letter to the Other'. Each member of the group should write a letter to whatever or whoever their 'other' is (Degree 1: Challenge Your Ism, page XX, will have helped you identify this). For me personally, I have a severe intolerance for intolerance, but with that comes a certain level of self-righteousness, of which I think many of us on the progressive side can be guilty. This is something I am constantly trying to work on without losing my convictions. However, I can't be asking you to challenge your isms without doing the same myself. You can read my own 'Letter to the Other' at www.Diversify.org.

- If we want the fair, inclusive society that we espouse, the one that our forebears fought and died to bring about and that we feel may be under threat, then we need to be an active part of that society. Ideas like tolerance and diversity aren't defeated because people vote one way or another; they are only lost when we stop believing in them and stop practising our beliefs. If we care about these things, then we have a variety of means to protect them so that they endure. Yes, we can march and demonstrate so that our feelings and allegiances are clear to the world. The world is a crowded place now and social media has made it possible for us to connect with almost any part of it, but most of us can have the greatest impact in our own neighbourhoods, friendship circles, homes, and, most importantly, within ourselves.

IF you have a week, a month – or a lifetime:

- Think about what you can do to challenge your own thinking: the inbuilt assumptions you have that may be limiting your thoughts on what is possible. Get to know other people who think differently to you. Understanding other people helps you to start the conversation we all need to have and to keep it going.

• Encourage and empower those closest to you to do the same. This may well impact on where you choose to send your children to school, with whom you decide to create a friendship or family, and who you see when you look in the mirror.

• Travel and experience how other people see the world and see if your perspective changes. Travel can play a very important role in understanding the 'other'. In a study of over 7,000 people from 18 countries by travel website Momondo, the key findings were as follows:

  • 76% said travel made them look at diversity and difference more positively.

  • 76% said travelling gave them a more positive view on other cultures in general.

  • 65% said they believed there would be less prejudice if people travelled more.[*]

Of course, new approaches are not easy. We often seek change for the better, but we also resist it because of uncertainty and discomfort. Some may still see a celebration of diversity as political correctness or part of a simple zero-sum game where gains for 'others' are a loss for them. Even so, the same rules apply. People who resist diversity are themselves part of a group who face barriers and should also be recipients of the same approach of dialogue and empathy. Be prepared to listen and talk to people who don't agree, and keep listening and talking with an open mind and an open heart. Even those who don't understand or see the need for diversity are still part of it and shouldn't be excluded from the conversation.

* The Value of Travelling by Momondo: https://www.google.co.uk/search?q=momondo+travel+survey&ie=utf-8&oe=utf-8&client=firefox-b&gfe_rd=cr&ei=B21GWampNoHVXpPQsYgO

Yes, we want inclusion for the excluded, but change is not for their sake alone – it's for all of us. Communicate what can be achieved for everyone in a more open and empathetic society. If we are able to understand and accommodate the circumstances of 'others' so that they can contribute fully to society, then we will be better placed to improve the rules of the past and present to create a better future.

PART SEVEN

THE OTHER VIEW

'So then let us pursue what makes for peace and mutual upbuilding.'
Romans 14:19

The Old Way

In 2012 I was invited to An Evening with Bill Clinton. The event was organized by the Policy Network in conjunction with the Center for American Progress, and was supposed to be a conversation between Bill Clinton and Tony Blair, moderated by the Center for American Progress (CAP) founder John Podesta. Due to his father falling ill, Tony Blair was forced to pull out of the event at the last minute, so the conversation ended up being a double header between Clinton and Podesta. Clinton made two salient points that would turn out to have a significant impact on his wife's electoral defeat four years later.

The first was that he spoke of concerns about the growing political divisions in America, eloquently describing how one of the largest divisions we have today is not race, gender, or even religion, but politics: 'We have gotten over living next door to someone of a different race, a different religion. The only people we don't want to live next to are people who vote differently to us.' He also lamented the 'breaking of the hearts' of white working-class men like those he had grown up with in Arkansas; he flagged that they had been left behind and there was a brewing hopelessness within them. Clinton waxed lyrical in his jovial yet commanding style and his words struck a chord with me, as he was the first high-profile politician I had seen raise this issue.

The warning signs were clear. This conversation was moderated by the man who would go on to spearhead Hillary Clinton's presidential campaign, and yet, for whatever reason, these warning signs were not heeded and were not one of the central messages of that campaign. And we know what happened next. It just goes to show how vital it is that we listen to the 'other' view, and how perilous it is to ignore it. This is perhaps the hardest part of learning to diversify – but it's also the most important. With a little patience and a lot of open minds, we can do it – and we must.

CHAPTER ONE

The Argument for Debate

'Emotions heal when they are heard and validated.'

Jill Bolte Taylor

Throughout this book I have been urging you to challenge your isms and imbedded intolerances, yet in order to move beyond societal divisions we have to somehow learn to agree to disagree. Anyone who knows me will tell you that I love a good debate, and I've been fortunate enough to be in the company of some of the best thinkers and debaters from the worlds of politics, philosophy, and the arts, but even I have struggled at times to listen to and accept the 'other' side of the argument, so it's little wonder that historically we've always found this somewhat tricky.

In Britain and America we have long been divided by our ideas, with many of these disagreements defining our whole identity – as Unionists or Confederates, Royalists or Parliamentarians, Catholics or Protestants, even Yorkists or Lancastrians at our most medieval. These competing ideas have led to internal wars that have been anything but civil. We have fought and killed each other, willingly and under duress, for the sake of our differing views. But fast-forward a few centuries – through two world wars, a civil war or two, a couple of bloody revolutions, and a gun powder plot for good measure – and we have arrived at Destination Democracy, with religious and political freedoms hard-won and the right to express our views through the ballot box rather than the barrel of a gun. It's this emphasis on debate that keeps that democracy alive, so if we want to maintain all our ancestors fought and died for, we must persevere, no matter how frustrating it becomes, and discuss the issues until we're blue in the face – until progress is finally made.

Create a safe space for debate

There is an old British saying that advises, 'Never discuss religion or politics at dinner', but for the majority of us, this is the most natural place to discuss these things. This exchange of opinions and objective exploration of various points of view supports intellectual growth and enhances the education of children especially. It develops our ability to communicate, to analyse information, and to make decisions, but, more than that, for many it is an enjoyable pastime. Some of our best schools, colleges, and universities are hubs of debate, where friendships and bonds are often formed from opposing sides of an argument. Within democratic society we have found that arguments can indeed be civil, and there is almost uniformity in the idea that we can agree to disagree. In the past, if there was a divide it was probably between the more affluent, who had the time and inclination to debate ideas, and the less affluent, whose most pressing concern was likely putting food on the table. This inequality of access to discussion has helped reinforce a class divide where there is a perception that working-class people are unable to process complex debates and understand nuanced arguments. As a result, they've traditionally been excluded from careers in politics, communication, media, and strategy – anywhere those intellectual abilities are valued.

Growing up in a West African household there was a limit to my exchange of views. In African culture, we defer to our elders on pretty much everything, to the extent that if there is a disagreement in the home between parent and child/adolescent, then family elders are usually brought in to give their view and mediate. So the youngsters have the numbers stacked against them, literally. I did learn from the elders in my community, but I also tested the ideas and views I found beyond it. I was fortunate that my journey from my teenage years put me in touch with a variety of people from different backgrounds, helping to inform my own ideas from a wide range of perspectives. Had I been prevented from having these experiences, my views might have been more limited.

That said, I equally understand that some parents may feel a sense of losing a connection if their children take on ideas different to their own. The family household is the primary unit of society, so how we deal with opposing views at home is an indicator of how we will deal with opposing views in society. A home that can manage opposing viewpoints and debate them to a happy compromise or consensus is a household that will raise children best suited to grow and contribute positively to society. Sadly, this isn't always the case. There are plenty of families out there currently divided by politics, religion, and generation, even though our homes are supposed to be a refuge where we can safely express or challenge views. As a child growing up in the former rather than the latter, I can say that households that do not expose and explain different viewpoints to children are not only stifling them, but also encouraging them as adolescents (who are impressionable and naturally curious) to seek answers outside of the home. Without parental guidance and a framework with which to evaluate and analyse other viewpoints, young people especially are vulnerable to those with more radical views.

On the flip side, if they are encouraged to investigate new ideas and bring them home for further discussion without rebuke, they will be better prepared to accept and deal with conflicting views. They will also have the ability to align home viewpoints with more mainstream views, or alternatively make family-held views better understood outside of the home. We are all conduits between mainstream concepts and home beliefs, but children more than most. Most of our ideas are handed down to us from our parents, who similarly had ideas handed down to them from a different time and place. Children and adolescents will be the ones to bring new ideas into their homes that they access via the media, Internet, education, and wider society. Not all the new ideas that come home will be progressive, but it's better that they are brought home and debated rather than kept secret, festering in bedrooms and fed by the Internet and outside influences.

Some of these new ideas can change the whole trajectory of that young person's life. I count myself as someone who has followed my own ideas and pursued the path less travelled much to my benefit. Then of course there are younger family members whose enthusiasm can change the thinking of their parents and grandparents, as millennials did in influencing their elders to vote for President Obama – twice. Admittedly, in the UK, millennials were unable to pull off the same feat during the EU referendum, but given the effect they had on the Labour result in the 2017 General Election, who knows what they might achieve in the future . . .

Find the middle ground

Growing up in a working-class neighbourhood during the 1980s, I saw a normally apolitical local community become very political under the shadow of the Cold War, Apartheid South Africa, and the de-industrialization of Britain. International and domestic battle lines were drawn. It was difficult to have a polite exchange of views when whole industries were being dismantled, which were the lifeblood of not just a community but of generations of families. I watched as the factories that had been the main employers in my area all closed, one after the other, due to the market-orientated political views of Ronald Reagan and Margaret Thatcher. The stakes were high and the exchanges were personal. Views and positions became solidified. Left versus right, the Communist East versus the Capitalist West, and the needs of the economy versus the needs of society. Both sides saw the need for their views to win the day as imperative – the other side had to be defeated.

In this climate, ideological camps were forming and there appeared to be no middle ground or compromise on either side. Political views became linked to identity once again. If you were on the political right you were for limited government, the free market, a hardline on communism, and against sanctions on South Africa. If you were on the political left your views were the exact opposite. The left held the idea that government was necessary to ensure society was protected from the extremes of the free market, and democratic socialists had some sympathy with the anti-imperialist, egalitarian ideas of communism and were intolerant of Apartheid South Africa. These were iconic battles of ideas, underpinned by significant moral questions. You were on one side or the other, with heroes and villains on both sides depending on your point of view.

Society was fragmented and the challenge was set for one side to find a centre ground that brought together views from the right and left. During the 1990s both the Labour Party in the UK and the Democrats in the US found success and managed to unite a majority around a set of liberal ideas that secured consecutive electoral victories. These victories did not just happen on election day. Difficult conversations had to take place with friends in which cherished ideas and beliefs were challenged. Both left-of-centre parties started moving towards the centre to appeal to voters who would normally have voted against them. 'New Labour' was able to keep core support and adapt to reach out to voters whose views they would have previously been at odds with.

In the political sphere of ideas, a type of '*Pax Liberalis*' was established that we could all sign up to. Sexism and racism were relegated to the margins, class warfare was suspended, and religious conflict became the stuff of bygone eras. We could now accept disparity in wealth as long as equal opportunity was offered to all. By incorporating ideas and compromising some principles, there seemed to be something for everyone. In this new order where progressivism and its ideas reigned supreme, it did feel like peace in our time. And although the systems were still flawed and the cracks eventually appeared, there is a lesson we can take from it. That this is something we, as individuals, will also have to learn to do: reach out to those with whom we may disagree and consider the merits of their position, because until we do that we cannot move towards each other and achieve a consensus.

Never be complacent

The cracks that eventually appeared in this *Pax Liberalis* came in the form of complacency. The 'liberal elite', as they were soon to be termed, forgot that surface tolerance could hide opposing viewpoints. Different sides of the argument stopped making the effort to reach out and listen to people who had reservations about this new consensus of ideas. In the UK, the moment liberalism fell victim to its own intolerance can be seen no more clearly than during the 2010 General Election, in what came to be known as the 'Gillian Duffy' moment. The then prime minister Gordon Brown was campaigning when one of his own supporters, an older working-class woman, questioned his Labour government's immigration policy and why there were now so many Eastern Europeans in the country. She asked Gordon Brown where all the immigrants were flocking from. In a typical politician-like way, he politely responded without really addressing her question and moved on. But then, when safely back in his car (or so he thought), the Prime Minister became irritated, calling Gillian Duffy a 'bigoted' woman and chastising his staff for allowing him to be put in a situation where he had to respond to someone with a different point of view.

Unbeknown to him, this exchange was caught on a TV interview microphone that he had forgotten to remove. This, of course, was picked up by the press, who gleefully ran back to Gillian Duffy as fast as their heels could carry them to play the recording back to her. Duffy appeared more shocked than angry. In her view, she had just had a friendly exchange of opinions with a leader she was intending to vote for, only to hear that he found her and her views 'bigoted' and would rather not have spoken to her at all. When Gordon Brown discovered what had happened he sped back to see Ms Duffy to apologize, but the damage had been done. Labour went on to lose the election. The Gillian Duffy story is symbolic of the wider perceived arrogance and complacency of the 'liberal elite', who refused to engage or hear the disparate views of their own traditional supporters.

I have to admit that I've been guilty of this myself. Having committed myself to equality of opportunity, freedom of expression, and the celebration of difference – the things that I believed those of us on the left were fighting for – I soon discovered that my desire for these things was limited. I found that I couldn't stand to listen to those who were against the values I believed in. I found the different viewpoints of others offensive. How could you be in support of 'The Free World' of liberal democracies and be against imposing sanctions on a country that denied freedom to its majority black population? How could you sacrifice social justice for economic prosperity for a select few? Why would you be more concerned over the freedom of markets than the freedom of our fellow human beings? I couldn't see how we could ever meet in the middle and find that common ground.

This image of the aloof leftie crept into public consciousness and impacted the EU referendum in Britain and the presidential election in the US in 2016. The failure of progressives to engage with different views, even within their own camp, was to prove costly and ultimately led to a return of the old regressive right. An exchange of views is vital if we're to achieve the compromise that has saved us from deep divisions in the past. Instead, thanks to an environment of mistrust and miscommunication and a lack of cohesion, some of the xeno-phobic, racist, and sexist views commonplace in my youth – presumed defeated and discredited – have re-emerged like zombies from the grave, seeping into modern discourse.

Face the challenge

The challenge, then, is to take on these views and not to dismiss them or run away, no matter how uncomfortable they make us. Yes, it's more comforting to believe we have won these arguments and to refuse to listen to views we consider outdated. But as we've discovered recently, if not adequately addressed, old views don't die – they just go underground and, like weeds, sprout again when the political ground is more fertile. Education is key here. Children who are taught to critically analyse and evaluate various viewpoints are better able to apply this type of thinking in adulthood. I think we need more of this and from a younger age, so that future generations develop this ability to analyse, engage, and respond to views that may be different from their own. I also believe that restricting the exchange of views on, for example, university campuses is wrong, even when they are distasteful. Your private domain can be a safe space, but you shouldn't be afraid to hear views you disagree with outside of that space. I accept that some views are dangerous and inciteful and are rightly prohibited where they inspire violence, but when views are expressed in a non-threatening manner they can and should be given a platform, as long as they are scrutinized and chal-lenged.

I appreciate that it can be difficult to engage with views we find offensive, but this is something we all need to be prepared to do in a liberal democracy. Even when views are offensive they will speak to fears, desires, or values, and we need to argue for a better way to address or mitigate these concerns. Yes, there may be instances when we lose the argument and the public takes the opposing view, but that feedback should inform us and enable us to improve our argument even more. Being on the losing side of the EU referendum, I know this is easier said than done, but what we mustn't do is vilify the other side. We need diversity in ideas as well as diversity in people to make democracy work.

ACTION POINT: Visit the website of a political party you would never vote for. Try to read their policies with an open mind and consider rational counter-arguments where you disagree.
DISCUSSION POINT: Can there ever be an objective 'right' or 'wrong'?

CHAPTER TWO

Burst the Bubble

'If you never change your mind, why have one?'

Edward de Bono

We may think that social media has altered the way we express opinions and engage with different concepts. It's certainly true that the anonymity that platforms like Twitter and Facebook allow has emboldened some to communicate in a manner they wouldn't dare use in person. And the types of views espoused are those you might not come across in your everyday existence. However, the preference settings on some of these platforms mainly attract views you support or agree with, to create a social media bubble where we gravitate towards news, views, and individuals that think like us.

There have been cases, though, of people managing to break out of their respective bubbles to find some civil common ground, despite their wildly opposing views. In her TED talk, Megan Phelps-Roper, who left the infamous Westboro Baptist Church in Kansas after having been brought up as a member, describes how she and her husband met on social media, passionately disagreeing on a range of subjects but still becoming close friends. She comes up with some tips for how to talk and, more importantly, listen to people you don't agree with:

- Don't assume bad intent.
- Ask questions – this helps us map the disconnect between different points of view and signals they are being heard.
- Stay calm – it's okay to pause and revisit a contentious subject.
- Make the argument but don't assume that your point of view is valid just because it's the point of view that you hold.

These tips are certainly useful when it comes to our personal relationships, but they can also be helpful in the workplace and in the wider political sphere. And if progress is to be made, we need to avoid the echo chamber that comes with interacting only with those who share our own views, burst the bubble, and cross the divide in all three of those areas.

Love, not war

There is an ever-growing distance between Conservatives and Labour, and Republicans and Democrats, as political parties move away from the centre ground. And according to the Pew Research Center, it isn't just the fact that they think less alike; the way they feel about each other has also been impacted negatively. Supporters of one side feel angry and fearful about the opposing party, and this is problematic for the country and the parties themselves, which have to govern in the interests of everyone. In fact, the same study shows that the number of individuals identifying as Independent has grown, suggesting a disdain for the encroaching prevalence of identity politics,[*] and an aversion to having the difficult conversations that would bring us to a more moderate position.

---

[*] Pew Research Center: http://www.pewresearch.org/fact-tank/2016/06/22/key-facts-partisanship/

But this divide goes even deeper, to the most personal level and to the very heart of the life choices we make. For many people, political affiliation dictates not just who they vote for, but who they choose as a life partner. Eitan Hersh, an assistant professor of political science at Yale University, has studied this phenomenon and found that younger people in the US were more likely to marry across party lines than older voters. One couple who bucked this trend were leading Democratic strategist James Carville and respected Republican consultant Mary Matalin, who both worked on multiple presidential campaigns and administrations for the left and right respectively. The pair met in 1991 when they were on opposing campaigns for the Clinton versus Bush election race. Carville was Clinton's winning campaign manager and Matalin was one of Bush Sr's leading advisers. According to a CBS interview with the couple: 'While she was denouncing Clinton she was dating Carville.' During the campaign their relationship caused a media furore, with Matalin stating, 'The media does not know how to cover an unprecedented relationship.' Two years later the couple made their across-party-lines union official and were married in New Orleans. Two decades later they are still happily married and have two grown-up daughters. A regular fixture on major cable news networks and Sunday-morning political chat shows, they continue to oppose each other's political views while loving each other as a couple. Their strategy was explained in *Love & War*, a book they wrote together dubbed the 'political equivalent of couples' therapy'. Carville and Matalin describe how they not only agree to disagree but actually love and disagree.

Of course, it goes the other way too. One recent case of a bipartisan couple who haven't been able to successfully put aside their differences are the McCormicks, who split after 22 years of marriage when the Democrat wife found out that her Republican husband would vote for Donald Trump. Mrs McCormick was quite clear in her belief that voting for Trump was a relationship deal-breaker. 'Death us do part' was replaced with 'until Trump tears us apart'.

'It totally undid me that he could vote for Trump,' said Mrs McCormick. 'I felt like I had been fooling myself,' she added. 'It opened up areas between us I had not faced before. I realized how far I had gone in my life to accept things I would have never accepted when I was younger.'

A few years ago I found myself faced with my own 'inter-political' relationship conundrum. Everyone who knows me well knows that I try to be as open-minded and inclusive as I possibly can, and this even applies to my love life. I am an equal-opportunities dater: I have dated rich and poor. I have dated from my own Afro-Caribbean background, and I have dated white, Indian, Christian, Hindu, Jewish, Muslim, atheist (for the record these are not all individuals – some of them have crossed categories!). However, up until a few years ago, I had never dated a Tory (Conservative). Politics is such a major part of my life that all of my serious relationships have been with men who have shared a similar worldview – even if we were of different backgrounds, race, or religion, the one thing we had in common was our political affiliation. So you can imagine my surprise when a close friend tried to set me up with a leading Conservative supporter.

I still can't help but laugh when I recall how my friend pitched him to me: 'I have a great guy to introduce you to. He's handsome, smart, and successful, but there's a but – he's a Tory.'

'Okay,' I replied incredulously, and then added, 'When you say Tory – how Tory are we talking?'

'Quite Tory,' she replied in her most convincing voice.

What the hell! I thought. I couldn't claim to be a dedicated diversity advocate and then turn around and discriminate against a prospective partner without even meeting him. Our first date was enjoyable and we found much common ground and also much to debate, but our second date was absolutely hilarious. I thought nothing of it when he invited me to join him as his date to the annual Carlton Club dinner. Unbeknown to me at the time, the Carlton

Club is an elite gentleman's club that proudly describes itself as the 'oldest, and most important of all Conservative clubs'. It's aligned with the more right-wing arm of the Conservative Party and is a formidable fund-raising machine for their coffers, therefore their annual dinner is a must-attend event for all leading members of the Party, even if they don't fully agree with the Carlton Club mandate.

The dinner was held in the grand ballroom of a swanky hotel in London's Park Lane, and the first thing that struck me as I walked into the room was the sea of grey suits and older white male faces. Diversity certainly wasn't on the agenda that night – there were hardly any women there at all, apart from a couple of senior members of the then cabinet, such as Theresa May, who at the time was Home Secretary, and Justine Greening, who was the Secretary of State for International Development. It was a few months before the 2015 General Election and the main topic of conversation in the room was how the Tories could secure an overall victory and rid itself of the 'constraints of a coalition government' – this was the central theme of the keynote speaker Prime Minister David Cameron's speech. It was defiant and clear in its message: all-out Conservative victory at the upcoming election.

My date had bought tickets for one of the top tables and luckily we found ourselves sat next to the magnetic Ruth Davidson – this was pre-election and before her Scottish Conservative electoral campaign success, which would catapult her to national stardom. I had an absolute blast waxing lyrical with Ruth, debating issues and questioning her about how she could be Scottish, liberal-minded, openly gay, and yes, you guessed it, Tory. Ruth was quick to chide me about my assumptions and explain how her fiscally conservative values were not at odds with her socially liberal morals – indeed, for her the two were complementary. As I argued my points further, Ruth looked over at my date and whispered in his ear: 'You'll never convert her.' It was a wonderful evening of debate, contrasting views, mutual respect, and much laughter – and it taught me a strong, and dare I say it enjoyable, lesson: that, with a bit of mutual listening, debate, and understanding, opposing viewpoints need not be a barrier to forging rewarding new relationships.

Work together

But what of crossing this divide at work, where the atmosphere is inevitably a little more formal and the codes of behaviour a little more strict? I recognize my own fortune in being able to express my views so freely as part of my job – most people at work are unable to do so and actively avoid expressing any uncomfortable view at work. Of course, there are many instances when an exchange of views is not appropriate among colleagues and customers/clients, so perhaps there should be a regular forum or an anonymous medium where this can happen, to inform organizations of their colleagues' and employees' views.

Many of the 'isms' I've spoken of in this book will manifest in the workplace, so it's appropriate that they should also be addressed in the workplace. This is hard, of course, because in our office culture we continuously modify what we mean and are rarely plain spoken, and staff often don't want to be seen as challenging the management. However, I do think there should be a way of expressing a different point of view in a way that doesn't bruise egos or undermine leadership. Opposing views put our arguments to the test and help us to refine them, whereas hidden views can be demoralizing and affect productivity, so it inevitably will benefit staff, managers, and the company as a whole to have a means of communicating all views freely.

Cross the party divide

Working on the Remain campaign was such an interesting real-life case study for me of what it means to work across party lines. Even though my side lost the referendum, the whole process opened my eyes and challenged the tribal outlook I had of politics. It was a cross-party campaign, even on the ground, which in itself was no easy feat as the parties had just been campaigning against each other in the local elections. Our Remain campaign board meetings brought together friends and foes from across the political spectrum, and naturally there were heated debates – to be expected when you have Craig Oliver (Director of Communications for the Conservative prime minister David Cameron) and Peter Mandelson (Lord and Labour minister under Tony Blair and Gordon Brown, and EU Commissioner) in the same room. But even Sadiq Khan and David Cameron managed to temporarily put their differences aside after the London mayoral campaign where they had been on opposing sides, for the simple reason that we were all united behind the common cause of keeping the UK in the EU.

This is sadly a rare thing in politics. The current political discourse has become incredibly vitriolic, and the 2016 US presidential campaign was a clear case of this. Both candidates struggled to come up with a quality they admired in each other when the question was posed in a TV debate. This was the one question that Donald Trump actually answered better than Hillary Clinton when he conceded that she never gives up. Hillary Clinton could only manage to praise Donald Trump for his children. She had already attacked his supporters as a basket of deplorables, and both were subject to personal attacks and threats previously unthinkable in mainstream politics.

In the UK, political shows and even Parliament's Prime Minister's Questions is conducted in such an aggressive manner that it is near impossible to reason or understand the 'other' view. No one feels able to admit that the opposing side might have a point, unless they want to 'borrow' each other's rhetoric or ideas for their own gain. The only time there seems to be any temporary respite is when tragedy strikes, as was the case with the tragic murder of my friend,

Labour MP Jo Cox, and the death of former Liberal Democrat leader Charles Kennedy. Should we really have to wait for such events to take place before we can see our common humanity? Surely we should have realized by now that, when the shouting and bickering and the party colours are stripped away, we have 'more in common' than that which divides us?

ACTION POINT: Follow 10 people of opposing views to you on social media for a month, or buy a newspaper you would never ordinarily buy.

DISCUSSION POINT: Could you be in a committed relationship with someone who had the opposite views to you on key issues? Maybe you are – if so, how do you make it work? Do you avoid topics on which you disagree, or confront them?

CHAPTER THREE

Doing the Interfaith Work

'So powerful is the light of unity that it can illuminate the whole earth.'

Bahá'u'lláh

Religion was the original means of us finding common humanity beyond the traditional demarcations of region, nation, or political affiliation. I think we can agree that the results have been mixed. Religion managed to reach beyond the personal power of an individual leader or the institutional power of a state or empire to maintain a hold over the way individuals viewed their world long after the leaders and their empires had perished. Religions are meant to promote peaceful co-existence, unity, and a common point of view, and yet to achieve this, brutal wars have been fought, whole populations have been murdered or deported, and dogma has been enforced at the point of a gun or sword. On some occasions, though, religions have managed to spread their word without violence and division. The wisest religious leaders have won hearts and minds through incorporating diversity and encouraging debate. And it's this tactic we need to employ now to help us transcend the cacophony of differing viewpoints through the unifying principles of faith.

Preach love, not hate

Christianity is certainly responsible for its fair share of holy wars, but as the largest religion in the world, it's also uniquely placed to show us how religion, the ancestor of political ideology, can adapt and incorporate diverse views to appeal to a wider audience. It started out as a persecuted minority religion, but by introducing Egyptian, Greek, and Roman ideas, Christianity became a stronger brand across three continents. The Romans then elevated it to the official religion of their empire, but somehow it survived the decline and fall of its imperial benefactor. Again, early Christian leaders displayed a remarkable ability to incorporate the ideas of pagan Europeans by mimicking their solar feast days – Christmas (winter solstice), Easter (rise of the new Sun) – and even anglicizing the names of the first Christians. (Yes, you would have a hard time finding a Peter, Paul, Mathew, John, or James in first-century Palestine.) From Africa to South America to Asia, these populations have been able to adapt the religion to their own culture, and encouraging this diversity has allowed Christianity to grow and thrive.

However, Christianity has always had, and continues to have, its less tolerant viewpoints. In recent years this has been expressed more so in the US than in the UK or the rest of Europe. During the last century, the views of the religious right were in tune with those of southern white Americans in favour of segregation, as these were the churches that many of them worshipped in. And in the late 1970s, Conservative evangelical churches in the US began to align themselves with many of the views of the political right. This movement developed a real stronghold in the early Eighties through Jerry Falwell's 'Moral Majority'. Falwell was a prominent evangelical Baptist minister who is credited with helping to secure Reagan's 1980 victory. The Moral Majority were known for their hard line on issues like LGBT rights, abortion, stem cell research, and insistence on teaching creationism rather than the theory of evolution. This is the alternative Christian view that doesn't reach out to other faiths and other views, and fortunately it is not shared by the majority of Christians. I say this because in an age where faith is being used as a means of dividing us, we need our religions to respond in a way that is able to unite us in defiance instead. A version of Protestant Christianity that talks only to other Protestant Christians is not going to bring us together, especially in a world where Islam is likely to be the world's largest religion in terms of followers by the end of this century.* Undoubtedly, we need to reach out to Islam and to other faiths, and vice versa.

One American Christian evangelical minister who is doing precisely this is the enigmatic preacher Reverend William Barber from North Carolina. Reverend Barber was one of the breakout stars of the 2016 Democratic convention – his urgent call to action for a 'Moral Revival' brought the whole convention to its feet in rapturous applause, and evidently the same was true for the viewing television and online audience who took to social media to heap praise on this emerging moral leader of our times. Preaching in a style reminiscent of MLK or Bishop C. L. Franklin (the man with the 'million dollar voice' and Aretha Franklin's father), Reverend Barber declared it was time for a moral force to 'shock and resuscitate the heart of the nation':

> *We are being called like our forefathers and foremothers to be the moral defibrillators of our time . . . That is why I'm so concerned about those that say so much about what God says so little, while saying so little about what God says so much. And so in my heart, I'm troubled. And I'm worried about the way faith is cynically used by some to serve hate, fear, racism, and greed.*
>
> *When we fight for 15 [on minimum wage] and a union and*

---

* According to the Pew Research Center

universal health care and public education and immigrant rights and [LGBT] rights, we are reviving the heart of our democracy.

When we develop tax and trade policies that no longer funnel our prosperity to the wealthy few, we are reviving the heart of our democracy.

When we hear the legitimate discontent of Black Lives Matter and come together to renew justice in our criminal justice system, we are embracing our deepest moral values and reviving the heart of our democracy.

Before his DNC speech, Reverend Barber had already been gaining popularity for his 'Moral Mondays' movement – a grassroots organization whose Monday meetings aimed to 'help redefine morality in American politics'. Having already gained considerable traction in his home state, Barber and his moral comrades set about taking their message nationally, debating in local churches and arguing the case for a moral link between the anti-LGBTQ rhetoric often espoused by the religious right and the conservative fiscal policies that penalize the poor. Barber was motivated by the belief that 'God's dream' required 'a new justice movement to save the soul of America'.

'Saving the soul of America' is also how Dr King and leaders of the 1960s civil rights movement described their mission. Fighting voter suppression of low-income communities in the South has been a main focus of the work of Moral Mondays. In a *New York Times* op-ed, Barber wrote: 'Allowing this kind of retrenchment on voting rights sets a dangerous precedent, especially in the South. We cannot allow this level of political power to be determined by discriminatory voting laws.' Reverend Barber is an incredibly important unifying voice that can help subdue the current climate of growing intolerance and fear. As Ryan Grim and Julia Craven wrote in the *Huffington Post*: 'Barber has a rare ability to bring a fire-and-brimstone style yet still appeal to secular liberals, connecting the social justice tradition of the black church to the broader left, but also explicitly making room for non-believers and activists of other faiths – or, unusually from the stage of a national convention, especially from the mouth of a preacher, those who have no faith.'

Take the multifaith approach

One of our oldest religions, whose followers have been targeted since antiquity, is Judaism. Unfortunately, once again, we are seeing a worrying rise in anti-Semitism at the same time as we are seeing a rise in Islamophobia. Followers of these two religions may take opposing views on the Israeli-Palestinian conflict, but as minority faiths in America and Europe they have common cause in promoting tolerance and religious freedom. I'm reminded here of the poem 'First they came . . .', written by German Lutheran pastor Martin Niemöller, about how different groups were persecuted in Nazi Germany and the failure to speak out or provide a united response. The result being that when eventually the author of the poem becomes a target no one is left to defend his freedoms.

The Chief Rabbi of Russia and President of the Conference of European Rabbis, Pinchas Goldschmidt, is one who is not willing to make the same mistake. Commenting in the *Guardian*, he stated that the hostility in Europe and America towards Muslim refugees and the European Court ruling allowing employers to ban the wearing of religious symbols or clothing should concern Jews as well as Muslims. He acknowledges genuine fear over terrorism and also highlights that Jews as well as Muslims have been victims. With this common purpose understood, the Conference of European Rabbis, Islamic Relief Worldwide, and the Islamic Council for the Federal Republic of Germany came together to launch the Muslim-Jewish Leadership Council in September 2015. This body cites its purpose as follows:

To promote greater understanding and respect for minority religions, the MJLC will enable information exchange about the local and national communities' needs, concerns, challenges and the day-to-day experience of living a minority religious identity in Europe. The Muslim and Jewish communities share a common heritage, and have been connected by many bridges in the past. The Council will serve to build more bridges between and among these communities in future.

I would argue that this not only helps Muslims and Jews, but also everyone who has an interest in a democratic multifaith society where religious freedoms are valued and protected. These freedoms have been hard-won and so they need to be defended with equal tenacity. If the outcome we want is a harmonious multifaith society, then the approach we take should be just that.

Former UK prime minister Tony Blair has also been doing a lot of work to build bridges between faiths through his Institute of Global Change and previously through his Faith Foundation. The main thrust of their work is around countering extremism and populism on the left and right in defence of liberal values and globalization. The Institute is nonpartisan but supports politicians who wish to take on the populist arguments against globalization, and supports schools and teachers to engage with students to tackle extremism. This work in schools allows the extremist narrative and its perversion of faith to be tackled early on, before it can pollute impressionable minds, and crucially fosters the ability to debate and analyse different viewpoints – a key skill that all young people need to learn.

Tackling extremism

Extremist views should be exposed to critical analysis and evaluation like any other. If we exclude extremist, populist, or radical views on the right and left from the argument, we let them fester in the dark, away from the light of scrutiny and debate. Within the realm of democratic liberalism, we've been guilty of doing exactly that. We've set limited parameters of debate where we only take seriously views that are deemed credible, regardless of how much support they are getting out of sight. Many have argued of the dangers of giving a platform or publicity to people who hold illiberal or extreme views, but I would argue that it's just as dangerous to keep them in the shadows unchallenged. A clear example of this is the demise of the BNP (British National Party). Between 2005 and 2010 they had a local-election winning spree and in some cases won enough to actually take over councils in a few low-income communities. For years British broadcasting laws prohibited interviews with proponents of 'hate', but once these laws were liberalized and BNP leader Nick Griffin started appearing on television and having his racist dogma challenged, the mystique surrounding the Party quickly began to evaporate and the vulnerable communities who had been swayed by their propaganda stopped voting for them.

Crucially, in our mission to tackle extremism, we must also be careful not to tar everyone with the same brush – something that is happening far too often in the current climate. Less than 48 hours after the tragic Westminster attack in March 2017, while citizens were still mourning this horrific incident, the alt-right Twittersphere exploded with memes of a Muslim woman at the scene of the atrocity apparently looking 'indifferent' while walking past the injured. A few days later a group of predominantly Muslim women gathered on Westminster Bridge to condemn the attack. Responses like this are important to show the world that real Muslims condemn terror attacks, as we all do. But do law-abiding British Muslims need to apologize for terrorists who have hijacked their religion?

Unfortunately, minority groups often don't receive balanced reporting. So, when an individual who identifies with a certain group does something wrong, the wider members can be made to feel guilty by association – this 'collective guilt' is something my parents' generation had to deal with (back in the day) when any black person was found to have committed a serious crime. They almost felt as if they had to show the rest of society that we weren't all like that. I'd like to think that Britain is sophisticated enough to appreciate that sharing a colour, ethnicity or religion does not make you all the same. So, for example, I don't feel the need to apologize for the murderers of Lee Rigby, even though they were black, any more than a white person feels they need to apologize for the crimes of Ian Huntley or Jimmy Savile. For me, when an Islamist cites religion as a reason for committing a terrorist act, it's the same perversion as when a white supremacist cites the Bible or national identity as the reason for attacking a black church or a synagogue.

The best example is probably the fact that during the years we experienced IRA terrorism, we did not associate all Irish Catholics in Britain with the IRA or expect them to distance themselves from every attack we experienced. With this in mind, I think it's time we all got to understand the difference between Islam and Islamist extremism. When the problem comes from a misinterpretation of the religion's teachings, then undoubtedly conversations need to be had within each and every religion about how its followers should be taught to understand its usually ancient scripture in a modern context. But until we see all people of faith as having an equally valid viewpoint and an equally important contribution to make, and that the actions of one do not represent the many, we make the issue worse, not better.

ACTION POINT: Find out what the next holy festival is – whether it's Christmas, Diwali, Eid. Find out the story behind it and how it is celebrated.

DISCUSSION POINT: Is organized religion a good thing?

The Other Way

'Pluralism is no longer simply an asset or a prerequisite for progress and development, it is vital to our existence.'

Aga Khan

Liberalism on its own can no longer be the only acceptable 'ism'. We need a pluralism to take on populism and extremism. We need to take on this argument in a way we have failed to do until now, and take on the view rather than the view holder. Yes, it is hard to separate the individual from the views they hold, especially if those views are personally offensive or make us feel threatened. I know I would find it hard to debate someone with overtly racist or xenophobic views, but this is where we must be at our boldest and not be afraid to challenge. Even if your approach is purely motivated by wanting to bring people round to your way of thinking, we cannot hope to persuade anyone of a different path unless we are prepared to take the time to understand why they are on that path in the first place and provide a counter narrative for them to consider.

I've experienced first-hand how this can happen. Some of my own views have changed over the years due to people who have challenged my point of view, one example being the Brexit vote. Before the referendum I was unwilling to contemplate why anyone would see voting Leave as a sensible and viable option. But, like many Remainers after the referendum defeat, I was forced to open my mind and understand the motivation of the communities outside of London who helped to tip the vote. Understanding the genuine disaffection felt by people within these communities is something I had been oblivious to prior to the referendum. I now fully understand why they would vote to leave, even though I still disagree.

I'm not saying that everyone can be persuaded to a different point of view, but if you can find the right person with a pluralist outlook and engage them, I believe that some can. I am reminded of the slogan after the Westminster attack: 'We are not afraid'. And we should not be afraid of those with other views – we should challenge them.

We need to talk to people we would not normally talk to – just as the British government had to do with Sinn Féin to achieve peace in Northern Ireland. We need to increase the range of political and religious views we are willing to debate. Our liberal democracies were founded on principles of political and religious freedom, but we have decided to limit the views we will tolerate to only the ones that support liberal values and democracy. This is nothing short of hypocrisy. We can't propagate that we're proud of our liberal democratic values if we are afraid to practise them. If we can accept that excluded political and religious ideas growing in the shadows are a far greater threat to our way of life than a pluralist approach where we expose these divisive ideas, then we can begin the debate, find out what we can agree on, and fight for the hearts and minds of those who lean towards the 'other' view.

PART EIGHT

THE OTHER WAY IN ACTION

'The secret of change is to focus all of your energy not on fighting the old but on building the new.'

Socrates

The Other Way in Action

Throughout this book, I have looked at how we can live together and thrive by celebrating our different backgrounds, abilities, and views. I have made the case for diversity, outlining not only the social and economic benefits, but also the necessity of embracing all of our differences to safeguard future success. I want to use the final section of this book to further explore this 'other way' – the real alternative to how we do things now – by trying to answer the biggest questions of all: what does a truly equitable and inclusive society look like? What is the destination and how do we get there? In addition to our Six Degrees of Integration, this is where we get proactive – I'll present some FAQs, and some tips on how to apply tools in your personal, professional and public lives. Then, we'll travel through a hypothetical life – from birth to old age – and examine how the 'old way' compares to the new.

For inspiration, we can again turn to Martin Luther King's powerful words. His 'I Have a Dream' speech gives us a clear picture of the destination, the challenges, and, most importantly, a roadmap on how we get there:

> *We must forever conduct our struggle on the high plane of dignity and discipline. We must not allow our creative protest to degenerate into physical violence. Again and again we must rise to the majestic heights of meeting physical force with soul force . . .*

. . . even though we face the difficulties of today and tomorrow, I still have a dream . . . I have a dream that one day this nation will rise up and live out the true meaning of its creed: 'We hold these truths to be self-evident: that all men are created equal.'

It's true that getting from the fractured, unequal, restricted society we have now to the cohesive, equitable, fair, and free society that Dr King and others dared to dream of will be no easy feat, but we have to believe it's possible. If we do as we have always done throughout history – leave the fight for justice and equality to a brave minority – then it's unlikely we'll ever get there. However, if we all decide to actively pursue an 'other way', a more progressive way – one that begins with listening to and understanding the counter-argument, and leads to making tangible, practical changes in our personal lives, our businesses and our public policies – then sustainable change begins to take hold at every level of society.

CHAPTER ONE

FAQs

'Sometimes, reaching out and taking someone's hand is the beginning of a journey. At other times, it is allowing another to take yours.'
Vera Nazarian

No argument for diversity can be complete without giving the 'other' view a hearing and meeting it with the 'other' way. The arguments of the 'other' view are grounded in a perception of a cynical reality, which is as powerful as it is uncomfortable. They tirelessly argue and act against diversity through a belief that it's a fine idea in theory but doesn't work in practice. They might refer to it as the 'uncomfortable truth'. And they are entitled to their viewpoint, just as I have the right to beg (no, demand) to differ. As we've seen in the previous section, we must have a healthy debate, and it's imperative that those of us who believe in a diverse, inclusive society take on the opposing arguments head-on, so that we can progress with the 'other' way. All of us will be familiar with many of the counter-arguments, and so in this section I've decided to tackle them in the style of 10 FAQs – frequently asked questions, based on hypothetical scenarios. It's easy to imagine all of them being prefaced with an acknowledgement of diversity as an admirable idea, followed by the all-important 'but' – a thought that probably creeps into people's heads much more often than it is verbalized, although it's heard frequently enough nonetheless.

Yes, I'm all for diversity, but you can't get away from the fact that . . .

Q: We all prefer people with whom we have common points of reference and feel familiar, rather than those who are different. I manage a team of finance professionals who cater to the needs of HNIs (high net-worth individuals), and as much as I would like to have a wonderful diverse team, I know that clients will be more comfortable dealing with staff who understand and appreciate wealth and privilege and what it takes to maintain it. Unfortunately, we are in a climate where individuals who have managed to create and increase their financial worth will not always feel comfortable discussing their wealth with someone from a background devoid of wealth.

A: Yes, it's true we often have a preference for familiarity, but we are bored by it as well. The almost universal love of travel shows that we are intrigued by new experiences and meeting people different to those we already know. If you take a narrow definition of wealth, measuring it only in financial terms, then you may make the mistake of undervaluing a member of your team who hasn't experienced it. But that individual might well have a wealth of life experience that could offer your clients a fresh perspective on how they can maintain, improve, and use their wealth to create a legacy that will outlive them.

You also make the assumption that those from less affluent backgrounds don't understand the discomfort of privilege, when in fact anyone from a state school who has managed to find their way into your team would be acutely aware of this – 'bright' students often find that their ability causes uneasiness in an environment where the spectrum of educational achievement is broad. So, not only might the team member you have decided to exclude from your clients have more empathy with privilege than you might think, but the relationship with the client could also be enriched by their different backgrounds.

Yes, I'm all for diversity, but you can't get away from the fact that . . .

Q: Men and women are different; they have different strengths and different functions in society. Straight men will notice a woman's appearance before they notice anything else, which can lead to awkward situations at work and accusations of sexual harassment. Why don't we accept the reality and do what we used to do in the old days before political correctness, and steer boys and girls to jobs most appropriate to their gender? In reality this already happens to a degree – roles such as teaching, social care, child-care, personal assistants, charity work, and sectors requiring a softer skill set are dominated by women and they will often thrive in these settings, progressing further than their male counterparts, so perhaps there is no getting away from nature. To be honest, having women in the workplace has actually been detrimental to the family – children lose out as a result of the primary carer being unavailable to provide the nurture required.

A: Yes, there are differences between men and women, and yet you will find men that make amazing teachers and women who make fantastic engineers. There are teams in all sectors that are richer for having a gender mix, reflecting the diversity of their customer base. I would also argue that straight women notice the appearance of men as much as men notice women. I'm not advocating that we change the reality of attraction, simply that we behave in a respectful way towards each other at work and pay men and women equally for the same job. Men and women are both parents and we undermine the importance of having both of them feature equally as a child's carer, and of having a diverse workforce, at our peril, so it's in the interests of families and industry sectors to have flexible and generous maternity and paternity arrangements.

Yes, I'm all for diversity, but you can't get away from the fact that . . .

Q: Black or Islamic-looking men make us feel unsafe. It's a stereotype that unfortunately rings true that black men have a propensity to violence, evidenced by the shootings and stabbings in predominantly black communities. Muslim men are extremists who perpetrate horrific terror attacks and also have a derogatory view of women, evidenced by the control they exert over their wives, daughters, and sisters. I confess that I can't fault the police for targeting them, because they honestly do appear and behave threateningly.

A: You will have read earlier in this book how I had my own experience of feeling unsafe around a man who looked threatening. When we fail to engage or foster a relationship with anyone who looks different, we fail to develop a new positive point of reference – we leave rational thinking behind in favour of fear, based on stereotypes and symbols. I might see a Union Jack tattooed on the arm of a young white male with a shaved head and come up with a whole set of unfounded assumptions about him. And this sort of stereotyping is not just a problem with individuals; it is institutionalized, evidenced by the fact that black and Asian men are disproportionally discriminated against by the criminal justice system. These narrow viewpoints will continue dividing us unless we learn to diversify our circles to dispel stereotypes with actual experiences. And if we do have negative experiences, we should understand that there are good and bad apples in every group.

Yes, I'm all for diversity, but you can't get away from the fact that . . .

Q: If we didn't have Muslims we wouldn't have terrorists and we would all be a lot safer. Letting foreigners into the country has dangerous repercussions. I don't have anything against Muslims per se, but we don't know which ones will turn out to be terrorists. Radicalization is a Muslim epidemic, so as horrible as it sounds, we need to ban people from Muslim countries coming here for all our sakes. We need to close down certain mosques and keep a closer eye on all Muslims. What they are teaching their kids makes their young people so susceptible to this poisonous doctrine. None of the other major religions have people killing themselves in order to indiscriminately kill innocent people. We need to give the security services all the powers they need to monitor the communications and activities of Muslims. Forget civil liberties and political correctness – what good are those to the dead or maimed?

A: Neither Islam nor terrorism is new to the West. Britain has endured religious terrorism for centuries – the English Catholic Guy Fawkes tried to blow up the Houses of Parliament way back on 5 November 1605 after all. And although Islam's roots in the West are relatively recent compared to Christianity, there are a significant number of Muslims that have been born in the West, and only a small minority of these have become radicalized. These individuals do of course need to be dealt with, but by banning all Muslims from abroad, Western governments would be amplifying the extremists' call to arms, breathing life into their rhetoric that Muslims and non-Muslims cannot live together. I totally understand what terrorist attacks do to us; I have seen my home city of London – a beacon of diversity – attacked and it does test our resilience and tolerance, as it is designed to. The aim of the extremists is clearly to bait Western society into turning on Muslim citizens, pushing more of the most marginalized into their arms. This strategy is an abhorrent one, and it can only work if we respond in the way the extremists want.

A more appropriate response would be to target the individuals who preach and distribute this hideous ideology, which purposely grooms (mainly young) Muslim men to carry out acts of terror that the espousers are unwilling to carry out themselves. A more inclusive approach to Muslims in general would keep us safer than any ban; engaging with young Muslims is key to identifying and preventing radicalization. And to do this we need to show that we welcome the input of young Muslims in our fight against the extremists, and taking that path isn't consistent with removing their civil liberties on the basis that they might be extremists.

Yes, I'm all for diversity, but you can't get away from the fact that . . .

Q: It's too expensive and time consuming to fully integrate people with severe disabilities into the mainstream education system and workplace. We've done quite well so far with things the way they are.

A: Actually, it's far too expensive for us to waste their potential and have them languish on welfare. In fact, when you take into account what the untapped talent of these individuals could have brought to the economy, alongside the hidden costs of exclusion, such as the impact on mental health and the financial burden on the wider family, the cost is immeasurable. I concede that things have improved in terms of inclusion for disabled people, but one thing I have learnt about the journey to equality is that it is just that – a journey – and we must keep moving, because when we stand still we can become complacent and lose what we have gained.

Yes, I'm all for diversity, but you can't get away from the fact that . . .

Q: Immigration doesn't work because a lot of immigrants don't want to integrate. I preferred our country when we had an identity that we could be proud of, rather than this multicultural confusion. What we need is uniformity rather than diversity.

A: Yes, we all need to work harder at integration, and yes, there are barriers for new immigrants, many of which stem from language issues, inequality, and sometimes ignorance. But no Western society has ever had a singular uniform identity. Immigration is as old as life itself – far older than the modern nation state. America, for example, is a melting pot of Native Americans plus practically every other nationality on the planet. And Britain boasts a maritime past that saw it influence and absorb countless different cultures, contributing in no small way to the migration and globalization that is a reality of the modern world. It also has no less than three indigenous languages, of which English is just one. And that language is one of the most diverse on earth – a hybrid of German, Latin, and French.

Immigration is part of our DNA, and we can't go back, even though some of us might like to. Immigration has enriched our countries with new ideas and fresh talents, and there needs to be a recognition by both newer communities and more established communities that isolation works for nobody. We all need to be prepared to open up our networks, circles, families, and hearts to those who are different. Only then will our societies thrive and continue to be the envy of the world.

Yes, I'm all for diversity, but you can't get away from the fact that . . .

Q: Men are men and women are women. I feel we are going too far with this ambiguous gender and sexuality agenda. It confuses our children and distorts what a family is supposed to be.

A: What we cannot get away from is that the traditional model of gender and family does not fit everybody, so many children were already confused about why their physical gender didn't match their thoughts or emotions. Diverse versions of families have existed for a long time, since even before the traditional version. The idea of the nuclear family is a product of industrialization when families had to become more streamlined and mobile to fall in line with the demands of new kinds of work. In the modern era, even as houses and wages have improved they still mainly cater for a nuclear family of two parents, both working, with two or three children at a push – hence 2.4 children – a very limited set of criteria that doesn't reflect everyone. Families are indeed the building blocks of society and we need to support them, whatever form they come in.

Yes, I'm all for diversity, but you can't get away from the fact that . . .

Q: Some people are born to lead and some are born to follow. PC policies gives responsibility to people who are not equipped for it. We get the best people from our best universities and you dilute that at your peril. We have to accept that human beings are naturally discriminatory. There will always be a hierarchy; it's human nature.

A: Yes, some are born to privilege, but that does not mean they are entitled to lead. Even in the UK – one of the few countries to still have a hereditary monarch – actual leadership has been relinquished in favour of democratic leadership. Once upon a time we believed that our leaders were anointed by God, that this was the natural order of things and always would be. But after centuries of bloody wars and civil unrest, what many of us now realize is that we need a diverse meritocracy to utilize the talents of people from all backgrounds with a range of experiences. If we rely on too narrow a pool, we remain stagnant, and are left with the damaging ramifications of the mass exclusion of society. It is in our interests to equip everyone to their fullest potential. We don't have to accept the status quo because, actually, we never have.

Yes, I'm all for diversity, but you can't get away from the fact that . . .

Q: As the world moves on, older people are not able to contribute to the tech revolution, so it doesn't actually make sense to have anyone over the age of 60 on my team, and even that's pushing it.

A: We have an ageing population. The tech revolution is still about providing a service to a public that includes a range of ages, which should be reflected in your team. Technical skills can be taught, but experience is what it really takes to connect with people and experience comes from a life lived. Age blesses you with experiences that can't be taught or bought.

Yes, I'm all for diversity, but you can't get away from the fact that . . .

Q: Society will never change. They don't respect us. They 'tolerate' us, but they don't really want us in their places of work, in their friendship groups or in their families, so why should I bother when the odds are clearly stacked against me?

A: Society doesn't change by itself; it requires all of its members to make the change. It requires pioneers like the first group of black British MPs in the UK or the first African-American president. It requires gate-keepers at every level to ensure that everybody is given equal access to education and networking opportunities to support and develop them within a chosen field. But there is one other requirement: anyone seeking to overcome the barriers has to at least turn up in good faith, willing to contribute and earn their place. There are inherent inequalities in our society and we all need to work continuously to level the playing field. Those of us with opportunities need to bring them to the schools and communities that need them, and those of us in those schools and communities need to make sure we engage with everyone and take up every opportunity that we can.

CHAPTER TWO

The Three Ps:
Personal, Private, and Public

'Yesterday I was clever, so I wanted to change the world. Today I am wise, so I am changing myself.'

Rumi

Throughout the Six Degrees of Integration, I've spoken of what we can do as individuals and how we can reach out to those who seem different, but I'd like to explore further the transformations we all need to undertake, not just in our immediate sphere but also in a wider context.

With the combined efforts of what I like to call the Three Ps – the Personal (individuals), Private (businesses and corporations), and Public (policy makers) – we can bring about the change we so desperately need – but each requires a different approach.

Personal

Life is ephemeral; our only certainty is that one day we will no longer be here, so when that day comes, what is the impact that you personally wish to have made on the Earth? This is a topic I was fortunate enough to discuss in detail with Indian spiritual leader Prem Rawat when I moderated an evening talk with him, and his response was this: *'First make peace with yourself, then make peace in the world, not the other way round.'* In other words, the biggest and most fundamental change begins with us, and no one else. So how do we become a better version of ourselves?

'Treat others as you wish to be treated.'

This message is almost as old as humanity itself, and it's known as the Golden Rule. Throughout the ages it has been reiterated in many forms: Confucius, in ancient China, was the first person credited with documenting it, and since then ancients, philosophers, and religious leaders have all preached its wisdom. Its message is ingrained in our DNA, and even though we don't practise it enough, we all know we should. Religious scholar Karen Armstrong names it as the core principle of her Charter for Compassion, describing it as the absolute bedrock of human society: *'Look into your own heart, discover what it is that gives you pain, and then refuse under any circumstance to inflict that pain on anybody else . . . This is civilization. The golden rule is the basis of civilization.'*[*]

We have all been given this rule to follow in our respective cultures, value systems, and faiths, and it has been passed down through the ages and translates virtually unchanged. I believe the Golden Rule is hard-wired within us, but our fear of others and our collective lack of faith in humanity holds us back. Yet if we fail to live by this rule we miss out on a golden opportunity to experience the best version of ourselves. Admittedly, it's not easy, and we may not enjoy the process of change, but in doing nothing we maintain results we know we don't like.

These results of not living by the Golden Rule are visible all

* http://www.pbs.org/moyers/journal/03132009/transcript3.html

around us. Many of us have been shocked by the rise in prejudice and xenophobia in society and politics, especially towards the vulnerable and victims of circumstance. We had assumed that such feelings had been banished and discredited. Heroes and legislators from our past had done the heavy lifting so we wouldn't have to . . . or so we thought. We became complacent and felt that if we took care of ourselves, society would take care of itself. And as if that weren't bad enough, the results are costing us economically, spiritually, morally, socially, and emotionally. Unfortunately, an individualist approach can fail just as fantastically as a collectivist approach. So without each of us making that conscious decision to be our better selves, we will ultimately be disappointed with the results.

The good news is that as individuals we can choose to buck the trend and inspire the change we want to see. We have this opportunity every single day in the choices we make and the way we treat others in work, in business, in the street, and at home. As individuals, we can follow the Six Degrees of Integration, or similar practical steps, to remove barriers and bring us all closer together, or we can remain as we are, hope for a better future but feel we have no control over the outcome and resign ourselves to the status quo. If you've read this far into the book, I'm willing to wager that you're more inclined to remove barriers than accept things as they are. So challenge yourself to create this sincere, authentic change, to be your better self and to live wholeheartedly by the Golden Rule. There may well be times when we get caught up in the otherness of another person, but that should never be allowed to delay our journey towards inclusivity and finding true comfort with diversity.

'A great man is one sentence'

In Daniel Pink's bestselling book, *Drive: The Surprising Truth About What Motivates Us*, he asks the reader to consider two life questions daily as a way of self-improvement. One of them is based on a conversation between John F. Kennedy and politician and US ambassador Clare Boothe Luce, and a pertinent piece of advice she gave him when he became president. At the time, he was trying to achieve too much politically and she urged him to focus on a couple of key achievements that he wished to be remembered for: '*A great man is one sentence.*' Abraham Lincoln's, for example, was, 'He preserved the Union and freed the slaves.'

Boothe Luce's advice is a philosophy we can all apply to our lives. What do you want to be remembered for? Perhaps a slightly morbid question, but also a practical one. Our time here is limited so if we want it to have had wider significance then it is a question we must ask. You don't have to be trying to change or challenge the world to be satisfied with your answer. In fact, it's better that you narrow your focus rather than spread yourself too thinly. Otherwise you may end up with one extremely long sentence that is too incomprehensible to have meaning.

'Was I better today than I was yesterday?'

The other question that Daniel Pink puts forward as being vital for self-improvement is: '*Was I better today than I was yesterday?*' Again, you don't have to change the world, you simply need to make an effort to improve your environment and those you share it with and then ask yourself: did I do better than yesterday? But how does one make that effort? Well, you start with empathy, always, as advised by the wise teachers of the past. Show humanity and lead by example. Challenge the daily small injustices you witness or encounter personally either at home, at work, or in the street. If you are unsure what merits being classed as an injustice, it can be any action that makes someone else feel less than others or excludes them unfairly, even without their knowledge. If you see or hear loved ones or friends behaving in a way that perpetuates these injustices, suggest an alternative and explain your thinking. Be prepared to express and defend your view, promoting the benefits of diversity and highlighting the negative impact of exclusion on us all. Judge the tone of the mood in how you express these views – don't be overly self-righteous; nobody responds well to being preached to. Reflect on the choices you make and ask yourself what motivates you. Always consider the effects and potential consequences of your words and actions. Do they represent what you really feel and who it is you wish to be in the world?

'Before we pursue world peace, we need to achieve living-room peace'

A few years ago I interviewed the respected theologian Miroslav Volf. Volf is Professor of Theology at the Yale Divinity School and hailed as 'one of the most celebrated theologians of our day'. We talked for hours – or, more accurately, he talked while I eagerly lapped up his captivating wisdom. Volf has spent most of his adult life living and working in the United States. Even so, he still has a deep affinity with his country of birth – Croatia. Having asked about his feelings regarding the Croatian War, our conversation moved on to modern-day terrorism and the Iraq War, which was still ongoing at the time. I then naively asked this respected theologian how we could create 'world peace'. He looked over the rim of his trademark Clark Kent glasses, smiled at me and said simply: *'Before we pursue world peace, we need to achieve living-room peace. Most people live in a war zone in their own homes – sometimes we need to look closer to home first.'*

I was struck by the simplicity yet profoundness of Volf's observation. It's very true: the cold civility and small cruelties, which are the norm for far too many people, impact the whole in more ways than we can imagine. How we behave in our own lives to those we love, work with, or simply encounter can have all kinds of ramifications in the wider world. Ask yourself how your own thinking, beliefs, and actions are influencing the collective. Are there changes you can make to ensure that you are influencing the whole in a manner that is helping to move humanity in a more peaceful and unified direction? Even if your answer is yes, is there more you can do?

Community matters

Be an active citizen and make your voice heard. Take part in local and national political debates and processes. Encourage others to do the same, especially those who feel unheard, excluded, and therefore removed from our democracy. The more people are excluded and the fewer people participate, the weaker our democracy is, both as a domestic system and as an example on the international stage. As you travel around your city, community, or neighbourhood, take note of your surroundings, observe the trials and triumphs of your neighbours and those you share space with who may be different from you. Take the time to try to understand the barriers they face and what attributes they also have that enable them to triumph or just survive adversity. Yes, this may require interacting with strangers or starting an awkward conversation from nothing. Not sure how to break the ice? Well, there's always the weather – this tried-and-tested conversation starter works! The alternative is to join social groups or volunteer with community organizations that reach out to support the vulnerable or excluded in your local community. If these community groups don't exist near you, then you have the option of being the first to set one up, and getting out there to find who needs help to remove barriers and become included.

'The unexamined life is not worth living'

The most uncomfortable thing for all of us is to engage with people outside of our comfort zone. This is our own barrier that we must seek to address, while also helping to remove barriers for others.

Karen Armstrong argues in her book, *Buddha*, that in order to do this we need to follow the Buddhist doctrine of making sure that our benevolence isn't only reserved for our family, kin, tribe, class, religion, or race, and that instead this goodwill is spread to everyone we encounter.* This has to be the way forward, and yet we are currently in a situation where some of the world's most influential countries have taken the opposite approach.

We appear to be in an era of nativism, when some of our great diverse nations are being led to reduce themselves to narrowly defined tribes of 'deserving' citizens that are supposedly ancestrally indigenous (though clearly not in the case of the US). In doing so they want to exclude the very people who helped make those nations great. The nativist narratives of 'building the wall', 'France for the French', and 'a citizen of the world is a citizen of nowhere' are all deeply flawed, because with their narrow reach and tribal bonds, they will not be able to address the global issues that affect us all, regardless of national boundaries – issues such as climate change, global instability, terrorism, and inequality. The irony is, of course, that it's exactly these issues that fuel the immigration, international interventions, and higher cost of living that the nativist populists hate. But they have no solutions because they lack the empathy and compassion required to deal with the issue. They see empathy and compassion as weaknesses when they are in fact strengths.

However, people who think differently from us are still part of us, and we need to engage in the debate rather than despair or continue in complacency. Our minds will not only need to be sharp; we will need to listen and empathize to understand the other point of view. We will need the better version of ourselves to challenge the view, not the person. We need to reach out to all the 'others' to build an inclusive coalition, even those who oppose us.

* *Buddha* by Karen Armstrong (Weidenfeld & Nicolson, 2002)

In doing this we may examine our life and our actions without shame or regret. It was the Greek philosopher Socrates who said at the end of his life that the 'unexamined life is not worth living'. I would say that all life is a gift made for living and that in self-examination, and in the examination of the opposing view, with the aim of continuous improvement, we make that gift all the more special.

The collective consciousness

It's easy to feel that our own individual efforts are futile when the tide is pulling the other way, but there are powerful theories out there that would suggest that every little thing we think and do has an impact. French sociologist Émile Durkheim was the first person to introduce the concept of the 'collective consciousness' – the idea that all individual thinking shapes the collective, which in turn goes full circle so that collective belief systems then influence the individual.[*] What is in one is in the whole, and what is in the whole is in one, as it were. The idea of a universal mind and our ability to influence that mind with our own has been a long-standing area of conflict between science and philosophy. Albert Einstein, however, saw the two as inextricably linked:

> *A human being is a part of the whole called by us universe, a part limited in time and space. He experiences himself, his thoughts and feelings as something separated from the rest, a kind of optical delusion of his consciousness. This delusion is a kind of prison for us, restricting us to our personal desires and to affection for a few persons nearest to us. Our task must be to free ourselves from this prison by widening our circle of compassion to embrace all living creatures and the whole of nature in its beauty.*

[*] *Wisdom for the Soul: Five Millennia of Prescriptions for Spiritual Healing*, Larry Chang (2006) p.525

If we can shed this delusion, that each of us is an island, then perhaps we can find a new kind of empowerment in our thoughts, beliefs and actions, no matter how small and insignificant they may seem.

Keep on running

This journey is not a sprint, it's a marathon. We are not running against anyone, we are running for and with everyone. Many before us have run long and hard, enabling us to jog along at a more comfortable pace, but as we've seen over the course of time, ordinary people can make extraordinary things happen. Such was the case over half a century ago when Richard and Mildred Loving, a poor, working-class couple from a small town in Virginia, would go on to change the course of American history. In 1958, their inter-racial marriage was illegal in Virginia. They were sentenced to a year in prison, and their fight to have their conviction overturned and their marriage lawfully recognized would lead all the way to a ground-breaking Supreme Court ruling in 1967.

Like many other trailblazers, Richard and Mildred Loving were not running just for themselves; their landmark 'Loving vs Virginia' victory would go on to pave the way for millions of other Americans to love across racial boundaries. Indeed, if Richard and Mildred Loving had not shown such immense courage, 'a skinny kid with a funny name' born to a white Kansan mother and black Kenyan father might never have been born and America would have missed out on its first African-American president.

By championing diversity over barriers and inclusion over exclusion we, too, can inspire change in other individuals. They don't need to be major steps like Richard and Mildred Loving's, it can be as simple as changing the way we treat others we perceive as different. With that change, we start conversations, which connect us to other people. Those connections form bonds, which unite us in empathy, humanity, and common cause. Within that unity, we understand that what affects one or some of us, affects all of us. We then all have a vested interest in an improved society for everyone. Anything less than that is not an improvement. Once you are part of that common understanding then you have taken a step towards unity. That unity will become an irresistible movement, which if the rule of 'better than yesterday' is applied, will grow continuously and take on other views, find solutions, and change the world and the way it is run.

Private

I now want to talk about how those who are or want to be leaders or influencers within private business – a vital breeding ground for change – can bring about the improvements in our societies that we want to see. In the private sector, the ability to impact decisions or bring about progressive change is weighted not so much by the individuals you bring to the table but by the amount of financial resource those individuals bring with them. However, the collective rule still applies, so multiply your potential financial footprint by working collectively as consumers, investors, even workers. Companies do not generate money by themselves – they require high volumes of consumers with spending power to patronize them regularly. They require institutions and individuals to invest capital and workers to invest their skills and time. This makes the private sector more responsive than one might assume. Just as we should demand accountability and progressive changes in society from our governments, so we should also demand the same from our businesses. Social-impact businesses must become the norm in the future – 'profit with purpose' is the only viable business model to sustain through the global challenges that lie ahead (read the business case studies of Viacom in the US and Metro Bank in the UK at www.Diversify.org to see how these companies are spearheading the way with this principle). Big business has been the cause of many of the problems we face, but it can also be a big part of the solution.

In the office

As an employee of a company, which the majority of us are, you are a part of its internal workings that dictate who has access to jobs, careers, and promotions – the component particles of social mobility. As an employee, you perhaps feel less influential and more vulnerable than investors, stakeholders, or consumers, but you do have an insight into the culture and practices of the workplace that the others do not. If you are reluctant (understandably) to challenge the prevailing culture and practices by yourself, then act collectively within a company network, employee forum, trade union, or a professional body. Raise issues that are affecting the ability of the business to recruit and retain talent from a diverse pool and help create an environment of compromise where the established culture and practices are updated and reformed to become more inclusive. Sponsoring, mentoring, buddying, or coaching can help diverse individuals integrate into a company's culture while also enabling them to positively impact the culture.

Even in the smallest of ways, we can all do our bit to boost diversity and promote a peaceful environment at work. Query behaviour and procedural practices that exclude or increase division. If you witness that colleagues, clients, or contractors are made to feel 'less than' because they are an 'other' and receive inferior treatment as a result, address this in a manner that is appropriate. In either case, you will be helping both parties, as even unintended actions can have an unforeseen impact, which we might have preferred to avoid. Look at your existing relationships with fresh eyes and each new encounter with a fresh approach.

In the case of workplace discrimination, if you see something, say something; if you experience something, say something. Harassment, bullying, or subtle exclusion over a particular person's or people's difference can lead to an unproductive and mistrustful environment, as well as a deterioration in mental health and home life, and possibly a more pessimistic view of society. The impact of this kind of exclusion may not manifest itself for years, and when it does it can be unpredictable in its reach and impact. Exclusion causes a wound to the recipient that we would not want for ourselves, so in the interests of empathy and common humanity we all need to take practical steps to avoid this. If you are fortunate enough to wield some influence at your workplace or have the ear of someone who does, offer to discuss and work with others to address the issues that might be hidden in plain sight.

Yes, there is always an element of competition in the workplace and we want to see advancement on merit rather than as a result of a quota; however, so far the *laissez faire* approach has failed to deliver the social mobility and integration we've been trying to achieve. This will not be changed overnight, as those of us who more visibly reflect the culture will have set ideas of which attributes constitute value and risk in our colleagues. Let's be honest: diversity can be uncomfortable. There are changes that need to be made within a company's culture to fully accommodate it, but once we understand the true value of those changes, we accept that the discomfort is worth it.

I would suggest that companies with more than 50 employees undertake a diversity audit and look at each area of the business to identify the diversity gaps, and then set goals and targets in this area. Make sure that all existing employees understand the benefits and why this is important. I believe that we have now reached the extent of the swing of the progress trapeze. We can in this moment take a leap of faith towards greater equality and accept the discomfort that comes with that leap, or hold on to where we are, pay lip service to diversity, and find ourselves swinging back to where we were previously. If we make that leap, as uncomfortable as it might be, we reach for the prize of a greater future. The one that others have dreamed of and fought for.

A new business model

Taking a fresh look at where we stand is an ongoing task for every nation. Business, the driver of all wealth and prosperity, is good for society and even better when it takes ownership of its social impact. Proper regulation is the way to ensure that businesses provide a sustainable benefit to wider society, answering to empowered consumers who increasingly demand ethical business practices. In the twenty-first century, this responsibility must be enshrined in the ideals and structures of capitalism in order for the benefits of business and entrepreneurship to be recognized and felt by all members of society.

My friend Mark Florman, a businessman and the co-founder of the Centre for Social Justice, believes we need an inclusive model that not only creates increased equality in developed countries, but also fosters fairer trade with the developing world. Mark has created the 'Equilibrium' – a 12-point model that lays out a framework for the future of business:

> We must use the lessons of the Old World to foster an environment in which thriving business creates the conditions for social good, and by so doing, carries every member of their nation up with them – not just those who wield power.
>
> A new balance now needs to be sought out and struck. Equilibrium is the state of balance between opposing forces; and for the first time, there is a chance to achieve true balance by drawing on the lessons of the Old World and the New. Harnessing these lessons will require new leadership governed, on both sides, by realism, reason, and respect, and minds open to how the world is changing. We need to look beyond our own nation state to understand globaliz-ation and how it will affect us in the next generation.

Mark's Equilibrium 12-point plan comprises 12 key actions – six each for the developed and developing world:

A. Developed World

1. Empower job seekers with better training and wages
2. Reduce business regulation
3. Education and skills top priority
4. Skilled immigration
5. Financial advice for the poor
6. Free trade with the developing world

B. Developing World

1. Build institutions
2. Invest in women and girls
3. Universal education to age 16
4. Invest in artery infrastructure
5. Property and intellectual property (IP) rights
6. Trade zones to attract foreign direct investment (FDI)

If you are an investor, as an individual or as part of a company, then by using Mark's plan you can open your mind to the wider considerations of a company's practices. Is the path that the business is taking going to deliver a sustainable return on your investment as well as a social return? If you want that social return in addition to a financial return, then as an active shareholder you must hold your directors and board members to account. Engage fellow stakeholders and investors and consider the longer term and wider societal implications of a particular strategic direction. If you have a position of influence within your sector or sphere, use it in a positive way for good. Leverage your position to bring about equality of opportunity. Make yourself aware of what decisions will have a positive impact on society as well as the company itself. Begin to think of the fortunes of the business as indivisible from the society it exists in. In terms of us pushing for a fairer and more equitable society, it is achievable because the majority of us still desire it. The heavy lifting has already been done for the most part to get us to where we are today – all we need now are individuals of conscience to influence businesses, institutions, and governments to deliver on the dreams of our predecessors.

Public

Experience shows that in the public arena, the key society- and government-led institutions also require a high degree of uniformity, discipline, and submission to diversity to be effective. The building blocks here are a shared identity and common recognition of the leadership, structure, and purpose of the institution.

The American philosopher, journalist, novelist, and diplomat Michael Novak was one who championed the notion of 'unity in diversity'. His view was that: 'Unity in diversity is the highest possible attainment of a civilization, a testimony to the most noble possibilities of the human race. This attainment is made possible through passionate concern for choice, in an atmosphere of social trust.' The idea is that far from making a nation weaker, cultural diversity makes it stronger. That different cultures working together, united and with a shared identity, but at the same time valuing each of their separate contributions equally and allowing them freedom and individuality, can result in a truly cohesive society. This is not simply a utopian idea; this is actually how the model is supposed to work in both the public and private spheres, and it can be applied to everything from the smallest of institutions to a coalition of nations.

Unity in diversity

Historically, the state and its associated institutions have imposed uniformity on people over diversity, using a combination of bribery and coercion (carrots and sticks). The creation of early empires and kingdoms came about from essentially a series of takeover bids, where one state sought to absorb the resources of another. But even so, they saw that there was power to be gained through diversity. A victory over the opposing side was literally only half the battle. Elites with specific skills that the victorious side needed (such as local knowledge and access to resources) would need to be won over. These new resources would then increase the diversity of the enlarged state, making it a more formidable force.

Keeping this force together would be a delicate balancing act, though. The key to creating an effective and enduring state was not only the ability to enforce, but also the capacity to offer benefits if one 'bought in' or 'signed up' to the new order. And key to this offer was that if you did sign up, you could retain some of your local/regional identity. This was the case with the spread of the Mongol empire, Roman power and Christianity in Europe, and it's in part why they were so successful – enough to provide a model for the basis of European unity.

However, unity is hard to achieve and even harder to maintain when there are competing visions, as the unionist protagonists in America, Europe, and Britain have found. The architects and mandarins who desire the union of diverse states need to offer a grand shared vision of being better off together and weaker apart in the face of a considerable external threat. In modern times, the established wisdom has always been 'the economy, stupid' – after all, it was the threat of economic instability for Scotland if it split from the UK that saved the union during the referendum in 2014 – but crucially this didn't work when it came to Britain's membership of the European Union, so clearly we need a new kind of wisdom.

This is why, beyond the arguments of stronger together and weaker apart, there also needs to be a wider offer of advancement to individuals in the new order, regardless of their affiliation. Successful states and their associated institutions have always rewarded 'others' who bring their talents and loyalty to the shared national cause. In the decades following the suppression of the Scottish Jacobite rebellion against the Hanoverian monarchy in the eighteenth century, the

British began to incorporate significant numbers of Scotsmen into their armed forces. These Scotsmen would rise to become military leaders, securing territory for the British Empire around the world and gaining high-ranking political offices, something which still remains to this day. The federal government in the US similarly incorporated white men from the former confederacy into the military and federal institutions after the end of the American Civil War in 1865. Neither the Scots nor the southern white Americans were compelled to renounce their respective regional identities; they simply had to sign up and contribute to the shared vision. So should this not be our starting point for inclusion of all 'others' within the public realm?

Dare to dream

Martin Luther King and other visionaries have, through their actions and oratory, given us an insight into what this new unified society could look like. But although many of us have taken the ideas of King, Gandhi, Mandela, and others into our hearts, we haven't yet truly acted upon their visions, and so our complacency has reduced them to poetic odes – a utopian ideal, rather than a practical and realistic objective for our government institutions.

The problem we've had is the inability of these government institutions to adapt in good times to meet the challenge of diversity, in anticipation of our future needs in a competitive globalized world. The architects of post-Civil War America and Georgian Britain knew they would need the talents of their former adversaries to achieve their expansionist ambitions. Public sector institutions need to do the same with the diverse pool they now have. The failure to do so up until now has resulted in a stark inequality of access to opportunity, a lack of cohesion and the missed opportunity of a greater vision for both America and Britain.

Sure, we have come a very long way. The 'White Only' signs that Dr King spoke of are no more, and all 'others' do, in theory, have the right to vote. But when governments tolerate any form of inequality of opportunity based on race, class, gender, or religion then we are simply allowing those signs to remain by other means. If, for example, there are social and economic conditions that mean there are more 'other' men sitting in prison than in our top universities, then the signs might as well have stayed where they were.

Social inequality needs to be tackled by our institutions with the same vigour that segregation and racism were in the latter decades of the twentieth century. We need to charge the arms of our government machinery to work together and more effectively for the common good. We need to challenge an education system that fails a large section of society and sets them on the path to financial instability and sometimes criminality. We need, instead, an education system that provides a clear path to employment, social mobility, and financial stability for everyone. This must also apply to our prison system, so that we offer rehabilitation to give ex-offenders a second chance – the opportunity and ability to contribute and reap the rewards of honest work.

Solving multifaceted challenges like these is where diversity comes into its own, because they can only be met by bringing in a wide range of advocates, all signed up to the common cause, but with different opinions and experiences. Our public instructions need to reach out to informed and talented teachers, police officers, prison staff, prisoners, and ex-offenders who will all have valid input into what needs to be done. As it stands, what happens is that there may be some minor consultation with these individuals, but decisions, processes, and delivery will be left to politicians and civil servants. With visionary leaders, this can change – barriers can be broken down and a more inclusive approach adopted.

Social trust

The public bodies that represent us need to be more diverse than anywhere else if we are to achieve the atmosphere of social trust that Michael Novak spoke of. Change should come from those inside, but more likely it will come from pressure from outside, as is usually the way. Government institutions are tasked with protecting our freedoms and facilitating inclusion, but these were never their primary duties – they were given these charges thanks to pressure from those who fought for freedoms and the right to be included, recognizing that a level playing field means we all benefit. Equally, when these freedoms are denied to any section of society, we are all less free and excluded from the promise of a democracy.

So how do we remain hopeful when it may seem that society is moving backwards? How do we hold on to our vision of the future? We've got to the stage where we certainly pay lip service to equality but don't necessarily act upon it – and even though that is not good enough, we have to see that in itself as progress, as not long ago inequality was not only 'fair' but also natural.

Our democratic institutions have given us a means of pushing for change through collective efforts that are organized and targeted, such as demonstrations, lobbying, voting, and campaigning. Great oratory and an optimistic bias towards the arc of human progress has given us cause to believe that things can only get better. But they can also regress if we are not all contributing towards the outcome and we shy away from making changes in the face of resistance. That is why those of us who are part of organizations of influence, lobby groups, political parties, trade unions, faith and community groups need to keep diversity on the agenda, so that the decision makers reflect the people they serve, otherwise these institutions remain stagnant as society changes. Those who fear change may prefer this outcome, but if institutions like legislative bodies are allowed to become distant from those they represent, voter turnout falls and the democratic mandate is lost.

We cannot afford apathy any more than complacency. This has never been an affliction for nativists and special interest groups – they have built strong alliances both inside and outside of government institutions that diligently lobby for policies that benefit them – so we must do the same. The alarm has gone off loud and clear for all of us on the progressive side of the argument, and we must wake up to it.

CHAPTER THREE

A Timeline of Progress

'In the democracy which I have envisaged . . . there will be equal freedom for all. Everybody will be his own master.'

Martin Luther King

The opportunities to choose the 'other way' occur throughout a lifetime. We are a part of the social system from the minute we're born, and the attitudes and decisions of that system can hugely affect our lives until the day we die – from the care and education we receive to the opportunities and prospects available to us. So let's explore the timeline of a life lived the 'other way' and see just how different things could be.

0 Years

The Old Way: A child is welcomed into the world via a mother whose access to the best healthcare is affected by her economic and social status.

The Other Way: The child's social status has no bearing on the treatment she receives. As an advocate of the 'other way', whether you are a member of the family or simply an acquaintance, you feel a vested interest and pledge to support the child's growth. All nations have a fair and robust healthcare system that provides new parents with the best pre- and postnatal care, regardless of income. The child is cherished and welcomed not just into a family but into a local community and a country that celebrates its arrival as someone who will grow to make a significant contribution to society. The child is not measured by its physicality, gender, physical or mental ability, but by its boundless potential.

1–5 Years

The Old Way: This is a lonely one for the new family. Child-rearing is the sole responsibility of one or two people, who may also be coping with other pressures, such as finances and time. In some cases the child feels like a burden, and parents struggle to ensure that the child develops to the best of its ability.

The Other Way: New families are supported, allowing parents of both genders the time to engage with their child and develop a diverse network of family and friends that will support the child throughout its life. The 'It takes a village' mentality has been firmly reinstated and the child is very aware that the community around it plays an active role in supporting his or her wellbeing. As an advocate of the 'other way', the fewer attributes you share with the family, the more determined you will be to engage with them. Parents who advocate the 'other way' will aim to expose their child to as much diversity as possible, and at the same time ensure that their child sees positive images that reflect them. Advocates of the 'other way' within the media will also support this endeavour.

6–11 Years

The Old Way: The child is put in a school with other children from the same socio-economic class, with gender roles, views and 'other' identities becoming crystallized in the eyes of the child and the society they exist in.

The Other Way: All schools are diverse and able to cater for children from any background or ability. If you advocate the 'other way' and are a parent, a teacher, or are involved with children, you avoid judgements on gender roles and sexual orientation and dissuade other children from doing so. You provide as many opportunities as possible for children to engage safely with people who identify and think differently to them. By the time the child hits double figures they have been exposed to diversity in their society and are comfortable with it. Children, after all, see no reason not to authentically engage with people who are of a different social background, religion, generation, ability, or gender from them.

12–16 Years

The Old Way: The imbalance in resources within our educational system means that by the time a child reaches adolescence, clear differences are emerging in their educational attainment depending on their background.

The Other Way: In an imagined future, countries are interconnected and citizens expect their leaders to keep their countries united (they will be quickly replaced if they do not). Therefore the need for astronomical defence budgets is lessened, and the extra funds have been redistributed to education, the government's number-one priority. The private and public sectors constantly work together in a way that benefits the many, not just the privileged few. The private sector informs policy makers of the innovations of the future and works with them to create an education system that prepares children for the jobs of the future. There is no need for a private school system because the state system is adequately funded to provide the best education possible for all children. Schools are viewed not only as vehicles for job preparation but also for citizen creation; they provide support to parents and kids through education about alternative views, gender roles, identity, and sexual orientation in a non-judgemental, non-stereotypical way. Older people who advocate the 'other way' engage with teenagers as grandparents, surrogate grandparents, or mentors and are actively deployed in schools to act as wise elders for the community. Employers, businesses, and charities also actively engage with schools, mentoring young people and providing work experience and opportunities to learn how to access various career sectors. The 'other way' supports the emotional and mental wellbeing of young people by helping them prepare to make a contribution to society, regardless of their social background or educational attainment. And if you are a young person raised the 'other way', then you seek to take up any opportunity to contribute, knowing that there is a system in place designed to help you fulfil your highest potential.

17–21 Years

The Old Way: People who are 'others' are further marginalized at this point in their lives, by restricting their rights, access to employment, and self-identity.

The Other Way: Politicians and ministers create equality-based policies that are actually enforced. As young people become adults, these policies are extended to 16-year-olds and protect all forms of equality. If you are a person of faith, or a member of society interested in the welfare of young adults, then through the 'other way' you support and respect the rights of young people to make decisions about their bodies, sexuality, and gender. Furthermore, if you work in higher education or are an employer advocating the 'other way', you take action to increase the diversity of young people coming through your doors by creating pathways to success without restrictions that exclude diverse groups.

22–30 Years

The Old Way: In your twenties, adult life begins with the ability to contribute to society, earn an income, and maintain a household – these things are paramount to your identity as an independent adult citizen. The standard way has seen this aspiration become an unattainable dream for many.

The Other Way: The opportunity for young adults to contribute, earn income, and live independently is by design a realistic aspiration for all. With the 'other way', the private sector and politicians agree that market forces need to be harnessed to benefit society, not just shareholders – all businesses have profit with purpose at their core. In the 'other way', we change our mindset so that part of our own individual vocation is to ensure that every young person has the opportunities that we expect for ourselves and for our own children. As advocates of the 'other way' we work collectively and challenge our politicians, our employers, and the businesses we invest in and patronize, as well as ourselves, to remove any barriers that restrict anyone achieving these basic tenets of adulthood.

31–49 Years

The Old Way: These are pivotal years when most of us move from being individual adults to becoming part of a family unit that raises another generation. The standard way finds us becoming more insular, focusing on our own concerns and those of our immediate family. Under the standard way, we accept barriers, discrimination, or unjust treatment as normal and not something we as individuals can change.

The Other Way: These issues are our own personal challenge, and we form diverse alliances to address them, opening doors where we can for marginalized people and working to make sure they feel included and represented. With the 'other way', we see the importance of our children mixing with those different to them and we explain both the benefits and the challenges of difference. As a society we understand the importance and societal benefits of allowing parents more time with their children, and endeavour to make life and work as complementary as possible. Women make up 50 per cent of the workforce, for which they are paid equally; they have played a key role in redesigning the workplace, which now always features a kindergarten. Companies design this into their growth strategy, so parents are able to work near where their young children are educated. The traditional 'drop-off' therefore becomes the family commute, and family lunch breaks and daily playtimes are now the norm.

50–69 Years

The Old Way: As we pass the half-century mark our views start to harden and under the standard way we begin to look backwards with nostalgia and feel we have done 'our bit'. We become less tolerant of change as we look towards retiring, hoping we have made an adequate contribution to society.

The Other Way: We use this time to refresh ourselves with new ideas. We remain open-minded and utilize our spare time to explore different points of view and recommit ourselves to expanding our diverse circle of friends. We are respected as wise elders and seen as the moral guardians of society – our value is clear and revered by society as a whole. If our child-rearing years are over, we use the skills and experience we have gained to support other young families, not just our own. By doing this, we remain relevant and continue to grow and have a positive impact on society.

70 Years and Beyond

The Old Way: By now we have retired and often look back at the life we have led as we consider our own mortality. The standard way sees us become more isolated as we grow older and less in touch with anyone different to us. Despite a lifetime of contributing to the state, we are often left vulnerable, lonely, and unable to access or afford the social care we need.

The Other Way: Society will value, respect, and take good care of its older citizens with decent state pensions, compassionate social care, and active community programmes that encourage us to socialize and engage with others of all backgrounds. The 'other way' will also see us seizing that opportunity to engage with society and offering more to improve it, rather than withdrawing from it. Determined to save the best until last, we use our twilight years (when we have more time to ourselves) to apply our life experience and share it with progressive movements, pushing for a cohesive, equitable, fair, and free society.

CONCLUSION

'A dream you dream alone is only a dream. A dream you dream together is reality.'

Yoko Ono

Be the Change

We all seek to better ourselves and our environment, but we often struggle to know how to achieve this. Invariably, the answer that comes back to us time and again is that we, as Gandhi said, must 'Be the change that you wish to see in the world.'

If doing just that and taking the 'other way' takes a lifetime, it will at least be a lifetime well spent. And even if, like Martin Luther King, we don't get to see that promised land for ourselves, we would at least be able to see the incremental benefits of the 'other way', as every single positive intervention, no matter how small, will have an outcome that will perpetuate, just as every single neglect and exclusion, no matter how small, has regressive results with perpetual consequences. And we would at least be able to exit this world with the knowledge that we were leaving it a better place than we found it. King may not have seen that brave new world that he dreamt of, but he knew what it would look like:

When this happens. . .we will be able to speed up that day when all of God's children, black men and white men, Jews and Gentiles, Protestants and Catholics, will be able to join hands and sing in the words of the old Negro spiritual: Free at last! Free at last!

This sounds to me like a pretty great place in which to live. And I hope the arguments, examples, statistics, and case studies in this book demonstrate how we, as individuals, as business people, and as policy makers, can make this a reality. How we can redesign society so that people from all backgrounds are able to contribute, and we can all work together towards building a society where equality, diversity, and inclusion form the very heart of progress and eventually become the 'new normal'. We all have our part to play. It's time to figure out what our role is in shaping a better future – it may be how we hire, it may be how we create policy, it may be how we campaign, it may be how we love.

What it will be for all of us is how we think. How we think is what will create the future we all wish to see. We have to believe it, act upon it, and then we can live it. It's easy to be cynical, but like MLK we must all be dreamers in order to take a fairer future from a dream to reality. If we all endeavour to diversify our lives and move from six degrees of separation to enacting the Six Degrees of Integration, the 'other' will cease to exist and we will no longer define ourselves by what separates us, but rather by what unites us as human beings, just trying to make the most of the short time we have on this planet we all call home. The Other Way is possible and can be achieved – we all just need to play our part.

The Final Number

Throughout *Diversify* I have made the argument for a more inclusive and diverse society and have also proposed strategies and analysed the social cost and discomfort of change to individuals and to institutions. During the course of writing this book I also enlisted Professor John Hills and Professor Lucinda Platt and their team at the London School of Economics to undertake new analysis to add up how much people may be losing in total as a result of the income differences between less and more favoured groups.

The total cost of maintaining the status quo and refusing to invest further in inclusion and diversity according to the LSE is:

£127 billion pounds per year

The LSE found that men from ethnic minority groups and women from all ethnic groups would have extra incomes totaling £9,300 each on average (a total of £127 billion per year) if they matched those of white British men. This was just looking at people aged 16-59 who were already in work or looking for work, and not allowing for factors beyond gender and ethnic background.

Some of that astounding figure represents simple pay discrimination, where people with the same skills doing similar work are paid less than others. Some of it represents the lower incomes women in particular have than men, resulting from the way in which we organize our work and caring lives. Equalizing those wouldn't necessarily make us better off in terms of total national income – just a lot fairer.

But part of the number results from people ending up in jobs where we are not making the best use of their talents. That makes all of us poorer, with less production, and lower tax revenue from the lost 'others' who, if allowed to contribute to the their full potential rather than being excluded, would generate an extra to the treasury coffers. Of course, we also need to consider the cost of the benefit system, and the cost of criminality which, more often than not, is inextricably linked to lack of inclusion and opportunity. And we can't ignore the cost of a lack of integration to our precious National Health Service which we all want to maintain – people living in poverty are more prone to health issues such as obesity and diabetes. A detailed breakdown of the costs can be found at www.Diversify.org.

This figure forces us to face an uncomfortable truth. The prospect of social mobility has always been the fig leaf that shields the shameful inequality of our economic system. But, to maintain this system, you need an inclusive society which allows diversity at all levels and provides people with the belief that they can achieve a decent standard of living through their contributions. Over the past few years, experience and empirical evidence have shaken people's belief that this is still the case. Therefore, we face the prospect of growing poverty, civil unrest, disengagement, terrorism and criminality, all of which are expensive for tax payers and governments.

Ultimately, failing to address these issues is a cost we can no longer afford.

Acknowledgements

Now for one of the parts that I have looked forward to the most – the Acknowledgements! As they say no man is an island – well, no woman is one either. This book wouldn't have been possible without the help, support and wise counsel of some very special people who believed in me and shared my vision for fairer and more unified world.

First of all, I'd like to thank my darling cousin Reg, who spent hours brainstorming with me and providing his talent and unique perspective in helping to shape this book and all it turned out to be. I'm almost as lucky to have you for a cousin as Jayden is to have you as his Dad.

To the formidable and effervescent Caroline Michel (the woman I want to be): thanks for reaching out to me and encouraging me to write this book in the first place and then for connecting me with my HQ-HarperCollins Family – Lisa Milton, Clio Cornish, Sophie Calder, Claire Brett, Alison Lindsay and Louise McGrory. Lisa, thank you for your exemplary leadership and creating an imprint dedicated to giving a platform and home to female voices. Clio, what can I say? Apart from that it has been a sheer joy and delight working with you. From the day you walked into Caroline's office and spoke exactly what was in my head – I knew we were going to have a blast and here we are!!!!!!! To Holly and Kate: thank you for adding your literary stardust and tightening up my loose ends, your input was greatly appreciated. Charlie Redmayne – you rock, dude!!! I still have the mock-up you made for me, it's one of my favourite items.

To my MC Saatchi family – Lucy Bayliss, you are superhuman and the BEST agent anyone could ever ask for. Thanks for always going that extra mile and being such a ray of sunshine. Katie-Jane, what a great addition you have been to the family. Tory – you are the corporate queen and I feel lucky to be one of your princesses. Richard – ADORE you, honey.

My *Diversify* academic research partners have proved invaluable. I'd like to express my sincerest thanks to: Professor Anthony Heath, Dr Lindsay Richards and Dr Elisabeth Garrett from Nuffield College, Oxford University. Lindsay and Beth, you are both brilliant and somehow managed to simplify complicated research in order to make it accessible to as many people as possible – thank you for your effort, time and superbrain power. Iqbal Wahab, thank you for your excellent advice and for introducing me to Nuffield in the first place. Professor Stephen Kleinberg – loved spending time with you in Houston. Thank you for sharing your Rice University data and for shining a light on all that the city of Houston can be. Extra special thanks to Professor John Hills, Professor Lucinda Platt and Billie Elmqvist-Thurén from the LSE (London School of Economics). John, the work you do at the International Inequalities Institute is so important and vital in helping to inform policy makers, business and civil society on how we tackle inequality. It has been an honour to work with you, Lucinda and the rest of your team. To Dorothea Hodge, Jodie Gummow and Nick Colwill from Aequitas Consulting – thank you for all your help with the business and city case studies. Dorothea, thanks for being a wonderful friend and sounding board. Jodie – loved our interviews and data gathering expeditions. To Alan Milburn – thanks for all of your research around social mobility – really looking forward to making our movie!

Life is a journey of smooth paths and sometimes bumpy ones.

Having friends and family to share it with makes the journey all the more meaningful. To my parents (Mum and Dad) for their bravery in leaving with nothing and magically creating something special. Bec and The Girls: Tina, Sharon, Denise, Krista and Angela. Gerry DeVeaux, I LOVE you, baby, can't believe it's been more than twenty years – obviously we were both toddlers when we met! Margaret, you are one of the best human beings I have ever met and I am so grateful to have you as a friend and mentor. Waheed and Valerie, I grew up admiring you both and I still pinch myself that I get to call you both my friends. To my GIRLS: MT, Karen, Sofia, Verona and Lisa, I don't know how I would have survived the past couple of years without you guys. Words cannot express the depth of love and gratitude I feel to have you all in my life. Kanya and Diane – 100 Club Ladies!!!! David and Ashley, keep on changing the world. My NYC crew: Penny, Sara and Tristine, miss you, ladies, and the second-best city in the world. Virginia and Petteni clan, what a special family you are.

To Sammy, I miss you every day – thank you for the time we had, you are one of the best things that ever happened to me. Get ready, dude – I need your help from the other side. We've got work to do, buddy!

Lastly, to the future – I have no idea what's next but what I do know is that I'm excited and grateful to be alive to experience it!

The Ism Questionnaire:
How the Nation Responded

Attitudes towards other political views

1. As far as you are concerned personally, how important is it to try to understand the reasoning of people with other opinions?

   85% scored 5 to 7 (*Source*: British Social Attitudes survey 2014)

2. How would you feel if you had a son or daughter who married a Conservative?

   28% of those who identified as Labour: very upset (*Source*: YouGov/*The Times*, 2016)

3. How would you feel if you had a son or daughter who married someone who was Labour?

   19% of those who identified as Conservative: very upset (*Source*: YouGov/*The Times*, 2016)

Attitudes towards ethnicity and race

4. Do you think some races or ethnic groups are born less intelligent than others?

    22% say yes (*Source*: European Social Survey, 2014)

5. Do you think some races or ethnic groups are born harder working than others?

    47% say yes (*Source*: European Social Survey, 2014)

6. Would you say that some cultures are much better than others, or that all cultures are equal?

    56% say some cultures are better (*Source*: European Social Survey, 2014)

7. How much would you mind or not mind if a person from another country who is of a different race or ethnic group was appointed as your boss?

    27% score 5 or above out of 10 (*Source*: European Social Survey, 2014)

8. How much would you mind or not mind if a person from another country who is of a different race or ethnic group married a close relative of yours?

    25% score 5 or above out of 10 (*Source*: European Social Survey, 2014)

Attitudes towards gender, family life, and sexuality

9. All in all, family life suffers when the woman has a full-time job?

    27% agreed (*Source*: British Social Attitudes survey 2012)

10. A man's job is to earn money; a woman's job is to look after the home and family.

   13% agreed (*Source*: British Social Attitudes survey 2012)

11. A working mother can establish just as warm and secure a relationship with her children as a mother who does not work.

   77% agreed (*Source*: British Social Attitudes survey 2012)

12. One parent can bring up a child as well as two parents together.

   49% agreed (*Source*: British Social Attitudes survey 2012)

13. A same-sex female couple can bring up a child as well as a male-female couple.

   42% agreed (*Source*: British Social Attitudes survey 2012)

Bibliography

Ackroyd, Peter, *Queer City: Gay London from the Romans to the Present Day* (Chatto & Windus, 2012)

Axelrod, David, *Believer* (Penguin, 2015)

Baldwin, James, *The Fire Next Time* (Dial Press, 1963)

Brown, Brené, *Daring Greatly: How the Courage to Be Vulnerable Transforms the Way We Live, Love, Parent and Lead* (Penguin USA, 2012)

Campbell, Alastair, *Winners: and How They Succeed* (Pegasus Books, 2015)

Çatalhöyük *Research Project*, http://www.catalhoyuk.com

Clark, Glenn, *The Man Who Tapped the Secrets of the Universe* (The University of Science and Philosophy Press, 1946)

Coates, Ta-Nehisi, *The Beautiful Struggle* (Verso, Lonon and New York, 2008)

Collins, Jim, *Good to Great: Why Some Companies Make The Leap And Other's Don't* (William Collins, 2001)

Cox, Brendan Cox, *Jo Cox: More In Common* (Hodder & Stoughton, 2017)

Douglass, Frederick, *Narrative of the Life of Frederick Douglass, an American Slave* (Anti-Slavery Office, 1845)

Frankl, Viktor, *Man's Search for Meaning: The Classic Tribute to Hope from the Holocaust* (1946, Beacon Press USA)

Friedan, Betty, *The Feminine Mystique* (Victor Gollancz, 1963)

Goodwin, Doris Kearns: *No Ordinary Time: Franklin and Eleanor Roosevelt: The Home Front in World War II* (Simon & Schuster, 1994); *Team of Rivals: The Political Genius of Abraham Lincoln* (Simon & Schuster, 2005)

Hill, Vernon W., *Fans, Not Customers: How to Create Growth Companies in a No Growth World* (Profile, 2012)

Hills, John, *Good Times, Bad Times* (Policy Press, 2015)

Hodder, Ian, *The Leopard's Tale: Revealing the Mysteries of Catalhoyuk* (Thames & Hudson, 2006)

Jones, Owen, *Chavs: The Demonization of the Working Class* (Verso, 2011)

Klein, Naomi, *The Shock Doctrine: The Rise of Disaster Capitalism* (Random House Canada, 2007)

Mayer, Catherine, *Attack of the 50Ft Woman: How Gender Equality Can Save the World!* (HarperCollins, 2017)

Maynard Keynes, John: *The Economic Consequences of the Peace* (MacMillan, 1920); *The General Theory of Employment, Interest and Money* (MacMillan, 1936)

Morris, Charles R., *The Tycoons: How Andrew Carnegie, John D. Rockefeller, Jay Gould and J. P. Morgan Invented the American Supereconomy* (Times Books, 2005)

Obama, Barack, *Dreams From My Father* (Times Books, 1995)

Paglia, Camille, *Sexual Personae: Art and Decadence from Nefertiti to Emily Dickinson* (Yale University Press, 1990)

PAST (the Palaeontological Scientific Trust), is a South-African based public benefit organization that raises funds to support scientific research and education into the fossil histories of life and humankind in Africa. PAST's global All from One campaign uses the shared origins of humankind to promote tolerance and respect for diversity, and the shared origins of all living things to promote conservation of earth's natural environments and biodiversity. To find out more, visit: www.past.org.za

Ogunlaru, Rasheed, *Soul Trader: Putting the Heart Back into Your Business* (Kogan Page Limited, 2012)

Twain, Mark, *Adventures of Huckleberry Finn* (Chatto & Windus, 1884)

Vance, J.D., *Hillbilly Elegy: A Memoir of a Family and Culture in Crisis* (HarperCollins, 2016)

Wiesel, Elie, *The Jews Of Silence* (*Haaretz* [Israeli newspaper], 1966)

Yunus, Muhammad, *Building Social Business: The New Kind of Capitalism that Serves Humanity's Most Pressing Needs* (Public Affairs, 2010)

Index